INDIA
ON THE
EVE OF THE BRITISH CONQUEST

INDIA
ON THE
EVE OF THE BRITISH CONQUEST

A HISTORICAL SKETCH.

BY

SIDNEY OWEN, M.A.

Reader in Indian Law and History in the University of Oxford.
Formerly Professor of History in the Elphinstone College,
Bombay.

GYAN

Published by

GYAN

Gyan Publishing House
5, Ansari Road
Daryaganj, New Delhi-110002
Phone: 011-47034999, 9811692060
E-mail: books@gyanbooks.com

Distribution Network
gyanbooks.com
India, USA, Canada, UK, Australia, France

ISBN : 978-81-212-2446-8 (HB)
First Published, 1872

2nd Impression 2021

Printed at: Gyan Press, Delhi.

India on the Eve of the British Conquest
Author: Sidney Owen

INDIA

ON THE

EVE OF THE BRITISH CONQUEST.

A HISTORICAL SKETCH.

BY

SIDNEY OWEN, M.A.,

Reader in Indian Law and History in the University of Oxford.
Formerly Professor of History in the Elphinstone College, Bombay.

—"Mutato nomine de te
Fabula narratur."

LONDON:
WM. H. ALLEN & Co., 13, WATERLOO PLACE.
Publishers to the India Office.

1872.

"On croit nécessaire de dire à ceux qui pourront lire cet ouvrage, qu'ils doivent se souvenir que ce n'est point ici une simple relation de campagnes, mais plutôt une histoire des mœurs des hommes:—Le dessein de cet essai est de peindre les principaux caractères de ces révolutions, et d'écarter la multitude des petits faits pour laisser voir les seuls considérables, et, s'il se peut, l'esprit qui les a conduits.—VOLTAIRE, *Siècle de Louis XIV*.

PREFACE.

The following pages contain the substance of a course of lectures delivered at Oxford last year, and which had a threefold aim. First, to give such an account of the state of affairs in India, immediately previous to the establishment of British Rule, as seemed essential to a proper appreciation of our historical position in relation to that country and its native Governments; and as might facilitate, in some measure, the formation of just judgments on the character of our earlier Eastern policy.

A second object was, to trace the outlines of one of the most remarkable and dramatic revolutions which the world has ever witnessed—the rapid decline and dissolution of the Mogul Empire, and the rise and culmination of the Maratha Power.

Thirdly, it was attempted to survey this revolution not as an isolated and abnormal series of occurrences, but as forming, not the less because its actors bore strange names, and had (like Mahomet and Saladin) dark complexions, an essential portion of the history of the world; a portion closely akin, both in its phenomena and in their concatenation, to more popular and hackneyed, but not intrinsically more interesting or important passages; a portion suggestive of striking and instructive analogies to the leading circumstances, characters, and events of European annals, which it thus illustrates all the more usefully, if unexpectedly; and hence, in short, both claims and repays the attention of the general student of history and politics.

In recasting the lectures, the same objects have been kept in view. And with special reference to the third, more of the style of spoken composition has been retained, than would otherwise have seemed appropriate to what, in some sense, aspires to be a book; and historical parallels have been frequently suggested, without being worked out.

The materials available for the delineation or illustration of the period in question are very copious and miscellaneous. In using them, general impressions have been derived from too many works to be here enumerated, or even, in all cases, distinctly remembered. But for the details of events, it has appeared, on the whole, best to follow closely the lead of a few standard European authors, whose means of personal information were particularly good, and who have sifted with critical acumen the statements of others.*

* Thus, *e.g.*, little use has been made *at present* even of the *Seir Mutakherin*, though on the former account the writer of that curious book possessed great advantages.

Thus Mr. Elphinstone's high authority has resolved many doubts in the introductory historical chapters. Aliverdy Khan's career has been summarised chiefly from the contemporary biography translated and remodelled in Scott's *Dekkan*, (of which the account in Stewart's valuable *History of Bengal* is almost an exact transcript). Sir John Malcolm has been mostly consulted for the outline of Nadir Shah's portentous course.

Hyder Ally's rise has been traced almost entirely with the help of Colonel Wilks, whose discriminating and classical narrative corrects and explodes a mass of trash put forth on the same subject by half-informed or romancing writers, both European and Native.*

But the *pièce de résistance*, invaluable at every stage of the inquiry, has been the minute, luminous, sagacious, and scrupulously conscientious *History of the Mahrattas*, by Captain Grant Duff. This admirable work, being derived from native sources, now in too many cases irrecoverable, and from personal converse with actors in the events related, or their immediate ancestors, is an original and authentic *κτῆμά ἐς ἀεί*, of primary importance.

Much the same, though in a narrower field of investigation, may be said of Colonel Wilks' *History*

* Col. Miles, whose translation of one elaborate native life of Hyder has been here occasionally quoted, declines, not without ample grounds, to guarantee the accuracy of the narrative.

of Mysoor. And on this account, and because both are unfortunately—to the shame of Englishmen!—so scarce, these time-honoured but too generally neglected books have been here quoted freely.

No attempt has been consciously made to gloss over with the false halo of reckless hero-worship the moral turpitude of most of the prominent personages throughout the memorable period that occupies these sheets. But if, during such an epoch of disruption and anarchy, the tone of public morality was repulsively low in India; let it not be forgotten, that in England Charles the Second, Shaftesbury, Marlborough, and Walpole—and so much else implied in their names—still demand attention, without exciting unqualified admiration.

Should it be thought that too much stress has here been laid upon the influence of religion among the Marathas, it would be well to consult Sir Alexander Grant's account of Tukaram, the Maratha religious poet, in the *Fortnightly Review* (January, 1867.)

It would be childish to deprecate criticism. But, while the lecturer is very conscious of his own shortcomings; the difficulty of the subject, the pressure of other work, and the notorious intolerance of long discussions on Indian topics, must also be taken into account.

CHRIST CHURCH,

May, 1872.

CONTENTS.

INDIA ON THE EVE OF THE BRITISH CONQUEST.

CHAPTER I.

THE PHYSICAL FEATURES OF INDIA.

THE natural limits and the larger stereotyped divisions of India are strongly marked.

Wherever the sea does not wash its borders, it is at once connected with, and separated from, Higher Asia by the culminating region of the Stony Girdle of the Earth, or its lateral offshoots. The Himalaya, sweeping southwards at the Hindoo Koosh, is continued on a smaller scale in the Suleiman mountains; and the Hala range prolongs the barrier to the western sea. While on the east, the bold promontory of the Garrows and the Cossya Hills, determining and overhanging the valley of the Brahmaputra, are but a projecting spur of the Burmese mountains, which look down upon Aracan, feed the sources of the foreign Irawaddy, and separate India from China.

Hardly less distinct than its boundaries are the great regions, into which the character of its superficies naturally resolves the country. A vast, depressed, and typical area of river basins and deltas in the north; a mountain-girdled, and irregularly diamond-shaped table-land in the centre; maritime lowlands on either side, converging and communicating with each other at the southern extremity of the table-land; lastly a solid, wedge-shaped district in the extreme south, high in the centre, falling eastward and westward towards the sea, and having its apex at Cape Comorin;—such in the most general way seems to be an account of the country, however brief, not incorrect, or unimportant in relation to minuter geographical phenomena.

The Aravulli range, commencing geologically speaking in Kattywar, forms the eastern watershed of the Indus Valley; or rather ought to form it, but, from a circumstance which will be noticed presently, hardly fulfils the office. From the northern point of the Aravulli, the high land margin trends south-eastward, almost parallel to the Himalayas, until at the Rajmahal Hills it suddenly turns sharp south-westward, and continued through Orissa in the Nelli-green and other mountains, joins or rather becomes the Eastern Ghats. This great chain—The Ghats—though differing much in different parts, both as to character and elevation, is the continuous fringe of the table-land southward, across the Peninsula, (where the Neelgherries are its highest summits,) and again westward, till it once more approaches Kattywar, near the Gulf of Cambay.

The Neelgherries look down on a sort of funnel-shaped pass, the highest point of which is at Palghat, and which is called the Gap of Coimbatore.

Hence the triangular extremity of the Peninsula commences; and the Cardamum Hills are, as it were, the spinal cord of the land in this remote region.

In a general and comparative sense it is true, and for practical purposes useful, to describe the diamond-shaped central block as a table-land, girdled by mountains. But, while, on the north, the steep crest that looms over the Gangetic and Jumna Valley is not strictly a mountain range; this is almost equally true of many parts of the so-called Eastern Ghats. And even the Western, though the highest, and very abrupt towards the sea, are comparatively little elevated above the plateau which they fringe. Still more necessary is it, when we come to details, to discriminate clearly the varying elevations and depressions of the central table-land itself.

The highest region of all is the Neelgherries. The Western Ghats are considerably higher than the Eastern. The general slope of the table-land between them is decidedly eastward, and to a certain extent northward. But about the meridian where the

Peninsula properly so called ends, the geography is complicated, and both physical and political India are dichotomised, by several features, which have been reserved for what appeared their most appropriate place. If a line be drawn westward from Calcutta, and another southward from Allahabad, they will intersect each other at a point where the table-land reaches its highest elevation, except at the Neelgherries. Here, near the Hindoo place of pilgrimage Amercuntuc, the Mekal Hills collect the clouds, and disperse the waters distilled from the Dekkan in all directions. Hence the Sone flows northward to the Ganges; the Hasdoo, &c., feed the eastern stream of the Mahanuddy; the Wyne Gunga drops southward towards the far-off Godavery; while the Nerbudda strikes due westward to the Gulf of Cambay. So noteworthy is this wild region in a physical point of view; though in Indian history it is more conspicuous by its absence. Quite otherwise is the case with the famous river which it sends westward. Physically and historically, the mature stream of the Nerbudda and its confines are equally memorable. In the latter respect I will only now repeat a name which I formerly ventured to apply to it; and in calling it the Loire of India postpone any further justification or explanation of the term than is implied in the fact, that it separates Hindostan Proper from the "Region of the South"

—or in native phrase, the Dekkan. But as to its physical surrounding I must explain, that the barrier of demarcation between the North and the South is not single but five-fold. The northern bank of the Nerbudda is also the brow of the far-famed Vindhya mountains, which, continued in the Meyhar, the Kymore, and the Keinjua ranges, accompany the Sone in its pilgrimage to the Ganges. Again, the Nerbudda is overlooked, and separated from its companion westward stream, the Tapty, by the Sautpoora mountains, geologically a formation distinct from the Vindhyas. While, lastly, the Western Ghats, just south of the Tapty, are continued to the eastward in what ought properly to be called—though the term is hardly yet fully recognised—the Northern Ghats. Such is the remarkable and multiform line of separation between Hindostan and the Dekkan. For the present it may be assumed, that the southern table-land is tolerably equable in general elevation. But it must be mentioned, that while the whole tetragon enclosed between the Vindhyas, the range that borders Guzerat on the east, the Aravulli, and the southern crest of the Gangetic Valley—is a lofty region, this is specially true of the high table-land of Malwa; less so of the wild Bundlekund country; and least (I believe) of the eastern corner towards the Sone and the Kymore range.

From the nature of the case, as well as from what

has now been said, it may be inferred, that the subordinate geographical features of India may be described as deducible partly from the form and other circumstances of the Great Continent, partly from those of India Proper—or the Peninsula strictly so called. Or, in other words, paradoxical as it may sound, that India Proper and its distinctive geography begin, pretty much where Hindostan Proper, or that part more nearly related to Asia, ends. Thus, whereas it is a familiar coincidence that the line of highest elevation should be found to follow the direction of the longest land, the Himalayas fulfil this condition in the case of the Great Continent; the Eastern and Western Ghats in that of the Peninsula. So, too, both the origin, the size, and the general character and direction of the four mighty northern rivers are essentially Asiatic: whereas the chief Dekkan streams agree in rising far to the west—all but one in the Western Ghats—flowing eastward into the Bay of Bengal; being deep-channelled, yet shallow-watered, turbulent and unnavigable in the higher country; and in depositing a fertile and spacious delta at their respective mouths, mostly fringed and impeded by a heavy bar and a rough surf.

The Great Indian Desert again, on the east of the Indus, is but a continuation of its more widely diffused and famous western counterparts. I may add that the direction and position of the steep and lofty Western Ghats, the rock-bound coast, and narrow space of land at their base, the consequent absence of great rivers on that side (though small streams and torrents are innumerable), the direction of the rivers eastward, the wide expanse of low land on the eastern coast, and the deltas, are a combination of phenomena more or less exactly reproduced in America, Africa, Scandinavia, and in our own country.

The Vindhya, Sautpoora, and Northern Ghats, as well as the two rivers that run between them, though more obviously connected with India than with Asia, yet in their direction seem to ape the eastern and western *pose* of the colossal chain, that dwarfs them into comparative insignificance.

The great Asiatico-Indian rivers have certain points of resemblance. Fed from the highest water-shed in the world, they attest their common source by a volume of water, an impetuosity of current, a proneness to ramble and alter their channels, a copiousness of deposit, and an extent of periodical inundation, which recall the astonishment of Herodotus at the proceedings of the Nile, and which the New World hardly surpasses.

But the points of contrast are particularly worth attention, both on their own account, and in their historical and social bearings.

The Brahmaputra and the Indus, rising far to the

north, in the remoter regions of the Himalaya, and describing a vast snake-like coil around their Alpine home, pour their waters into the plain on the confines of the country; and seem never to be identified with its life, or endeared to the memory of its inhabitants, or intimately connected with its civilization. The shortness of its Indian course accounts for this in the case of the Brahmaputra. And two circumstances explain it in that of the Indus. First, the landward invader has ever come that way; and turbulence, devastation, idleness, sterility, and poverty have been the successive consequences of the fact or the dread of incursion. Secondly, how far the result of neglected human effort I know not, but a fact it seems, that a large portion of the Indus valley either has always been, or has relapsed into, a hopeless desert; and that within historical memory that desert has largely encroached on the once comparatively fertile country. Where works of irrigation are neglected or destroyed in a tropical climate, and the soil is thin, such a retrograde process goes on rapidly. Long and desolate sand hills occur between the Indus and the Aravulli. Salt pervades the ground far up country; and the streams that run westward from those mountains flow into a river, which does not reach the Indus, but either loses itself in the sand, or empties itself into the Great Salt Runn. The absence of tributaries from the east, after the junction of the

Punjnud—the united channel of the Punjab rivers —is probably connected with what appears to be the case, that the Indus has been gradually trending more westward. Thus between Sinde and the Aravulli, the large Province of Rajputana or Ajmir is mainly a desert, dotted with oases, in which the archaic Rajput communities still exhibit a striking resemblance to their ancestors, who in the same neighbourhood confronted Alexander. An earthquake, as lately as A.D. 1819, has greatly altered the mouth or rather the delta of the Indus. Possibly previous convulsions may have had much to do with the barrenness of the whole region. Cutch also is a country of volcanic origin. The hills in that insular region and in Kattywar seem to be (as I have already intimated) the geological commencement of the Aravulli range. At the same time, it may be observed, the form of both districts appears to favour the idea that, rounded off as they are, they may be relics of a vast, pre-historic delta district, when the Indus rolled its mighty waters further eastward, and battled with the sea and the united stream of the Nerbudda, the Tapty, and other rivers; and when the rocks or narrow islands of that day became gradually silted up and clothed upon:—until they were amplified, and almost completely attached to the main land.

The spaces between the Punjab rivers, the *Doabs* as they are called, differ greatly in fertility; and while the desert re-appears between the Chenab and the Ravi, the Julinder Doab, encircled by the Sutlej and the Beas, and far in the higher north-east region, is exuberantly productive.

It is difficult, in a few sentences, and without creating an impression of exaggeration, to convey a just idea of the manifold interest attaching to the Ganges, and its kindred stream the Jumna, regarded merely from a physical point of view. That this most sacred river has been to the Hindoo much what the Nile was to the Egyptian of old, and that its banks are crowded with historical cities and famous associations—are commonplaces. But it is also, as I have already said of these northern river areas generally, a typical study for the hydrographer. We speak of the Ganges as a single river. But it is rather, in fact, a geographical expression for a vast confluence of mighty streams, each many hundred miles in length, and fed from innumerable sources:—the whole forming an enormous and intricate system of Himalayan drainage, with contributions from the southern table land, less intricate indeed, but hardly inferior in the size and length of many tributaries; this prodigal accumulation of waters poured through a country everywhere adapted to profit by it; sloping gently and gracefully towards the Bay of Bengal; teeming with fertility; lubricated and enriched each year by the wide expanse and liberal deposits of the inundation; scored in the lower course of the stream by old and deserted channels and *jeels* or beds of lakes; ending at last in a wondrous region—*ἐπίκτητός τε γῆ, καὶ δῶρον τοῦ ποταμοῦ*—(as Herodotus expresses it of the Nile Delta,) so loamy that for 400 miles, it is said, not a pebble is to be found; so rankly and pestilentially fertile at its extremity the Sundurbunds, that human life can hardly be sustained, and, as Mr. Buckle would say, "nature," in this wild haunt of the tiger and the jungle fever, "dominates man." Such are a few of the more prominent characteristics of what may not improperly be called a unique river.

The extent and complication of its tributary system can only be appreciated by a study of the map. But one or two examples will illustrate how truly it is rather a confluence of mighty rivers than a single stream. The Sun Cosi from the east and the Gunduk from the west of Katmandu, the remote capital of Nepal, join at last, though at different points, the great gathering of waters. But while the former brings with it the added volume of many not unimportant rivers; the latter enters the Ganges almost at the same spot as the Gogra from the north-west, and the Sone from Central India. The Gogra again is a common term for a collection of large and long streams; and the tributaries of the great Sone are legion. Once more; above the junction of the

Ganges and the Jumna, or in the Doab Proper, the complication of northern waters becomes almost bewildering. But not to mention the long channel of the Betwa and other streams from the southern tableland, the Chumbul alone is in itself a host of rivers, and rivals in length the separate course of the Jumna.

Well may the Hindoo dread the Indus, and revere the Ganges. Nature and man have stamped for him the impress of terror on the former name: the latter personifies the vivifying and widely diffused powers of Nature; and has in every age been associated with facility of existence and communication, social prosperity, and political power. What the Danube was to the trembling citizen of Constantinople in the early middle ages, that and worse than that has been the Indus to the Hindoo. What Normandy in the later middle ages was to the French political arithmetician, that, and better than that, has been the Gangetic Plain to the exacting ministers of the Delhi sovereigns.

It is impossible to comprise, within the limits of this Sketch, even a general description of the ample and diversified block of highland that stretches from the Neelgherries to the Rajmahal Hills; and from the Aravulli Mountains to the Eastern Ghats. But a few characteristic particulars may be given. The greater portion of the north-eastern part of the region, or roughly speaking from the Eastern Ghats and the banks of the Godavery to the Mekal Hills and the Subunrika River, is, and apparently always has been, in a very primitive and indeed savage state; the bulk of the inhabitants being pre-historic races, under turbulent and ferocious chieftains, living in wild forests, possessing few of the arts of life, and little connected with the history of the Peninsula. The western portion of the block on the contrary teems, from north to south, with historical associations; has been the nursery, the base, and the battle-field of every indigenous Power (except the Sikhs) that for centuries has aspired to empire; and has been as closely connected with the military, as the Gangetic Valley with the industrial, life of India. And the complex political geography of the country still bears obvious traces of this fact in every direction. Thus, when defeated by the invading Mussulman in early times, the hereditary chief of the warrior caste, the representative of the Solar Dynasty, retired to the unfrequented country near the eastern slopes of the Aravulli; whence his tribesmen in after days went forth to contest vigorously the empire of India with Baber himself. And both the western desert and the table-land above, as well as the park-like Guzerat, are still tenanted by a host of gallant, haughty, dissipated lordlings, who present a striking contrast in character to the ordinary Hindoo type.

Thus again, when Baber's Empire was waning, the ignobler Jats made themselves strong in hill forts not far removed from the imperial city. And while no single place, defended by natives, ever resisted the English so stoutly, and frequently, and with such loss to our countrymen, as the Jat stronghold of Bhurtpore; this people is still represented in the same district, and at Alwar and Machery.

But the importance of geographical circumstances in war, and the extreme difficulty of reducing a mountain community under an able leader, were even more strikingly exhibited in the case of the Marathas. As I have already said:—" the sublime country of the Western Ghats, with its deep recesses, its umbrageous woods, its steep fastnesses, and the rugged and impracticable Concan at its base, furnished [Sivaji] with a secure and inaccessible retreat from pursuit, and a constant repository for his spoil; as well as with a race of hardy clansmen on whose fidelity he could implicitly rely, for among them he had been bred, and with their aid had performed his earliest feats.*" What Holland was to the Dutch against Philip the Second—that were the Ghats and the Concan to the Marathas against Aurungzib. Thus, after maintaining their independence against the Empire, this singular people proceeded to conquer a great portion of the highland, and not only

* *The Mussulman, the Maratha, and the European*, pp. 21, 22.

the Raja of Satara and the Peishwa, but all their great chiefs except one (the Guikwar) had their seats in this upper region—Sindia at Gwalior, Holkar at Indore, the Bonslay at Nagpore.

In connexion with the Marathas it may be mentioned also, that the valleys of the Nerbudda and the Tapty ineffectually sheltered their bad imitators the Pindaries from our arms. Nor need I dwell on the fact, that decayed and dismembered Imperialism is still represented in the transmuted Mogul functionary, the modern Nizam, who holds the centre of the Dekkan, and rules—or professes to rule—at Hyderabad.

What Sivaji was to Aurungzib, that Hyder Ally long threatened to be, indeed may be said to have been, to the English. And the connexion between the character of his country and his successful warfare against them is so close, that it may be well to add a few words on a subject so intimately affecting our own fortunes.

Mysore Proper is conterminous with the southern sweep of the Ghats; and is thus, so to speak, a vast natural fortress, surrounded on three sides by very formidable, though not impregnable, barriers, but exposed on the north, so as to be easily overrun by invaders from the heart of the Dekkan.

And the history of Hyder and Tippoo is strictly in accordance with these geographical peculiarities. Not to mention the occasional visits of the Nizam, the Maratha from the north is ever hovering on and over-passing the frontier; levying *chout*, pillaging and devastating the country, occupying the strongholds,—more than once assailing and beleaguering the capital itself.

While, on the other hand, from behind the screen of their hills, through the gates of their yawning and sinuous passes, from the vantage ground of their commanding plateau, working (as a soldier would say) on the interior lines of their central position;—the fierce and crafty barbarians inspire in the English at their feet a mysterious dread; watch and anticipate the movements of their antagonists; conceal their own operations till the time arrives for delivering the swift and terrible blow; elude pursuit in their lofty fastness; cross and recross the Peninsula, dealing their strokes alternately to right and left against dissevered armies, too scanty to co-operate along so extended a line of frontier.

A few remarks on the principal Dekkan rivers will complete what I have space to say on the central upland of India. They all flow (as I have observed) eastward into the Bay of Bengal; but may be distinguished as follows. The Mahanuddy is perhaps the shortest, but is the most navigable, and has on the whole the largest delta; flows through the wildest country; is most destitute of important tributaries;

and reaches the sea near one of the holiest places in India—Juggernath. The course of the Godavery is the longest, extending right across the Peninsula: it rises not far from Bombay, near that remarkablv feat of modern engineering, the Thull Ghat railway cutting; and forms, during the later part of its course, the northern boundary of the Nizam's territories; (the Pranhita, one of its larger tributaries, and the Northern Ghats completing that boundary line.) The Kistna has the largest drainage area, and the most numerous and celebrated feeders; one of them, the Bhima, rising a little south of the Godavery, and due east of Bombay, while the Tunga and the Bhudra, (whose united streams form the Toombudra, and join the Kistna at the extreme south of the Nizam's dominions,) and the Hugri have their sources far down in the western Mysore country. The Kistna also forms the boundary of the Nizam's territories on the south, until its final abrupt turn in the same direction. Lastly, the Cavery, though perhaps *positively* the shortest of the four, is fraught with the most interesting historical memories to Englishmen. Indeed it may be said to symbolize, as it were, inversely in its course the career of the British in India. At its mouth we first engaged with natives in a contest, which was the prelude to our long and obstinate struggle with the French, and which resulted in our acquiring there a post of much importance with a view to the later war. The chief scene of the Anglo-French struggle was at Trichinopoly, on the banks of the same river. Our next internecine war was with the Mysorean, whose capital was at Seringapatam, still on the Cavery; the capture of which place extinguished the Empire of Tippoo, and made us the strongest Power in the South. Yet twice more we had to vindicate our supremacy against the insolent challenge or the sullen opposition of the Maratha, whose starting point, like that of the Cavery, had been the Western Ghats, whence like that river he had advanced to meet the sea-born invader.

The smaller rivers, as the Palaar and the two Pennars, drain the space between the Kistna and the Cavery, and water the Carnatic Plain.

The triangular block with which the Peninsula comes to an end reproduces many of the features of the regions further north. The Palnai Hills, in which its highland culminates, confront and rival in elevation the Neelgherries, on the opposite side of the Palghat-Pass, or Gap of Coimbatore. The Cardamums, like the main chain of the Ghats, keep closer to the western than the eastern coast. Hence Travancore is narrower and more undulating, not to say precipitous: Madura and Tinnevelly are in general flat, river-traversed plains, in which the Vaiga, &c., repeat, on a diminished scale proportioned to the locality, the operations of the Cavery and the other Dekkan rivers. Some distance from Cape Comorin the Cardamums sink suddenly to 2,000 feet, and the Cape itself is (I believe) still not far short of 500. The whole of this block is abundantly watered both by streams and by the *monsoon* torrents, and exhibits the same exuberant fertility and, especially on the west, the same woodland characteristics that are found on the Malabar coast proper. While in the last century Tinnevelly was for years a fearful scene of anarchy,—hill chiefs and *colleries,* Mysorean irregulars and English Sepoys, revolted servants and relatives of the Carnatic Nawab, and soldiers of fortune who fought on their own account, reproducing in a coarser and more confused form the phenomena of the Great Coast War; this Province is now chiefly known among us in connexion with the remarkable progress of Christianity within its limits, and the social improvements which have been the steady result of that progress. On the other hand, across the mountain range, the primitive Rajaship of Travancore presents a hardly less satisfactory spectacle as a model Native State, under English protection and auspices, assimilating English resources, including University Education, but unannexed, and reclaimed but undevoured by English "civilianism," as it so nearly was in the last century by Tippoo's appetite for conquest.

Some of the characteristics of the coast line, and o

the lower lands between the Ghats and the coast, have been incidentally mentioned. But, at the risk of some little repetition, it may be well to attempt such a general sketch of their features as is commensurate with my limits. The sharply defined, continuous, and almost straight line of the western range contrasts obviously with the wandering and nearly broken course of the eastern crests. Also, the general proximity of the former to the sea, with the remoteness from it of the latter. Nor is it difficult to perceive that the western lowland is often no plain at all; while the eastern is in no small measure shaped by river deposits. But it must be added, that the double formation—the lower range or "Undercliff," and the final summits prevalent in the Himalaya—is repeated along much of the Eastern Ghats: that the deltas of the great Dekkan rivers rival in fertility, though on a reduced scale, the Gangetic plain: while the character of the coast, the silting up of the river mouths, and the occurrence of a violent surf along the whole eastern sea-margin, afford not a single good harbour between the Mahanuddy and Cape Comorin.

Nor are matters much mended in this respect, on the western side; for though the surf is not here prevalent, except off the southern coast, the character of the geology is fatal to the existence of spacious and landlocked havens. Estuaries indeed there are; but these are treacherous receptacles; and even

Bombay, though presenting from the hills which overlook it one of the most beautiful, indeed magnificent panoramas in the world, is by no means so readily accessible to the sailor as an unprofessional critic might imagine.

How far the Hindoo's dread and hatred of the sea are connected with this absence of good harbours, I must not now attempt to estimate. But I have on a previous occasion pointed out the important influence which, in concert with the monsoon, it exercised upon the course of the Anglo-French contest.*

And the peculiarities of the Malabar coast must

* "But the most serious impediment to warfare on the mainland, and a total obstacle to maritime enterprises, was the Monsoon. This prevails, on the Coromandel coast, from about October to December. It is ushered in generally by gales and thunderstorms of appalling violence: it swells the rivers with surprising rapidity and volume; fills the deep channels of the water-courses, and reduces the country variously to a lake or a morass. The comfortless chilliness of this dreary season, the effect of constant wind and an all-pervading atmosphere of moisture, alternating with capricious bursts of fiery sunshine, can only be appreciated by those who have felt it; and is a most trying experience, whether to a native or to a European constitution. Harbourless, and threatened by the raging surf that rolls ever on these shores, and most fiercely at such a time, the fleets were compelled to quit the coast and seek shelter at a distance, before the Monsoon broke; or to remain at the risk of being beaten to pieces at their anchorage in the open roadsteads, or to brave the perils of the mid-ocean at its wildest season. Thus the settlers were left to themselves and their own resources during a quarter of the year; unaided by that branch of the service on which they so much depended for their military efficiency, and even for their existence in the country of their exile."—*The Mussulman, &c.*, pp. 45, 46.

not be altogether ignored, even in so summary a sketch of Indian Geography as the present.

No maritime *plain*—strictly speaking—at all. A comparatively narrow strip of land between the sea and the Ghats; land broken up, contorted, writhing (as it were) from the rugged and indented sea-margin, till after preliminary gambols of a wilder character it shoots aloft in steep and terrific cliffs, and craggy summits, which I shall not attempt to describe, and whose beauty and majesty must be seen to be understood. Magnificent forests clothe these elevations, and spread far down into the wild country below, and extend their mysterious and treacherous shade for many a mile along the table-land above. Impetuous torrents leap from the mountain sides; rive, and still further diversify, in their headlong career seaward, the uneven and craggy surface of the coast land; and the hollow *nullahs* of the dry season are, on the approach of rain, transformed in a few hours into deep, furious, and impassable cataracts. The thunderstorms of these regions are terrific: the deluges of rain violent, copious, and frequent beyond all comparison elsewhere in India. There is a native saying that, on the Malabar coast the monsoon lasts nine months. Roads throughout the greater part of the country there are none; the character of the ground, and the luxuriance of the forests and jungles alike preclude them. Nature here (to use once more Mr. Buckle's expression) dominates man.

CHAPTER II.

THE EARLIER MOGUL EMPERORS.

BABER, the Founder of the Mogul Empire, was descended, on his father's side, from Timour, on his mother's, from Chengis. His early life was not unlike that of the conqueror of Bajazet, as described by Gibbon. He was but twelve years of age when, by the death of his father, he succeeded to the government of Ferghana, a principality on the Sirr, the ancient Jaxartes. His struggles and adventures during the next ten years are admirably described by himself, and read like a romantic tale of knight-errantry on a grand scale. His sturdy frame, his precocious and versatile abilities, his indomitable energy, his quick observation and lively susceptibility to the curiosities, wonders and beauties of nature, his warm heart and genial temper, and his constant cheerfulness under adverse circumstances, are most attractively displayed in his *Memoirs;* while in a style as far as possible removed from the popular conception of the rude Tartar, he records a series of victories and defeats, of hair-breadth escapes and daring achievements, which well illustrate the old adage, that truth is, after all, often stranger than fiction.

Eventually overmatched, routed, and expelled by the Usbeks, but undismayed and hopeful as ever, and with a select body of attached followers, he marches southward; and making himself master of the kingdom of Cabul, begins to meditate the audacious project of repeating in India, though in a better and more humane spirit, the exploits of his great ancestor Timour.

There the old Empire has long been dissolved, and many separate kingdoms, as usual, have arisen on its ruins. An Afghan sovereign rules at Delhi, and in vain attempts to arrest the impetuous course of the hardy and experienced invaders. A Hindoo Prince, the descendant of a hundred kings, and the hero of a hundred fights, next musters a vast host of his own people, the traditionally warlike Rajputs, and renews the contest, on his own account. But again Baber's fortune prevails: later efforts to resist or subvert his power, a power based not only on violence, but on the generous treatment of the conquered, prove equally fruitless: and just as the mediæval system is breaking up in Europe, and the Age of

Charles the Fifth is opening out an indefinite vista of change and reconstruction in the Western world, the refugee from Central Asia establishes his throne in Hindostan; and, having crowded into a comparatively brief span the experiences and achievements of a long career, expires most characteristically, in the full belief that he has offered his life, in exchange for that of his son, and that the offering has been accepted.

Such, in a few words, was Baber, one of the most fascinating characters in history. Mr. Elphinstone pronounces him to have been "the most admirable prince that ever reigned in Asia." And those who are disposed to dismiss him as a barbarian conqueror, would do well to glance at Lord Jeffrey's account of him, published in the *Edinburgh Review*, on occasion of the appearance of his *Memoirs* in an excellent English version.

If Baber's life, as related by himself, reads like a romance, his son Humayun's, full at once of startling disasters and terrible incidents, and of petty mortifications and grotesque perplexities, may almost be called a melodrama. *His Memoirs* are not an autobiography, though composed by a contemporary, and a follower of his chequered fortunes. Humayun's career has been compared to that of Charles the Second. But Robert of Normandy, or King Stephen, would seem to offer juster and more numerous points of resemblance.

The new Emperor is at once called upon to maintain his authority by the sword. He displays great gallantry, and remarkable though fitful energy; and is at first successful. But his personal defects, the difficulties inherent in his situation, the faithlessness and ambition of his brothers, especially of Kamran, who robs him of Cabul, the base of his military power, (which to stave off immediate hostilities Humayun abandons), and the ability of his Afghan rival, Shir Khan, ruin his cause: and after a succession of crushing defeats, spasmodic struggles on an ever-lessening scale to recover what he has lost, narrow escapes from imprisonment or death, and severe trials in the Great Indian Desert, the dethroned Emperor takes refuge at the Court of Persia. There he is at once patronised, insulted, and persecuted by the haughty king; and is compelled, in hopes of procuring assistance towards regaining his throne, to adopt the *Shia* peculiarities of garb—if not of faith.

With a Persian contingent he at length returns to India, soured by misfortune; wreaks, as he passes, a bloody vengeance on his brother Kamran—whom he regards as the original author of all his calamities; recovers Agra and Delhi, with a small district around those cities; and shortly after dies, from the effects of an accidental fall.

Humayun was by no means a commonplace man.

Some European authors speak of him with respect, if not with admiration. He had gained military distinction under Baber. And while his abilities were good, his temper does not seem to have been originally cruel. But his character, as well as his fate, was to a remarkable extent, a conspicuous foil to that of his great father, and of his still greater son. His energy was intermittent; he was constitutionally indolent and dilatory. "Good-natured"—in the same sense in which Charles the Second was good-natured, not otherwise—he was selfish, capricious, inconsiderate of others, flippant, and distrustful. Hence he was unequal to a sustained series of warlike combinations, or to a self-abnegating political conciliation of heterogeneous and clashing interests. He inspired neither enthusiasm nor respect: his supporters fell off continually; and his very servants slighted him. This during his first troubled reign. The darker hues of his character, on his restoration, must probably be set down to his misfortunes. It is impossible to say how far he might have improved, had his life been prolonged, and his dominion once more established on a less contentious basis—neither Kamran nor Shir Shah being now alive to molest and threaten him. Yet though, with every allowance, it is not easy to admire the man, the life of the adventurer is interesting and instructive. And it is far from improbable, that his successor profited largely by the experience of his errors and their fatal results, as well as by the lessons to be derived from the more prudent, engaging, and prosperous course of the firm, sagacious, and generous Baber.

Disappointing, rather than surprising, as is the sudden collapse of the young Empire under Humayun, its re-establishment, extension, and consolidation under his son present one of the most interesting and remarkable phenomena in history.

Baber, brilliant, like Cortes, as a successful adventurer, did not live to prove his capacity for organization; though his fame, his noble nature, and his judicious treatment both of friends and foes, were not lost upon his posterity, and were reproduced with more abiding results by his grandson.

Acber, the Charlemagne of the dynasty, was the real founder of the imperial system, in its leading and most distinctive features. He was a man well fitted for the purpose of evolving order out of chaos, in such a state of society, and laying deep in the hearts and imaginations of his miscellaneous subjects the well adjusted foundations of a dominion as stable as was compatible with the circumstances of his position, and the precarious event of finding fit and appreciative successors.

Powerful, athletic, and enduring in frame, incredibly active both in body and mind, brave to temerity, passionately devoted to field-sports, enterprising and skilful in war, undesponding in temper, and resolute in maintaining his authority over turbulent and ambitious followers; but temperate, calm, sincere, just, statesmanlike and profoundly benevolent; anxious to promote not only the limits and tranquillity of his dominions, but the welfare and improvement, material, intellectual, and moral of his people;—he stands forth in character and achievements at once as no inferior, in some respects indeed as a more favourable counterpart of the far-famed Frankish reviver of the Holy Roman Empire, and as the greatest and best sovereign of the Mogul, or perhaps of any Eastern monarchy.

Aided and tutored, at the outset, by an able but stern and overbearing captain of his father's lawless army, he assumes independence, and the personal cares of government, at the early age of eighteen. For fifteen years he wages incessant and obstinate wars to recover what he conceives to be the rightful territories of his House. In the course of this arduous struggle he displays great military qualities, the most adventurous gallantry, traits of touching and chivalrous nobleness, and an equally amiable and politic clemency towards his opponents, combined with a conspicuous absence of vindictiveness and cruelty. Save one Hindoo chieftain, (who baffles him by burying himself in the jungles and deserts of

Guzerat), every pretender to empire, north of the Nerbudda, has been permanently subdued, and all Hindostan Proper has submitted to his sway. Candahar and Cabul have been re-annexed. Cashmir has been seized—to become the luxurious Simla of the Mogul Emperors. A severe reverse sustained by his lieutenants, at the hands of the North Eastern tribes of Afghanistan, much resembling in its circumstances our own terrible disaster on the same border, has been followed by a partial reduction of the irreclaimable mountaineers. In the Dekkan, Berar and Candeish have become imperial Provinces; the capital of Ahmednuggur has fallen, after a long and heroic resistance; and the power of that State has been shaken to its foundations; though its complete subversion is reserved for a later time.

Such were the extensive and solid military triumphs of the reign. But though, personally or by his generals, Acber had wielded the sword with so much vigour and success, that his conquests did not require to be repeated, and were secured by the construction of fortifications, the maintenance, remodelling, careful inspection, and regular payment of a large and well-appointed army, and by improvements in the art and implements of war ascribed to the Emperor himself; yet this truly heroic king's heart was in the beneficent works of peace; and he might without hypocrisy have made the profession:—

> "We are brothers, we are men,
> And we conquer but to save!"

Henceforth he proves himself a father to all his subjects, by strict and just personal government, and by the careful choice and vigilant supervision of appropriate ministers and local governors; by removing a variety of unnecessary and obnoxious taxes, especially those which bear hard on the poor, and by reforming the land-revenue system, so as to make it, though from its purer collection more productive to the sovereign, less oppressive to the cultivator; by improving the currency, erecting buildings of general utility, and introducing regular and expeditious posts; by assembling all classes to witness in holiday harmony splendid spectacles, athletic sports, and animating beast-fights—the mimicry of war; by employing Hindoo and Mussulman alike in his service, both warlike and administrative; by keeping up an imposing and accessible Court, frequented and guarded by officers and chieftains of every race, tongue, and creed throughout his ample realm, but refraining (it is *said*) from the usual practice of receiving from those whom he delights to honour the gift that blinds the king's eyes, and tends to impoverish the giver; by treating his Mussulman officers liberally, while strengthening his hold over the Hindoo, through the favour accorded to the gallant and faithful Rajput, and the practice now introduced of imperial intermarriage with the ancient and noble houses of that tribe; by discouraging sectarian fanaticism and religious persecution, attracting to his Court eminent scholars, writers, and teachers, fostering schools and general culture, and encouraging especially the study of *comparative* religious literature, friendly controversy, and serious speculation:—by such means did Acber justly rival the undying fame of Charlemagne, secure the lordship of the soil which his prowess had won, initiate institutions, and infuse a tone, which preserved his Empire in vigour for a century after his death, and deserve the gratitude of his own people, and the reverence of mankind in after ages.

Though a highly-cultivated man, the great Emperor seems to have left not a line of his own composition.* But in his beloved friend and devoted admirer, Abul Fazil, he had an Einhard, who both wrote his life, and compiled in the *Ayeen Akbery* an invaluable and very curious account of the Empire, its topography, administrative arrangements, military resources, the ordering of the Court in all its branches, the Emperor's principles of government, his instructions to his officials, and many interesting particulars connected with his character and habits.

* Ferishta says that he wrote poetry. If so, did it survive him?

Besides other authorities, his son Jehangir's *Memoirs* also throw much additional light both on the man and on the reign.

It remains, after all, more or less problematical, how far the peculiarities of his eclectic religious system were due to the bent of his own speculative temper, how far to a long-sighted policy. His father's enforced conformity to the *Shia* sect may have had something to do with it. Baber himself, too, was a very cosmopolitan religionist. Acber's desire to conciliate the Hindoos undoubtedly told in the same direction. Especially was he anxious to smooth down differences with the Rajputs. But it is hard to believe that his proceedings in this matter were due to policy alone. He had a genuine interest in religious problems for their own sake; a broad sympathy with what he esteemed rational piety and moral excellence, under all forms; and an equally cordial antipathy to what he considered not only mischievous—but perverse, self-opinionated, and unphilosophical exclusiveness. On the whole, those only who are prepared to pronounce with confidence and precision on the balance of motives, and the spiritual condition of Theodoric and the Emperor Frederick the Second, will perhaps feel justified in reading the perplexing riddle of Acber's faith and religious conduct. He died, it seems pretty clear, an ostensible Mussulman. But if so, does this fact meet and answer the main question?*

The excellence of Acber's institutions was attested by the continued prosperity of the Empire under his two immediate successors. Jehangir's reign was indeed at times a troubled one, and exhibited many of the familiar and unfavourable features of Oriental despotism At its opening, one son revolts, and though, on the failure of the attempt, his life is spared, he is never forgiven, and dies in captivity, while his followers are executed by hundreds with barbarous severity. At its close, another son, the future Emperor Shah-Jehan, is goaded into rebellion by the too apparent design of supplanting him in favour of a younger brother. The latter crisis was precipitated by the over-weening influence of the world-renowned Empress, Nur Jehan, a woman whose character was hardly less remarkable than her beauty, or her strangely romantic story. Nor was she satisfied with setting the father and the son at variance. Jehangir was led by her to distrust and ill treat one of his ablest and most powerful nobles; who thereupon, by a *coup de main*, seizes the person of the Emperor in the midst of his camp. But the artful and dashing Sultana contrives to rescue her lord; who, however, does not long survive these agi-

* Is it more conclusive than the final offering of a cock to Æsculapius by Socrates?

tating scenes; and Shah Jehan reigns in his stead, and Nur Jehan is heard of no more in public life.

Candahar too, that perpetual bone of contention between Persia and India, is again lost under Jehangir; and though Shah-Jehan, while still heir-apparent, completes the reduction and conciliation of Rajputana, and makes great progress in the Dekkan, the fruits of his labours in the latter quarter are forfeited by the effects of the rupture with his father.

Thus the first aspect of the reign is not re-assuring for the stability of the dynasty; and it almost seems as though Humayun's cycle of ruin both to the Emperor and to the Empire were about to recur. Yet this impression I believe to be, in reality, most erroneous. Acber had effectually and finally disposed of all the older claimants to the throne of Hindostan. An Oriental monarchy, if otherwise well organised, can stand much strain in the way of what, while we cannot but pronounce them to be civil wars, are regarded in the East as inevitable, —not to say normal—family quarrels, of a violent perhaps, but by no means necessarily of a very dangerous, much less destructive tendency to the *raj* itself.

They are the Asiatic form of the *Fronde* cabals and tumults. Or, to take an earlier illustration, the Anglo-Norman Power was not dissolved, how far was it imperilled, or even weakened, by the contests between the Conqueror's sons? However that may have been, certain it is, that more general and more radical causes of decay than the *simultates* and *jurgia* of the Zenana were required to shake a dominion, that had now attained a steady and strong hold on the imagination, if not on the affections, of the natives of India, and that was skilfully adapted to foster the interests both of the native, and of the foreign adventurer. It is equally clear, that the world outside India—including Europe—now looked with admiration and awe upon the august fabric of Mogul Imperialism; and contemporary evidence of this fact is both abundant and precise.

This double aspect of the reign is reflected in, and explained by, the personal character of the Emperor—

"Nil fuit unquam
Sic impar sibi."

Jehangir has been compared with his contemporary James the First—"the wisest fool in Christendom" —who sent a formal embassy to the court of his Asiatic brother. And certainly a considerable resemblance between the two men may be traced. Their exalted theories and well-rounded periods about the divinely delegated functions of sovereignty, their passionate and pedantic indignation against subjects convicted or suspected of disaffection, their amusing pride in petty devices of kingcraft, their lingering belief in magic, their notable displays of selfishness and puerile meanness, their favoritism and maudlin sentimentality—especially in their cups, their shrewd and coarse sayings, and frequent lack of self-respect, poorly compensated by an affectation of dignity in public:—these and other circumstances may be observed, in which poor human nature, aspiring to a God-like attitude on two such different stages, exhibited contemporaneously, in either case, an equally extraordinary and grotesque falling off in practice from the sublime ideal.

Still Jehangir, though gossiped over and laughed at privately in his capital, sustained in an atmosphere congenial to the freaks of despotism the character and power of the Great Mogul, far more successfully than James was able to hold his own as King of England.

For, on the other hand, the character and conduct of the Asiatic monarch present, on a closer inspection, a much more favourable appearance. He undoubtedly had a high view, not only of his privileges, but of his duties as a sovereign, and a sincere desire to rule his people well. It is impossible to believe that the political disquisitions and pious sentiments on this subject, which abound in his rambling autobiography, however overstrained, rhetorically amplified, and too often forgotten in actual life, are mere cant. Nor was his administration, on the whole, either oppressive or imbecile. His admiration for his father's great qualities and wise dispositions was both profound and salutary. Even his occasional fits of revolting barbarity were not wanton, but were prompted by his sense of the propriety of maintaining unimpaired his legitimate authority. And they diminished in frequency and violence as he grew older, in which respect he contrasts favourably with too many tyrants both Oriental and Occidental. His passion for Nur Jehan was inordinate, and, as usual, her kinsmen were great gainers by it. And he had originally cleared the way for her becoming his consort by a foul, Uriah-like murder of her former husband. But his uxorious devotion to her was *toto cœlo* removed from the contemptible, nauseous, and pernicious fondness of James for Buckingham and others. The destined Empress was a highly gifted woman both in personal charms, in taste, in intellect, and in moral resolution and courage. Nor, where her ascendancy was not in peril, does she seem to have been otherwise than actively beneficent in her influence. Her courage she at once proved by resenting so strongly the fate of her husband, that, though Jehangir had consigned her to his harem, it was long before he ventured—or was inclined—to raise her to the contemplated dignity. After becoming his wife, however, she ruled his heart alone, and to the end. And her power, in spite of the final troubles excited by her jealousy, seems to have been beneficial both to the character of her husband, and to the interests of his subjects. Her father was a capable and honest minister. And her brother dissociated himself from her schemes, and aided the accession of Shah Jehan.

The graceful adornments of the Mogul court, which long continued to attract the admiration of Europeans, were not a little due to her; while, unlike most fine ladies, she was economical as well as tasteful in her devices. It was not in her company that the Emperor indulged in the private drinking bouts, which she probably did much to render less frequent, instead of sympathising in the practice, after the fashion set at the English court, and described by an eye witness not less graphically, than Sir Thomas Roe has recorded the incidents of his *petits soupers* with Jehangir. The Emperor, too, though a more decided Mussulman than his father, was lenient and tolerant, and is even said to have had affinities with Christianity.

On the whole, Jehangir seems to have been by no means a bad king, judged from an European point of view; and very much above the average of Oriental sovereigns; while the disturbances of his reign were episodical, and of short duration.

Under Shah Jehan the Empire attained its zenith. At no other period was it so tranquil, well-ordered, and thriving in its older Indian Provinces; never were the feudatory princes of Rajputana more zealously devoted to the imperial service: never was the Court more splendid, or the Emperor more powerful, wealthy, or generally respected. Nor was the conventional idea of the Great Mogul—as the Sovereign of India, and of India alone—ever so near being realised. For while, after a partially successful effort to recover the extra-Indian territories of his ancestors, Shah Jehan finally, in the spirit of Hadrian, abandoned regions too difficult, costly, and unproductive to be profitably retained; on the other hand,—*Southward*, the course of empire held its way. The monarchy of Ahmednuggur, which Acber had assailed, and Shah Jehan himself, during his father's reign, had been on the point of annihilating, was now finally extinguished, in spite of the gallant efforts of its last champion, Shahji, the father of the great Sivaji. Bijapoor and Golconda, the two remaining Afghan kingdoms of the Dekkan, were reduced to tributary States; a Mogul party was established in each; the Prime Minister of Golconda transferred his obedience and invaluable services to the Emperor; and Shah Jehan began to talk the language of a master, interfering with the internal policy of Golconda, and the question of regal succession at Bijapoor. Yet it does not appear that he contemplated the extinction of these kingdoms—at least at once, and before that step could be prudently taken.

The imperial Provinces in the Dekkan were now elaborately surveyed, and the revenue system of Acber was introduced into them.

Unremitting, till towards the close of his reign, in

his personal attention to business, the Emperor was most happy also in the choice of his servants (among whom Saad Ullah Khan is pronounced by Mr. Elphinstone to have been "the most able and upright minister that ever appeared in India"), and in the employment of his sons, who for many years implicitly obeyed and cordially served him, fighting against the common enemy on the frontier.

Shah Jehan was a rather stricter Mussulman than his father. But, though the Mahometan was encouraged, the Hindoo was not molested.

Nur Jehan had been handsomely pensioned off; and a formidable rebellion early in the reign was promptly quelled. After which mildness and graceful munificence became the general order of the day.

That Shah Jehan was able, without imposing new taxes, or resorting to other oppressive measures, to lavish on one occasion alone largesse to the estimated amount of £1,600,000; to maintain his royal establishments on an unexampled scale of magnificence, and a regular army of 200,000 horsemen; to construct the most beautiful and costly edifices in India, including the celebrated *Taj Mahal;* to build a new and splendid capital at Delhi; to devote to the decoration of the famous peacock throne, jewels, &c., variously valued at from four to six and a half millions sterling; and, after all, to amass a reserve treasure of some £20,000,000, will (even if some exaggeration lurk in the items) give a not unfair idea of his ability, resources, and reputation, before his abrupt and tota eclipse.

But this brilliant prospect was soon to be overclouded.

Hitherto five sovereigns had occupied the Mogul throne, each succeeding his father, and all exhibiting, in spite of strongly marked individuality, a decided, and on the whole a favorable family likeness. All had been men of ability, energy, determination, and (Humayun perhaps excepted, though great allowances must be made even for him) of notable governing qualities. All had been, so to speak, men of the world; for Orientals, at least, open and simple in character, hearty and frank in demeanor, straightforward and explicit in their general aims, mostly free from the cruel propensities and bloodthirsty practices commonly and too justly associated with the idea of an Eastern despot; tolerant in the delicate matter of religion; rather lax, to say the least, in their adhesion to Mahometanism. Such men were well adapted to sway the destinies, and develop the resources of such an Empire; and to retain a hold over the heterogeneous and sensitive population comprised within its spacious limits.

But the time had now come when a very different system was to be pursued by a Prince of a very different temper.

As Shah Jehan grew old, and advancing years and luxury relaxed the vigour of his faculties, the question of the succession became more and more serious. He had four sons, all of mature age, versed in affairs, ambitious, and little inclined to mutual forbearance and concession when the great prize of empire was at stake. Morad, the youngest, was a man of slender ability, and, though brave, an inveterate sensualist. Shuja, the second, was naturally clever, but had impaired his talents by self-indulgence, and his reputation and popularity with his co-religionists by leaning to the *Shia* sect. Dara, the eldest, was a bold, open-handed and open-hearted Prince, but rash and overbearing. He was also still more un-orthodox than Shuja, and had committed himself by broaching, in writing, an eclectic scheme for uniting the Hindoo and Mahometan religions. He was, however, a favourite with the Hindoos.

Aurungzib, the third brother, was not only a singular contrast to the rest, but a novel and unique phenomenon in the Mogul House. Gentle, unassuming, even humble in manner, courteous and considerate in his general intercourse, yet dignified and princely on occasion; simple and self-denying in his daily life, austere in morals, and a sincere zealot for the *Sunnee* faith, but secretly glowing with unquenchable ambition for the highest worldly station; wary, calculating and cold-blooded, yet susceptible of enthusiasm both on the secular battle-field, and in the subtler and more ideal contest for the ascendancy of Islam; sedulous in attaching to his interests the unpronounced and the wavering, in detecting and allaying germinant opposition, in perplexing, dividing, and confounding open adversaries; dark and devious in his own machinations, consummately cunning in penetrating and over-reaching those of others, and infinitely suspicious of all men; inflexible and utterly untrammelled by moral or humane considerations in the pursuit of his objects, and while, like Philip the Second, gaining support and enlisting partizan devotion as the Champion of the Faith, ready to risk the exhaustion and dismemberment of the Empire itself, rather than forego the attempt to enforce his religious formula; like the same sovereign, indefatigable in attention to the minutest details of business, and capable of heroic perseverance in a losing game, but equally destitute of broad statesmanlike views, and profound insight into the more general and permanent workings of human character, the unwritten limiting principles of government, the complexion of the times, and the consequent possibilities of things; well trained and well informed in the craft of regular warfare, and ever ready to incur toil, hardship, and danger when great personal or public interests summoned him to the field, but little conscious as yet that peculiar circumstances and the extemporised devices of genius might ultimately prove too strong even for such a general, wielding the whole force of the State;—such was Aurungzib, a man percisely adapted to gain the day over all his brothers; to track his unfaltering way, through a cloud of mysterious intrigue and a sea of blood, to a throne which had hitherto been regularly and peacefully transmitted in his family; to reverse the traditional and characteristically mild policy of his predecessors; to rule the empire with energy and dexterity; and, in the end, through the influence not only of his cankering and infectious vices, and his uncompromising and fatal prejudices, but even of his very virtues, to break it in pieces like a potter's vessel!

CHAPTER III.

THE MOGUL GOVERNMENT.

A SHORT account of the imperial system will make the following narrative more intelligible.

The power of the Emperor was theoretically absolute. The property, the liberty, the lives of his subjects were at his unconditional disposal. According to the received courtly doctrine, he was the exclusive owner of the whole soil of the Empire. He could impose, enhance, and abolish taxes at his pleasure. He could establish monopolies, and regulate and prohibit commerce and manufactures. He could compel the people of one district to migrate to another. He could exact military service, and levy military contributions, to an indefinite extent. Patronage, both civil and military, was entirely in his hands. He could raise a man of the lowest class, and of no experience, to the highest rank, and to the most important functions. And the most exalted officials he could degrade *suo nutu*. He could punish any of his subjects with the most capricious and extreme severity;—fine, imprison, torture, mutilate, put them to death, on mere suspicion, or in the indulgence of mere passion.

The extent of his territories, the pomp of his Court, the vast number and splendid equipments of his armies, the conventionally submissive tone of his ministers, his provincial rulers, and his generals, the hyperbolical lordliness of his swelling titles, and, in most cases until the decline of the Empire, the ability and vigour which he displayed in his personally conducted government, combined to give an impression of awful reality and unfaltering force to these formidable prerogatives.

Nor could it be otherwise, seeing that the sword had given the Mogul the empire of India; that no permanent landed aristocracy, such as has arisen in Teutonic communities, for some time existed, to make constant head against Imperial despotism; that collective popular organization for a similar purpose was quite out of the question; that the social compact was an unhistorical European speculation, the first conditions of which were inconceivable to an Asiatic; that neither the principles of Islam nor the precedents of Oriental rule favoured the limitation of the powers essentially reserved to a sovereign who, from the nature of the case, was peculiarly and permanently in the position (as Dr.

Arnold would have said) of the general of an army of occupation in a conquered country.

But if the ideal power of the Emperor was so unrestricted, the actual checks on its exercise were numerous and effective. The general circumstances of his political situation,—as a Mussulman alien in the midst of a vast Hindoo population, a large proportion of which was by no means unwarlike, and a Mogul ruling over fiery and turbulent Afghans, the memory of whose domination was fresh and suggestive; his dependence for the maintenance of his authority, and the execution of his decrees, upon ministers, satraps, generals, and ultimately upon his troops; the public opinion, at least the general and well-ascertained sentiments and the strong prejudices of his subjects, whether Mahometan or Hindoo; the constantly impending danger of insurrection, or of violent attempts to redress public or avenge private grievances, if not to remove the despotic author or favourer of them; the continuous tradition of moderate, and on the whole equitable and beneficent rule, established even in the heat of conquest by Baber, developed, systematised, and rationally expounded under Acber, and strengthened by the almost superstitious reverence commonly paid to custom in India; and last not least, the strong sense, forbearing temper, and liberal views of most of the Emperors, obviated many of the evils of despotism, and combined not so much to cramp its energies, as to give them a safe, if not always a humane direction.

Though internally the Empire was rarely, before the time of Aurungzib, disturbed by commotion and revolution, the work of conquest went on steadily, almost unceasingly, on the frontiers. Rebels were crushed, at times, with merciless severity, (for the generous and bold policy of Acber in forgiving even *such* offenders was not always in vogue:) criminals were dealt with both summarily and severely: capricious and revolting cruelties towards individuals were not unfrequent on the part of the less enlightened and virtuous sovereigns: and mere suspicion was too often pretext enough for degrading and oppressing distinguished officials. Still the general conduct of the Mogul Rulers not only exhibited no approach to the proverbial standard of Oriental tyranny, but would (I suspect) sustain a favourable comparison with that of too many European Cæsars, Saviours of Society, Heroes of *coups d'état*, and Paternal Despots, whether in ancient or in modern times.

Nor must it in this connexion be forgotten, that Aurungzib himself died before we were well rid of the danger of Stuart restoration; and more than a century before our Statute Book was purged of laws, the ingenious cruelty of which would have excited the astonishment and contempt, if not the horror, even of that stern and unscrupulous sovereign.

It may be well to develop a little more fully the nature and operation of each of the above-mentioned checks on the otherwise unlimited power of the Great Mogul.

Foremost among them was, of course, the danger of assassination and insurrection. It is not only in Turkey that irresponsible despotism is tempered by the fact, or the fear, of the bow-string. The elaborate precautions as to the cooking, serving, and pregustation of his food, which occur in Abul Fazil's account of the imperial kitchen, betray a jealous fear lest the Emperor might be poisoned at his meals. The absence of any notice of such attempts,* during the great period of the Empire, is a tolerable proof that the government was neither tyrannical nor cruel. This, as well as a rank crop of other bad practices, flourished in the decline of the dynasty; and Orme, early in his narrative, records a whole string of murders of rulers in the South, too closely corresponding to similar events that I shall have to mention at Delhi.

But besides the summary way of assassination, the more devious, but equally dangerous avenue of rebellion, lay ever open to an ambitious chief, or an

* Baber gives a long account of an attempt to poison him, contrived by Sultan Ibrahim's mother.

outraged and oppressed people. The same circumstance that made Theodoric lenient and fair, or as bigots would think, over-indulgent to the majority of his subjects, and very circumspect in his general conduct, operated in the case of the Moguls. They differed in religion from the bulk of their people; and they were the intrusive leaders of hosts of northern barbarians, whose taste for plunder and oppression needed no stimulating, and might, by the infection of bad example, soon become ungovernable. To ill-treat the Hindoo was dangerous. To encourage a war at once of race and of religion, between the conquerors and the conquered, was still more dangerous. Soon the practice of leniency being established, the temper followed; and the large-hearted Acber promoted a theological eclecticism, which was more successful in its political application, than in its general adoption as a religious system. Hindoos were exempted from the odious distinctive tax on "unbelievers," and freely admitted to both civil functions and military commands. After which any general oppression of the Hindoo race and religion, as such, would have been, of course, indefinitely more rash and impracticable than before, and would in all probability have overthrown the dynasty in any age, and however otherwise just and wise the administration might have been. And, in fact, what in the West would have been deemed a very trifling amount of such oppression, sufficed, under the powerful and highly-gifted Emperor Aurungzib, to alienate the Rajput, to exasperate the Jat, to give a plausible colour and vast help to Sivaji's schemes of independence, and eventually to sap the foundations of the imperial power.

Another check was found in the constitution of the government. As normally in the East, the great functionaries of the sovereign's ideally unrestricted will, were, in reality, only so far subservient to him, as either they chose to be, or as their circumstances and his personal character combined compelled them to be. By playing off one against another, and by securing either their attachment or that of their dependents, a clever and uncautious Emperor might reduce them to almost unlimited subserviency. But the extent of the power which he nominally wielded, was, in turn, entrusted in its degree to his ministers and lieutenants. And the very simplicity of administrative despotism favoured its overthrow, or its curtailment, by a resolute satrap or an ambitious commander-in-chief. A military government is always exposed to such military risks; and, to be secure, it must be forbearing.

Another check was one, which has been too often forgotten by those who have speculated upon Indian subjects. It has become almost a common place, that there was no hereditary aristocracy in the Mogul

Empire. That there was no peerage, of the same special character, and with the same constitutional rights, powers, and privileges, as that of our own and other European countries in modern times, is, of course, true enough. But if, in a Homeric community, *οἱ ἀμφὶ βασιλέα*—was an intelligible and allowable periphrasis for the King himself; if, in mediæval times, the conduct of great conquerors and feudal sovereigns, even when little prescribed by strictly constitutional canons, was to a very great extent dependent upon the sympathy and approval of his Comites, Duces, Witan, Earls, Council; if, in modern days, the important change in the form of government in British India from that by the Governor-General *and*—to that by the same officer *in* Council, has often resulted in little diminution of the influence exercised by his subordinates over the measures of the Supreme Government: so the Great Mogul, however careful to retain personally the reins of empire, and to decide for himself in the last resort, was accustomed to consult, and be greatly guided by the opinion of what we may venture, without any abuse or over-straining of language, to call his Great Council of Ministers, Omrahs, and other persons of position, distinction, or special knowledge.

Nor was this the only approach to aristocracy, and aristocratic influence on royal counsels, as they exist, or have existed, among us. Though the Emperor could raise the beggar from the dunghill, and set him among princes; and though the title and dignity of Omrah, Khan, or Bahadur, were, as much as those of definite offices, essentially personal, not family possessions, or (as we might say) titles of life nobility, created by royal grant on each occasion; yet four circumstances must be observed of a contrary tendency.

(1). As in Europe, in early times, according to Mr. Hallam, ancient and distinguished lineage was much considered; and such honours consequently had a constant tendency to run in the same houses; until, in the later days of the Empire, even purely official titles became strictly hereditary, and their holders, as in Europe, became politically independent.

(2). Even in the case of a *novus homo* who had faithfully served the Emperor in an important station, though on his death not only did his official appointment, but even his personal property, of right lapse to the Crown, and his honorary title of Omrah or otherwise expired; yet it became customary to forego or commute the rights of the fisc, on behalf of the family of the deceased; to employ his descendants in the imperial service; and, if not at once, after a time, to re-ennoble the house by a fresh creation in favour of the new *employé.*

(3). Liberal grants of land or its revenues in perpetuity were not unfrequently made by the Emperors, not only for charitable or religious purposes to corporations, but in return for distinguished services to individuals or families. Thus gradually, as in Europe, the great and historic houses became, in spite of the theory which gave all the land to the head of the State, rooted in, and the virtual, if not the technical, proprietors of the soil. And thus, by degrees, not only the owner of *Enam* lands, or those avowedly ceded in propriety; but even the *Jaghiredar*, or beneficiary tenant, if other circumstances were favourable, came to acquire much of the consideration, and to exert much of the control over the policy of government, of the mediæval baron, or the modern nobleman, or many-acred squire.

(4). And when, from the regular and completely incorporated Provinces of the Empire, we pass to the outlying Principalities, which were more loosely, though very really connected with it, we shall find that an almost exact counterpart of middle-age feudal society, and its vague but stout protest against royal absolutism prevailed, especially in Rajputana. Colonel Tod may, indeed, in confirmation of a cherished theory, and in his enthusiastic desire to enlist the sympathies of Englishmen on behalf of his favourite race, by extenuating the remoteness of their social condition from our own, have drawn out too elaborately the lineaments of a feudal constitution in Ajmir. But, if so, he has done little more than repeat the error which was fashionable when he wrote; the error of those, who by centuries have antedated the existence, have toned off most unhistorically the diversities, and have exaggerated or fixed far too rigidly the features, of Western feudalism. And the fact remains, so similar to what Guizot and others have pointed out as characteristic of the great days of aristocratic ascendancy in Europe, that the Rajput Rajas not only gave their daughters in marriage to the Emperor, and filled the highest offices in the State; but continued throughout, though tributary in money and men, otherwise virtually independent local sovereigns, or *haute noblesse* of the first order, and most unshackled condition; and transmitting all their patriarchal privileges from father to son, according to their tribal institutions, were also, from generation to generation, the proud and higly-prized mainstays of the monarchy, and the hereditary protectors of the Hindoo interest in the Imperial Council Chamber: and when, in an evil hour, Aurungzib estranged them, the power of his house received a mortal blow, and rapidly declined, to rise no more.

Directly, of course, the great body of the people had little or no constitutional power in the State. Their chief functions were to hear, to obey, to toil, and to suffer. They might, indeed, appeal against oppression; and the voice, even of the lowliest, was at times listened to and answered by the redress of evils inflicted by powerful officials or other great men, and even of hardships emanating from the Emperor himself. But such a remedy was too difficult, too precarious, and too dangerous, to be considered a practically effective privilege. Still the conventional and old-established usages of the people, especially in the matters of religious liberty, property, and the village constitution, however much the Emperor might be inclined to regard them as—in Stuart phraseology—"graces" rather than rights antecedent to, and in limitation of the imperial power, imposed considerable restraint on the exercise of that power. And what was to be feared from the determination and despair of those, whom European sciolism long afterwards was fond of calling "the mild Hindoos," when incited and combined by a man of genius, and organised under their own sympathising chieftain, will be seen as we proceed, and might have been anticipated by those capable of reading the profounder lessons of human nature, and the signs of the times in which Aurungzib and his predecessors flourished.

Though the general conduct of the Government towards its subjects was mild, not the less was the character of the Government itself primarily and essentially military. The Emperor was, indeed, the supreme civil magistrate and the source of all civil authority. He was also in some sense throughout, in a very real sense under such a prince as Acber, the

Father of his people. But he was more especially, conspicuously, and on all occasions the Generalissimo of the Empire. The sonorous titles which he assumed —as Conqueror of the World, &c.—were mostly military. The commander-in-chief of his armies was the most exalted of his subjects. The provincial governors were almost invariably, in better times, chosen for their military ability; and their office, like his own, was more directly conversant with military administration; resembling in this, not a little, that of the rulers of Themes in the Byzantine Empire, William the Norman's earls, Cromwell's major-generals, and Buonaparte's upstart kings. The *quasi*-aristocracy of the Empire, the body of Omrahs and Mansubdars contained, indeed, in the latter class especially, not only men who had gained distinction in war, but who, from services or merits of a different description, had been ennobled by being raised to the grade of nominal commanders of a specified body of soldiers. But the great passport to rank, power, and wealth was military fame. The high political position of the Rajput Rajas, the selection of their daughters to mate with the Mogul Princes, was no doubt due not only to their long descent and illustrious reputation throughout the Peninsula, but to the hereditary fighting qualities of the whole Rajput race, and the number of serviceable soldiers that were thus more securely bound to the imperial interests.

The Mogul Court, again, when stationary at the capital, whether at Agra or at Delhi, wore much the semblance of a grand military council chamber. And the very amusements of the Court savoured of war. Throughout the week large musters of troops, inspections of their equipments, inquiries into the state and deserts of their officers, were conducted periodically by the Emperor in person, or under his immediate eye. A vast number of half-military attendants was retained to fight publicly in the immediate precincts of the palace as gladiators, or against wild beasts. Not only did the pursuits of the chase keep up the combative spirit of the Emperor and his courtiers and officers, but the same animals made sport in the Durbar by their encounters with each other in time of peace, and were employed, during war, in serious field operations. Full particulars on this subject, as to the elephants and camels, are supplied in the *Ayeen Akbery*.

The imperial progresses, too, were substantially military promenades; so numerous and amply equipped were the attendant levies (including both heavy and light artillery), so elaborately organised was the order of the march and of the encampment. Except, indeed, in the number of regular troops employed on either occasion, there seems to have been little difference between a peaceful migration to Cashmir, or an equally peaceful inspection of the Provinces, and a campaign, such as Aurungzib's in the Dekkan, undertaken for the suppression of a formidable rebellion, or the prosecution of a grand scheme of conquest and annexation.

The same essentially military character is disclosed in the general conduct of the administration. The judicial office is constantly exercised in the style of a drum-head court martial rather than of a civil court. And not only were soldiers habitually employed where we should use policemen; but, as in India even under our own rule, not to say in Ireland, the ugly features of foreign occupation by the sword, and a too prevalent disposition to lawlessness, were revealed in the fact that the police themselves were at least half soldiers.

Thus, again, the vast resources of the State were in a great measure absorbed by military requirements; and when the disorders and loss of revenue entailed by the interminable Maratha war made it impossible for Acber's careful plan of punctually paying the troops and their officers to be maintained, the doom of the dynasty was sealed, and the fabric of government fell rapidly to pieces. It may be added that in the minute and comprehensive statistical survey of the Empire which was compiled by Abul Fazil, the most prominent and important point seems constantly to be the number of regular or irregular soldiers liable to be supplied by each district to the imperial service.

Lastly, the history of the Empire during its most

flourishing period is in strict accordance with the above view. Even the lazy and luxurious Jehangir bore arms, though with little credit. But all the other five Emperors were distinguished, indefatigable, and more or less successful generals. Circumstances, indeed, combined with grave personal errors, caused Humayun to miscarry in his contest with Shir Khan, and foiled all Aurungzib's attempts to subjugate the Marathas. And Shah Jehan in his later years became a man of peace, and suffered himself at last to be deposed without striking a blow to sustain his earlier reputation in war. But what royal dynasty can exhibit a prouder or more remarkable muster-roll of six consecutive fighting sovereigns, among whom the first is Baber, the precocious, ubiquitous, and irrepressible founder of the Empire; the third Acber, who re-founded and extended it in wars that may challenge comparison with those of Charles the Great, and who thoroughly remodelled the military system; the sixth Alumgir, who, a warrior from his youth upwards, wore out the last twenty-three years of a long and agitated life in one continuous and laborious campaign; and died (so to speak) in harness, and unsated with war, at the advanced age of eighty-eight?

So much for the general character and policy of the Government. Its form was, as usually among Orientals, extremely simple. The Emperor conducted the general administration through a variety of ministers, the chief of whom were the Vizier, or Prime Minister, the Amir-ul-omrah, or Commander-in-chief, the Dewan, or Chancellor of the Exchequer, and the Kotwal, or head of the police (or of the Home Office); who also collectively formed his Cabinet Council, and assisted him with their advice; though the ultimate decision of each matter rested, as I have said, absolutely with himself. To throw greater light upon important and intricate subjects, unofficial persons of consequence, and others who possessed special knowledge, were at times summoned.

From lower courts, from oppressive ministers, and from provincial governors, an appeal lay to the Emperor in person, sitting daily as Judge in the *Amkas*, or Great Audience Hall of the capital, or in its counterpart elsewhere.

I may mention, that he was also theoretically Caliph, and as such Pontifex Maximus, not to say Pope, over his Mussulman subjects; a function which justified, or seemed to justify, Acber in his religious innovations; though it must be remembered, that to Indian Mahometans of the *Shia* sect the Emperor, as a *Sunnee*, was in fact a heretic. This circumstance it is important to bear in mind, both because it still further illustrates what has been already said as to the expediency of moderate counsels suggested by the religious leanings of his subjects; and because it affords some semblance of extenuation for Aurungzib's rigorous and aggressive policy towards the Mahometan kings of Bijapoor and Golconda. Nor must the absence of organised ecclesiastical opposition to the imperial will, analogous to that of Popes and Prelates in the West, be forgotten, as due to the lofty pretensions of the Emperor, and the lack, among Musulmans, of any regular religious hierarchy. From time to time there were serious disturbances, even rebellions, raised by fanatical devotees and their followers. But continuous politico-ecclesiastical rivalry with the Holy Eastern Emperor was incompatible with the constitution alike of the State and of the Church.

Returning to purely secular matters, there were at the capital other Judges, who sat as assessors with the sovereign, or who separately pronounced judgment, assisted by a *cazi*, or expounder of the law.

A variety of new and empty official titles was from time to time, and especially in the decline of the Empire, extemporised at Court; either in obedience to the same instinct that produced a similar invention of grandiloquent appellations at the Byzantine capital in the Middle Ages, or to provide for the pressing claims to patronage and distinction of important individuals, or again to secure their resignation of some definite office, which it was thought desirable to commit to other hands.

Such is an outline of the central government and its functions.

The Empire was divided into Provinces, called *subahs*, each ruled by an officer termed originally *sipah-salar*. Under Acber there were fifteen of these Provinces: twelve north of the Nerbudda, three in the Dekkan. Aurungzib's conquests added three more in the latter region. In later times the *sipah-salars* became *nawabs* (or Nabobs as the English called them); and several Provinces were consolidated under one general *Subahdar* or Viceroy. Thus the whole Dekkan became the *subahdary*, or as the English again corruptly called it, the *subah*, of the virtually independent Viceroy, Nizam-ul-Mulk, known to us, once more improperly, as *The Nizam*. The Viceroy, in Mr. Elphinstone's words, "had the complete control, civil and military, subject to the instructions of the Emperor." He was removable at the pleasure of his august master; but in later times, as in the case just mentioned, he was apt, not only to retain his post for life, but to convert it into an independent principality. This happened not only in the Dekkan, but in Bengal and Oude, the ruler of the last being also, for some time, standing Vizier of the Empire.

Originally the Viceroys necessarily administered the Provinces themselves. But after Aurungzib, the corrupt and dangerous practice crept in of sending thither a deputy; while the Subahdar continued at

Court, enjoying there a luxurious life, receiving the liberal *douceurs* that he could always command for the exercise of his influence, or intriguing on his own behalf against the rivals and enemies who threatened to supplant him in the Emperor's good graces, and to procure his *recall* before he had actually set out for his neglected but lucrative field of labour. An equally objectionable custom arose about the same period, of allowing or acquiescing in provincial pluralities,—so to speak. Thus again, as we shall see, Nizam-ul-Mulk was at one period at once Viceroy of the Dekkan, and of Malwa, as well as Vizier of the Empire; and though he resigned the last post for another high-sounding title, yet he clung afterwards, until the course of events deprived him of it, to a third vice-royalty,—that of Guzerat, which he had acquired by expelling, in the Emperor's name, its former rebellious governor.

The imperial "edicts," says Colonel Dow, "were transmitted to every district; they were publicly read, and registered in the courts of justice." But how far were they observed at a safe distance from "the master's eye?" The Emperor, indeed, periodically dispatched emissaries, somewhat after the fashion of Charlemagne's *missi Dominici*, as commissioners of enquiry, with the object of bringing to light abuses and misgovernment, and maintaining the uniformity and healthy action of the whole imperial system. But Bernier represents them —under Aurungzib—as very venal, and as having played habitually into the hands of those upon whom they were intended to act as a check.

Under the *Subahdars*, as I have said, were the *Nawabs*, or rulers of single Provinces, who in turn presided over the *Foujdars*, or military commanders of smaller districts, "whose authority," again to quote Mr. Elphinstone, "extended over the local soldiery or militia, and over all military establishments and lands assigned to military purposes, as well as over the regular troops within their jurisdiction; and whose duty it was to suppress all disorders that required force within the same limits."

The *Subahdar*, the *Nawab*, and probably the *Foujdar*, had each a *Dewan*, or finance minister, who, in the first case at least, was, though subject to the authority of the Viceroy, appointed by the Emperor; and as such, and as being commonly a Hindoo, was probably designed to serve as a spy upon his superior officer. All functionaries, down to the lowest stage in the official hierarchy, were supposed to be nominated by the Head of the State, or at least confirmed in their office, after being selected and provisionally installed by their immediate superior. But here again, as the personal vigour and vigilance of the sovereigns diminished, the theory was habitually ignored; though it always supplied malcontents or provincial rebels with a pretext for disputing the authority of the more or less irregularly-created functionary, and his too assuming patron. This is the gist of the long diplomatic controversy between the French and the English in the days of Dupleix. As in that case, forged *firmans* of appointment or ratification from Delhi were constantly received with mock solemnity from a mock envoy, and impudently bandied about to deceive the unwary, to reassure the hesitating, and to strengthen usurpation with a false gloss of regularity.

With the limitations already mentioned, the absolute power wielded by the Emperor was delegated, in his more contracted sphere, to the Viceroy; and when his tribute was paid, the Nawab was, on a still smaller scale, almost equally unrestricted in the general exercise of his authority. Hence, although the ability, activity, and resolution of the earlier sovereigns to a great extent obviated the danger, there could not but be, in the very nature of such a government, a strong tendency to insubordination and ultimate dissolution And it is interesting to find, that a precaution very similar to William the Conqueror's plan of scattering his great barons' manors in different parts of the country, and in districts over which others than the grantees of those manors held sway as earls, was adopted by the Mogul Emperors. *Jaghires*, or beneficiary holdings, were assigned within the area of one *subahdary* to ministers, military commanders, or nobles, otherwise unconnected with the region. Thus the interests of the Viceroy and the powerful *Jaghiredar* were divided; each would be, to a certain extent, a restraint upon the other; and Orme goes so far as to assert, that the Emperors deliberately counted upon the discord thence ensuing, as a means of preserving their own power. Perhaps this is an afterthought. But certain it is that the later and more imbecile sovereigns went even further; and in the hope of retaining some fragment of an authority that was passing rapidly out of their hands for ever, habitually played off one ruler and commander against another; and secretly incited jealousies, rivalry, and hostility, each stage of which hastened the destruction of the whole political system. To such desperate palliatives for their enforced subservience to their own delegates were these degenerate monarchs reduced! *Nec vitia, nec remedia ferre potuerunt!*

In the better days of the Empire, both the satraps and their subordinates were carefully selected, and often exhibited a copy of their master's virtues. But even then, a bad choice must have been not unfrequent; and the people in such a case suffered cruelly. The remoteness of the seat of government from so many parts of the Empire, the difficulty and tardiness of communication, the practice of silencing the voice of the imperial itinerant commissioners by bribes, the terrorising and repressive influence of local power, and the eagerness of a ruler, whose tenure of office was uncertain and might be very short, to make the most of present opportunities, as well as the expensive habits and love of a large and costly following, combined to make the man, who ought to have been the protector, the taskmaster and plague of the unhappy provincials.

The evil grew at once more common and more severe, as the sovereign's personal rule was exchanged for that of ambitious and unprincipled ministers, successful military adventurers, and greedy and irresponsible favourites. For then the local governors came to be appointed under the same influences, often by direct bribery; and too faithfully acted in the spirit of their patrons, and of their own antecedents. Bernier, indeed, asserts that even in the earlier part of Aurungzib's reign the *subahdarys* were habitually farmed. But such seems not to be the view of Colonel Dow and other authors; and I suspect that the lively and thoughtful Frenchman has generalised too hastily on this, as on some other subjects.

In a descending scale, the oppression and extortion of the Subahdar were too often repeated by the Nawab, the Foujdar, the Zemindar, and the Poligar; though the constitution of the village communities, and the sentiments of their members, imposed a considerable check on the conduct of their headmen.

The Rajput Principalities, being self-administered, and in later times practically independent, were less exposed to these evils.

Ministerial employment, provincial rule, and military command, were the three great prizes of ambition. But though often prolonged or repeated, and often enjoyed, in one form or other, for life, they were essentially what we should call occasional appointments, or posts. As such, they were distinguishable from what—*mutatis mutandis*—I have ventured to term the permanent life peerages. These were the Omrahships, and Mansubdarys.

The two ranks are sometimes confounded, sometimes spoken of as distinct. On the whole, perhaps, it is pretty true to say, that Omrah was a general term for an ennobled person; while the Mansubdary was a military decoration (adapted to the military character of the Government), implying the nominal command of a specified number of cavalry; the actual amount of the Mansubdar's force, whether of horsemen or including infantry also, being always considerably below the estimate at which he was rated, and for which he received pay from the State. I shall return to this subject in connexion with the army.

There was also another title, that of Bahadur, or

Commander, which has been compared to knighthood among us.

Whether the Omrah and the Bahadur received pay directly as such, I am uncertain; but imagine that a *jaghire* would generally, if not as a matter of course, be assigned him, wherewith to keep up his dignity. It needs hardly be said, that the same persons who received any of these distinctions were also constantly in office, of one kind or other; and the Princes of the Blood were regularly created Mansubdars of the highest class. The military commanders rejoiced also in the affix of Khan, or if Rajputs, were usually termed Sing.

The chief sources of the proverbially ample revenue of the sovereign were: (1). the crown lands, which had not been either permanently alienated in *Enam*, or assigned in usufruct to individuals in *Jaghire* tenure; (2). the *caducæ hereditates* of government officers of various kinds, and according to some authorities of wealthy subjects generally. But I much doubt whether the latter class, that is those who were not employed by Government, were even in later times thus posthumously stripped of their mere personalty, much less of their incomes accruing out of the land—as *Zemindars;* though doubtless a heavy fine was imposed on the *hereditas jacens*. And, directly or indirectly, even government officials probably contrived to transmit a good deal of their property unchallenged to their posterity. What we may call the *allodial* lands of the villagers in the Regulation Provinces (to use an English equivalent expression), however strictly subject to taxation, were certainly not actually liable to appropriation by the sovereign; still less were those in Rajputana, and other tributary States of the same kind exposed to such a risk.

But to continue. (3). A third source of the imperial revenue was the proceeds of confiscation, which was at times inflicted in a very arbitrary manner. Jehangir, in his *Memoirs*, tells a grotesque but tragic story of the way in which he punished an over zealous and griping speculator who, to enrich himself by obtaining the farm of the tax, recommended the re-imposition of the *jezia*, or poll-tax on unbelievers. The Emperor, more mindful of Acber's policy than of Mahomet's precepts, closed with the proposition, farmed out the impost to the projector, exacted the money on the spot, and then cut off the unlucky fellow's head, for having had the shameless wickedness to tempt his sovereign to commit so criminal an act of intolerance! But he adds, sententiously, that he did not think it right to deprive the family of the rest of the victim's property. (4). Trade and commerce, both external and internal, yielded a large revenue in the way of regular taxes, and occasional presents of great amount, for the concession or ratification of commercial privileges and (I believe) of manufacturing monopolies. (5). The last item is connected with a fifth and extremely productive means of replenishing the royal coffers. The primitive habit of not approaching a great man empty-handed, especially when anything was to be sought or hoped from him, flourished in full vigour at the Mogul Court, though Acber is said to have received comparatively few gifts. Perhaps the fact was, that he took care to requite, or more than requite, what he received by counter presents. His benevolent and beneficent liberality to the deserving and the needy; his loans to those who were in temporary difficulties; his private and delicately ministered subsidies to those who were too proud to beg, and too poor to meet the claims of their position, are fully chronicled by Abul Fazil. But, in general, the Emperors seem to have been greatly the gainers on the balance between the gifts which they conferred and those which they received. A perennial stream of *nuzzurs*, or votive offerings, was lavished at the shrine of majesty; and, on great occasions, a plentiful shower of such gifts poured in, of the most miscellaneous character and profuse amount. The magnificent jewel collection in the imperial treasury and the brilliants which adorned the famous Peacock Throne are said to have been amassed in this manner.

(6). But the principal standing revenue of the State was derived from the land tax. This, estimated at a third of the produce, had been settled by Acber on very equitable and enlightened principles. It may be enough now to say that by his plan it was re-settled every decade, on a carefully calculated average of the previous ten years' annual amounts, that deductions were made for unfavourable circumstances, poverty of soil, backwardness of cultivation, fallow years, natural catastrophes, &c.; and that the estimated amount might, if the *peasant* preferred it (thus it was what we should call a *ryotwar* settlement), be paid in kind. Acber's system was retained by his successors and extended to the Dekkan; though local tyranny, as I have already implied, frequently prevented the enjoyment of its full advantages by the cultivator, even before the Marathas began to swarm over the country, and absorb its revenues.

Some account of the military force must conclude this sketch of the imposing political structure, which those originally despised freebooters eventually subverted.

The army was differently constituted at different times, and consisted of a great many classes and qualities both of officers and soldiers. The character of the sovereign, the consequent spirit of the government, and the geographical area and social condition of the Empire at various periods, were faithfully reflected in the successive modifications of the military system.

Baber's invading army was a compact, well appointed, and well handled force of some 12,000 men, mostly cavalry, match-lock men and archers, but provided with heavy guns, which in action he chained together, to give material solidity to his perilously small base. Thus he twice gained decisive victories by deploying a smart body of horsemen on both flanks of his opponents, and driving their vast masses inwards till they became an unmanageable and panic-stricken rabble; when he completed their discomfiture by assailing them in front with troops who passed through the intervals of the batteries, the chains being at the critical moment unlinked for the purpose.

Thus, in several capital points, Baber's tactics singularly resemble Henry the Fifth's successful devices, under very similar circumstances, at Agincourt.

Baber's army was, of course, entirely composed *at first* of extra-Indian ingredients. But this soon ceased to be the case.

Humayun, too, returned, and reconquered a portion of the northern Provinces chiefly with a foreign force, a Persian army, lent him by the Shah.

And throughout the whole period of Mogul domination, both generals, officers, and soldiers from Upper Asia, as well as from Afghanistan, which was mostly a Mogul Province, were employed in great numbers, formed the most efficient part of the regular army, and received higher pay than the natives of the country.

Aeber's conquests and organising tendencies opened an entirely new era in the history and character of the army, as in those of other institutions. Henee-forth Hindoo—espeeially Rajput—offieers appear in high and independent commands; and the patriarehal chiefs of the same tribe mustered their clannish levies under the imperial standard; though they seem to have preferred, and generally to have obtained, serviee in the open field, rather than garrison duty, for which they were less adapted than otherwise inferior forees.

The extended limits of his territory now supplied the Emperor with a much greater choice of native soldiers than of old. And he introduced striet regulations, both to enforee diseipline, to prevent oppression by the levying of pay on the *jaghire* system (preferring as far as possible the method of payment in cash direet from the treasury), and to obviate the collusive musters, whieh had too often enriehed the generals at the Emperor's expense, and erippled the effieiency of the army in the field.

He also, with the insight that, in so many departments, marked his extraordinary advanee upon the ideas and praetices of his age and plaee, discerned the importanee of infantry; and provided that each *Mansubdar* should maintain an equal number of footmen and of horsemen; and that, of the former, a fourth were to be matehlock-men; the rest might be archers. Yet he did not neglect to entertain a numerous body of the same description of high-class cavalry, that we have found so useful at the present day.

The Sinde horse, composed of Mahometan gentlemen, each taking service on his own account, requiring to be himself ridden (so to speak) with a somewhat loose rein, and therefore demanding, or rather admitting, few officers; but dashing, high-spirited, and susceptible of enthusiastic devotion, even to *Feringhee* leaders whom he respects, and who treat him properly:—a body of irregular cavalry so composed, which the genius of Napier extemporised, and the moral ascendancy of Jacob brought to perfection, is no inadequate reproduction of Acber's enterprising *Ahdis*, or, as they would have been called in later times, *Sillidars*.

Meanwhile the bulk of the regular army was mustered, in a rather loose and inexpert fashion, under the *Mansubdars*, who, like dukes in Europe in earlier times, at this period were essentially, and, it may be almost said, exclusively, military officers, rather than titular dignitaries.

The nominal number under the *Mansubdar's* command indeed now, as later, exceeded his actual contingent, except in the very lowest ranks. But serve he did in fact, and at the head of his appointed quota, though he might also be destined to one of the chief commands.

The great defect of the arrangement was, that there was no proper ramification of the vast host. There were generals and their deputies, nominated by the Emperor. And there were levies of men, each under his *Mansubdar*. But, according to the view of Mr. Elphinstone, "below the chief officers—there was probably no chain of subordination, except what arose from each man's authority over his own quota." This view seems confirmed by native and contemporary accounts of battles; and combined with the imperfect organization of the men in each quota, goes far to explain the constant fact, that on the death of a general, an Indian army was in the habit of melting away like a snow-wreath.

Acber's artillery, transport corps, *matériel*, assortment of weapons, and other military appliances, are all worth attention, but must here be passed over in silence. Lastly, however, it may be mentioned that he devoted much labour and skill to fortification,—his capital, Agra, presenting what were then considered model works of this kind; and that his provincial militia, according to the *Ayeen Akbery*, exceeded in number four millions of men. This vast estimate, however, probably refers to those who were liable to occasional service of a semi-military character, rather than to those who were actually, much less contemporaneously, called out to fight.

Such is an outline of this great sovereign's military arrangements, in the maturity of his system. However defective, judged by our present European standard, they produced, under the eye and through the inspiring influence of the first master of war at that time in the East, the most formidable and resistless machinery of conquest that India had seen since the days of his terrible ancestor, Timour. In this, as in other respects, it will be seen below that matters were much changed for the worse under the more sumptuous and pretentious, but less enlightened and practical Aurungzib.

CHAPTER IV.

AURUNGZIB IN HINDOSTAN.

The memorable and complicated civil war which resulted in the deposition and imprisonment of Shah Jehan, the judicial murder of Dara and Morad, the private assassination of their sons, the defeat and flight of Shuja, and his obscure death in a foreign land, and thus in the complete triumph and lonely pre-eminence of Aurungzib, forms one of the most typical passages of Eastern story. It has accordingly engaged the pens of many writers, from Bernier, who related it to his contemporaries in Europe with Herodotean picturesqueness, grace, and imaginative colouring, to Sir William Sleeman, who diversifies the multifarious interest of his charming *Rambles*, by dwelling upon it at considerable length.

But a very short summary must here suffice of a struggle, equally notable for the sudden and final degradation of the most powerful sovereign who had occupied the Mogul throne, the violence of the fratricidal rivalry, the religious character imparted to the contest by the fanaticism of Aurungzib, the series of catastrophes and crimes that followed thick upon each other, and by which alone the victor secured his prize, the dark memory of these events in the minds both of the sovereign and his subjects, and the complete and fatal change in the imperial policy attending the elevation of Aurungzib. Thus this remarkable crisis was, in fact, the beginning of the end, and contributed by no means remotely to the ruin of the House of Timour.

The scene opens with the sudden illness of the Emperor, which Dara, who has Shah Jehan's full confidence, and is conducting the central government in his name, in vain endeavours to conceal from his brothers in the Provinces (1657). Shuja in Bengal, and Morad in Guzerat, at once exchange the title of Viceroy for that of Emperor, and prepare to maintain their respective pretensions with the sword. Aurungzib, in the Dekkan, more cunningly dissembles his ambition; musters his forces; and professing the desire of devoting himself eventually to a life of religious seclusion, tenders his immediate services to the simple Morad—ostensibly for the purpose of securing *his* succession, and the righteous repression of the ungodly Dara. Thus he disarms the rivalry, and procures the co-operation, of one brother; while in the North the two others are left to waste their strength in mutual hostilities.

Shuja is presently defeated by the young Prince Soliman, Dara's son, and returns to Bengal.

Aurungzib's intentions towards the Emperor, who is now convalescent, but entirely in the hands of Dara, are still ambiguous. But having joined Morad in Malwa, he hastens to flatter the vanity, and confirm the delusion, of his credulous brother by every token of subservience; and the joint armies achieve a first success against the Rajput Jeswunt Sing, who has been commissioned by Dara to arrest their course, and whom Aurungzib fails not to brand as "an infidel" (1658). The Chumbul is soon passed; and the enfeebled and distracted Emperor in vain contemplates mediation, at the head of his forces.

He fails to restrain the reckless impetuosity of Dara, who without waiting for the succours which his son is bringing up, engages the allied brothers, and sustains a disastrous defeat. On this occasion, the energy, gallantry, and perseverance of all the Princes are equally conspicuous; and the fate of the day is decided by Dara's being compelled to dismount from his elephant, when he has almost succeeded in attracting victory to his banners. But the most significant circumstance is Aurungzib's real, or affected piety, and steadfast confidence in the protection of Heaven, both during and after the battle. Throughout he assumes, it must be observed, the tone of a champion of the Crescent, and an avenger of unbelief.

While the hapless Dara, fallen from his high estate, pursues his forlorn flight with a few thousand followers towards Delhi; the victors occupy Agra; and Aurungzib fruitlessly endeavours to propitiate the Emperor, and by plausible representations to acquire the place in his affections, so lately occupied by Shah Jehan's firstborn. Finding this hopeless, he proceeds to blockade the old man in his own palace; and soon after deposes him, and himself assumes the imperial title. But he does not blind or put his father to death.

Meanwhile Morad, having now served the turn of the wily and selfish politician, has been rudely disabused of his high hopes; imprisoned; and finally murdered with a hypocritical affectation of justice, and a mock condemnation for former cruelty in the exercise of his viceregal office in Guzerat.

Hitherto, with the cold and subtle schemer, lowliness has been young ambition's ladder. But Morad's pretensions being thus disposed of; their father deposed and a prisoner; their eldest brother a defeated and homeless fugitive; Shuja's rash attempt upon the throne having ended in his constrained return to Bengal; and Aurungzib's more deliberate claim being confirmed by his military success, and his possession of both the Mogul capitals, Agra and Delhi; he is able to assume the commanding tone of a recognised Potentate; and the waiters on Providence hasten to desert the setting for the rising sun.

Prince Soliman, at the head of a large army, still menaces Aurungzib. But, after a time, two Rajput Rajas go over to the new Emperor; Soliman's army melts away rapidly; he moves northward, with ever lessening numbers, to join his father at Lahore, but is out-manœuvred by Aurungzib: he then seeks refuge with the petty chief of Sirinagur, who after a decent interval of suspense, a prudent observation of the signs of the times, and a formal negotiation, surrenders the hapless Prince to the tender mercies of his uncle. Aurungzib exhibits the prisoner to the commiseration of the Court, in gilded fetters; promises to treat him well; and immures him, together with his brother Sepehr, who has also been captured, and a son of Morad, in Gwalior, the Vincennes of the Mogul Emperors; where all three soon after perish mysteriously.

Meanwhile the Emperor in person has pursued Dara, but has been recalled from the Punjab to the defence of his capital and throne against Shuja, who has again advanced with the army of Bengal. In the neighbourhood of Allahabad, Aurungzib's fate again trembles in the balance, through the defection of his formerly defeated antagonist, and recently reconciled ally rather than subject, the powerful Jeswunt Sing, Raja of Joudpoor. This chief has submitted too late to experience the attention that he conceives to be his due; he is also antipathetic to the orthodox Aurungzib, as a former friend of the heresiarch Dara; and his cold reception determines him again to change sides. In the darkness of the night he vehemently assails the Emperor's rear, while Shuja is to attack in front. But Shuja's dilatory movements, and the presence of mind, firmness, and skilful dispositions of Aurungzib baffle the plan; and in the general action which ensues, Shuja is decisively defeated, and once more retreats eastward (January, 1659). He still, however, protracts the contest against the imperial lieutenant Mir Jumla, and is even joined for awhile by the eldest son of the Emperor; but is eventually expelled from India, and retires with his family to Aracan; where they are all put to death as accomplices in some design of rebellion against the local government.

While Shuja retires discomfited to Bengal, Jeswunt, not caring further to share his fallen fortunes, or to cut himself off from his own strong country, marches homewards; and as he approaches Agra, is strongly suspected of an intention to restore Shah Jehan. A brief success, at least, would probably have attended such a move. But Aurungzib allows him no time to mature his schemes, or to brood over his personal wrongs. With his usual adroitness he detaches the Rajput from Dara's cause, by delicate attentions and liberal concessions. Nor is this done too soon.

Dara has rallied; raised another army; gained over the Viceroy of Guzerat, Shah Nawaz Khan (though the latter is Aurungzib's father-in-law); and is in command of that Province and all its resources. But the indefatigable Emperor again defeats his brother, and puts him to flight; Shah Nawaz is killed in the battle; and Dara's prospects henceforth are desperate, and his followers dwindle away; until, after a series of fitful and abortive efforts and melancholy wanderings, he too is betrayed and delivered up to his remorseless brother. Much feeling is testified for him in his misfortunes by the populace; but no movement for his deliverance, much less for his restoration to power, is attempted. And Aurungzib, maintaining to the last the character of an avenger of the orthodox faith, causes Dara to be tried and condemned as an apostate, and executed in prison (July, 1659). He has his brother's head served up to him "in a charger;" takes due care to ascertain that there is no mistake or collusion as to the identity of his political victim; and then—

> "Some natural tears he shed, but wiped them soon,"

if, indeed, they were natural at all!

It now remained to be seen how such a man, with such antecedents would thrive, as successor of Baber, of Acber, and of Shah Jehan.

It is not necessary here to enter upon the general merits of Aurungzib's civil government. These were, as may be inferred from what has been said of his character, in many respects unquestionably great and conspicuous, and have, in spite of his faults, justly entitled him to the admiration both of his own subjects and of foreigners. My present object is rather to trace the fatal influence of his intolerance in hastening the disruption of the imperial system.

His earlier measures in this direction were of a vexatious rather than a distinctly oppressive character. In Mr. Elphinstone's words:—"they tended to stir up a scrupulous and captious spirit, and to mark the line between the followers of the two religions which it had been the policy of former monarchs to efface."

Such were the appointment of a *mullah* (a sort of Mahomedan scribe) with a body of cavalry to restrain the licentious exhibition of the abominations of idol-worship; and the prohibition of fairs on Hindoo festivals, as well as of the music, dancing, and miming, that form such essential and marked features of the social life of the people. Again, in forbidding astrology, he approached very closely, if he did not actually enter, the region of positive religious persecution. He subsequently established a distinction very invidious and galling to the Hindoos by remitting half the customs duties due from Mussulmans. While the pride of the native race was thus hurt, their pleasures were curtailed, and their religious rites subjected to the obnoxious inspection and control of the official expounders of a hostile religion; the Court gradually assumed, in conformity with some of the above regulations, a puritanical aspect, most unlike its old genial character, and ill calculated to propitiate a people so much devoted to the splendid and turbulent entertainments hitherto exhibited by the Emperors for the public enjoyment.

Other and severer enactments followed. A most ill-advised though ineffectual attempt was made to exclude Hindoos from public employment. Thus the fundamental though implied compact between the House of Baber and the majority of its subjects was broken by the sovereign; and it remained to be proved how far such a breach was compatible with the security of the dynasty. The Great Mogul had openly renounced his noblest function—the Fatherhood of all the many "peoples, nations, and languages," that had hitherto co-existed and flourished harmoniously under the common shelter of a rule, absolute indeed, but free from partisanship in the exercise of powers availing for the general protection, and delegated alike to representatives of every race and creed. The Tartar Conqueror mistrusting and repudiating the services of his indigenous but well-affected subjects; the foreigner proscribing the traditional institutions, the popular recreations, the characteristic arts of the country with which his ancestors had done so much to identify themselves; the Mussulman inquisitor spitefully repressing, by police regulations, and by the agency of the hated interpreter of his own bald faith, the gladsome or awful pomp of the venerable Hindoo ritual, and the exuberant fervour of worshippers equally inveterate and demonstrative in their religious instincts; the arrogant head of a party, or in the native way of thinking and speaking—of a caste, cruelly and perfidiously abusing his power, by inflicting a financial stigma on the dissidents from his comparatively upstart society, and filling his coffers with the proceeds of his unkingly sectarianism; the insidious proselytiser scheming to cheat out of their religion the needy and the wavering—by the help of the tax-gatherer:—such were some of the altered aspects in which the Emperor now stood revealed to the susceptible imagination and profound prejudices of his Hindoo subjects.

The smouldering discontent waxed deeper and more dangerous, and at length amounted to positive disaffection. On the re-imposition of the *jezia* (1677) the cup of bitterness overflowed; and an ominous and many-voiced note of warning—a clamorous concert rather of murmuring and protest—was heard at the capital, and sounded into the ears of the Emperor himself.

The palace was beset with unavailing suppliants. The "hard task-master," who had succeeded the milder Pharaohs, insulted the abject complainants by forcing his unheeding way through the eager and obstinate crowd; and the constitutional practice of petitioning the sovereign in person for redress of grievances died away in unavailing groans and low-muttered execrations. The tax was levied in and around Delhi without further resistance.

This remarkable scene however was but the prelude to the real drama of popular opposition, which (as in mediæval England) could hardly be enacted without the aid of leaders of note and station.

Such were the Rajput chieftains, of whom not the least famous was Jeswunt Sing of Marwar or Joudpoor. He had, it will be remembered, alternately opposed and served the Emperor. But Aurungzib probably had never forgiven him; and on his death, soon after the exaction of the obnoxious poll-tax, his family were treated with a mixture of perfidy and severity well calculated to bring on a dangerous crisis. Ajit Sing, the young son of Jeswunt, through the devotion and valour of his servants, headed by Durga Das, escaped and lived to wage constant war against the wily Mogul, who had endeavoured to entrap him into his power.

But the outrage offered to the noblest House in India, the general character of the Emperor's policy, and the demand of the *jezia* from the Rajput States, produced the explosion that had been long impending. The chief of Jeipur was too closely connected, both locally and socially, with the Emperor to resist openly. But the Rana of Oudipur or Mewar, Raj Sing, combining with Jeswunt's children, hastened to repudiate the hateful and insulting tax, to throw off his allegiance, and to plunge into war.

Aurungzib took the field in person (1679); but, after some months spent in hostilities, concluded a peace with Raj Sing, which, though it bound the latter to abandon his allies in Marwar, virtually acknowledged an imperial failure as to the deeper and more permanent cause of quarrel. The *jezia* was remitted, or, in the language of the Government, commuted for a small district, which the Rana gave up, as a petty though noble Prince, who had confronted the Great Mogul, might well do without loss of honour.

Even this qualified success on Aurungzib's part was, however, only momentary. The people of Marwar were still in arms; and Ajit Sing seems to have lost no time in again assisting them.

Once more the Emperor in person approached the scene of action, and concentrated several armies under his sons and the Viceroy of Guzerat, to stamp out the audacious insurrection. An obstinate, cruel, and protracted contest ensued. Raj Sing, assailed on all sides, fled into the Aravulli, whither Prince Azim hastened to pursue him. The open country was, by the Emperor's express orders, devastated in a remorseless manner; villages were burnt, fruit-trees cut down, women and children carried off; terrorism, in its harshest form, was the order of the day. On the other hand, the Rajputs kept a large expeditionary force of cavalry in the low country; the refugees from the hills co-operated with their usual ardour; and, in reading such a summary account of their joint proceedings as the following, we seem to be already engaged in studying the course of Aurungzib's final discomfiture in Southern India. "They cut off convoys," says Mr. Elphinstone, "attacked detachments, defended favourable positions, and sometimes gained important advantages by surprises and night attacks."

Proud, fanatical, and reckless of human suffering, Aurungzib might close his eyes to the obvious lessons of the war hitherto; but the next move on the part of his able antagonist, Durga Das, could not be lightly ignored, and revealed unmistakeably the tendency of the Emperor's intolerance to plunge himself, if not his kingdom, into the pit of destruction.

That a Hindoo partisan leader, however distinguished, should have meditated deposing the Emperor, and such an Emperor, seems a bold and strange undertaking indeed. That Durga Das should have partially shaken the fidelity of Prince Moazzim, the heir to the throne; should afterwards have brought over Prince Acber to his plan; and that the latter, under Hindoo influence, should have assumed royal state, have found Aurungzib's Mussulman nobles ready to abet and take office under him; and the army passive in their hands, or rather ready to join in the treasonable design, is stranger still. Such, however, was the case. And when the Prince, with his Rajput allies, advanced at the head of 70,000 men against his father, the Emperor, taken by surprise, and with but a handful of soldiers at his side, was in the utmost peril. Such an emergency, however, was well calculated to exhibit his unrivalled skill in baffling combinations against himself. A single staunch adherent availed to tamper with and sow distrust and division among the rebellious Moguls. One chief went back with his brother, Aurungzib's emissary. Another was killed in the act of rejoining the Emperor. The soldiers followed, as before, the example of their leaders; and the Prince was soon left alone with Durga Das and his Rajputs. He escaped, faithfully escorted by a body of his Hindoo friends (1681); and we shall hear of him again at the Court of Sambaji, the Maratha Raja.

Thus, already, imperial bigotry had estranged the noblest and most devoted Hindoo supporters of the throne; involved the Empire in a difficult, inglorious, and protracted war; promoted rebellion among the Moguls themselves; and occasioning treason in the Royal House, had linked a Prince of the Blood in close league with the exasperated champions of persecuted Hindooism.

Meanwhile the war continued and became more and more envenomed. The devastations of the Moguls provoked the Rajputs to acts of ferocity and responsive bigotry, contrary to their generally mild, tolerant, and chivalrous disposition.

Like the Sikhs, not long afterwards, when exposed to a similar visitation, "they plundered the mosques, burnt the Koran, and insulted the mullahs."

Wearied out with the tedious and disreputable strife, and anxious to prosecute his grander schemes of aggrandisement in the Dekkan, the Emperor again consented to make peace with Raj Sing, on terms far more favourable than before, and which, in fact, amounted to a distinct confession of failure in both the original objects of the war. The *jezia* was explicitly abandoned; at least the cession in lieu of it was now formally demanded in expiation of the aid given to Prince Acber in his rebellion; and the haughty Mogul was fain to guarantee the restoration of his dominions to the son of Jeswunt, when the young Prince should attain his majority.

Even then, however, a momentary respite only was secured; the war recommenced; lingered on throughout Aurungzib's reign; increased his difficulties in the Dekkan; and, in the end, powerfully contributed both to lower his reputation, to exhaust his resources, and to undermine his power.

CHAPTER V.

SIVAJI, THE FOUNDER OF THE MARATHA POWER.

THE scene of the events related in this Chapter lies entirely in the southern, or more properly peninsular, portion of India, that is, south of the rivers Nerbudda and Mahanuddy; or what is called, using the word in its widest sense, the Dekkan, as opposed to India north of those rivers, or Hindostan.

The Dekkan itself is loosely divided by Hindoos into five great regions, Dravida, Carnata, Telingana, Gondwaneh, and Maharashtra. With the wild region and primitive tribes of Gondwaneh, east of the Wyne Gunga river, we have now no concern. Dravida extends from Cape Comorin to the Lake of Pulicat, north and south, and westward to the Eastern Ghats. Telingana lies north, Carnata north-west of Dravida, and both abut on Maharashtra. This last country, the home of the Maratha people, and chiefly the theatre of Sivaji's exploits, is bounded as follows: to the west, it has the Indian Ocean; on the north, it extends along the Sautpoora Range from Naumdode to the Wyne Gunga. This river limits it on the east, until the Wurda becomes the boundary as far as Manikdroog and Mahoor. Then the rambling Manjera separates it from Telingana; and speaking roughly, the Kistna and Malpurda are its southern confines.

Maharashtra is estimated to extend over upwards of 100,000 square miles. Its great determining physical feature is the steep and lofty range of the Western Ghats, or Syhadree mountains, which extend far beyond its southern limits, and give occasion to a threefold geographical division into the Concan, or the country between the mountains and the sea; the Ghat Mahta, or the mountain region itself, often very wide; and the Desh, or table-land eastward of the Syhadree chain. The whole of Maharashtra is more or less hilly, and four transverse ranges of considerable height intersperse the table-land; namely, the Chandore, now often called the Northern Ghats; the Ahmednuggur chain; that just below Poona; and still further to the south the Mahadeo hills, near Satara. The Ghats Proper rise far above the table-land, and are surmounted by majestic and precipitous masses of rock, which form natural fortresses of imposing appearance, vast size and very difficult access, especially when these original advantages are improved by the appliances even of rude native art. Long lateral spurs, and detached blocks of similar dimensions, penetrate far into the eastern upland, and enclosing deep and well-watered valleys, give an average of more than twenty miles in breadth to the Ghat Mahta.

These spurs and islands (as they would be called in Somersetshire), as well as the four principal transverse ranges already mentioned, were also crowned with a multitude of forts. The Concan varied in character; but especially below Bombay was mostly a rugged, broken, and impracticable country, the basement and buttress system (so to speak) of the soaring Syhadree Range, which sinking sometimes suddenly, sometimes more gradually towards the sea, poured down streams that in the monsoon became terrific torrents, and that have in all directions scarred and diversified the surface of the land, and increased the difficulty of road-making in such a region. Both the Concan and the Ghat Mahta were thickly wooded, particularly, in each case, the valleys and glens; and the prodigious and continuous rainfall, the steepness of the passes, the dense and pestilential atmosphere of the jungles, and the frequency of sublime and terrible thunderstorms, made all warfare in such a district, during several months in each year, almost impossible. The historian of the Marathas, himself a soldier, pronounces that "in a military point of view there is probably no stronger country in the world."

Besides the Nerbudda and the Tapty, which rising far to the east flow westward into the Gulf of Cambay, three of the chief Dekkan rivers, the Godavery, the Kistna, and the Bhima, descend from the Syhadree Range, and with their innumerable tributaries spread fertility in every direction over the table-land; though their deep-cut channels, and the comparative scantiness of their constant stream, prevent all comparison with the exuberant fecundity of Bengal, and other lower regions on the eastern coast. On the banks of the Godavery and its feeders, the Neera and the Maun, was reared a breed of horses unsurpassed for speed and vigour in any part of India.

The bulk of the population of Maharashtra was Hindoo, though Mahometan rulers had imported a considerable proportion of strangers in race as well as faith; and in the mountains, particularly towards the north, Bheels, Coolees, Ramoosees, and other primitive tribes abounded. Among the Hindoos, the sharply-defined fourfold caste classification of Menu had, as elsewhere, been replaced by a multitudinous subdivision on no intelligible principle, though not on that account necessarily the less rigid. The Brahmin, indeed, still retained both his name, his purity of blood, and his intellectual ascendancy; and in the person of the Peishwa was ere long to become virtually a secular sovereign. But he had for ages compromised in most cases his sacred character, and forfeited popular reverence by engaging in mundane affairs; and the spiritual director of the Maratha was often a low caste man, sometimes (oddly enough) even a Mussulman.

So, too, the saints held in honour throughout the Maratha country belonged to all classes and creeds. The votary of Islam, and of the Jain worship, the *pariah*, and the primitive barbarian, alike attracted the respectful homage of the tolerant and fundamentally pantheistic Hindoo. Again, as among Hindoos generally, the undoubted Rajputs still claimed to be the surviving or re-created military caste; so the higher martial class among the Marathas made apparently reasonable pretensions to Rajput descent, and justified on this ground the practice of secluding their women in the Mussulman fashion, unless where a lady had to undertake active public duties. Sivaji, it will be seen, boasted royal blood on the mother's side.

Learning was almost confined to the Brahmins, many of whom, however, were extremely ignorant. Sivaji, like Hyder Ally, could neither read nor write. The prevalent religious worship was that of Mahadeo or Siva, as denoted in the famous Maratha battle cry, *Hur! Hur! Mahadeo!*

At the time when our narrative opens, the Dekkan was in a more than usually disturbed and critical condition. On the dissolution of the older Delhi Empire at the end of the fourteenth century, a powerful Mahometan monarchy, called the Bahminy, had been formed in Maharashtra; while further south a rival Hindoo State took its name from Bijanuggur, its capital. The Bahminy monarchy had been subsequently resolved into five separate kingdoms, two of which had been soon merged in the three larger Mussulman sovereignties of Ahmednuggur, Bijapoor, and Golconda: and the Hindoo dynasty of Bijanuggur had fallen a prey to its own corruption, and the attacks of its neighbours. Still later, Ahmednuggur had tempted the annexing disposition of the great Mogul Emperor Acber: he had begun, and his successors had completed, the absorption of that kingdom. In the last days of the falling State, Shahji, originally a Maratha soldier of fortune, of humble birth, rose into importance in the public service; and contributed for a while to arrest the progress of the imperial arms. He afterwards made his peace with the conqueror (1636); transferred his allegiance to Bijapoor; and while the Emperor Shah Jehan's son, Prince Aurungzib, was meditating the reduction of the two surviving Mahometan Powers of the Dekkan, Shahji assisted his new sovereign in waging war in Carnata, and making precarious additions to a dominion, whose limits should rather have been restricted, and its resources husbanded, against the imminent hostilities of the artful, powerful, and encroaching Mogul.

Shahji was the father of the extraordinary man whose career it is now proposed to sketch.

Though the spirit of the hero is an original particle, an incalculable element in his composition, yet, as with common natures, his character is in a great degree formed, and the direction of his activity determined, by his circumstances.

> "The child is father of the man."

So it was with Sivaji. Born in the hill fort of Sewneree (1627), in an age when old political arrangements were being fast dissolved, and thrones were tottering in every direction around him; of a father who, after submitting alternately to three different sovereignties, helped to make war on a fourth; entrusted to the separate care of a doating mother, who proudly traced back her lineage to the former Rajput monarchs of Maharashtra, the victims of the older tide of Mussulman conquest; again and again, from his earliest infancy, the companion of that mother's flight from the Mogul arms; hidden away in the hills by some unknown but friendly hand, when his mother was at last captured by her pursuers; entrusted later to the charge of a wise, faithful, patriotic, and pious Brahmin, Dadaji Konedeo (the manager of his father's Poona *jaghire*), under whom he learned to excel in horsemanship, and in warlike exercises, to observe strictly the rites of his religion, and to glow with admiring and sympathetic enthusiasm at the recital of the exploits of Gods and deified heroes; climbing the steep crag, leaping the foaming torrent, and tracking the fierce tiger to his lair, in company with the hardy and daring mountaineers, and winning golden opinions from these simple people by his audacity, skill, familiarity, humour, and instinctive air of authority; gaining in his excursions a thorough knowledge of the country, of its paths, its strongholds, and their condition, and of its assailable and defensible points; venturing presently with his lax companions on Gadshill enterprises of a more than questionable character; warned back to more sedate and respectable avocations by his faithful mentor, and entrusted by him with civil functions, which enabled him by his engaging manners and conciliatory conduct to steal the hearts of the higher classes in the open country, as he had before captivated the rude hill-men:—such were the original circumstances and pursuits of Sivaji, which formed at once a natural opening and an admirable training for his after career.

The precocity of Oriental heroes is often remarkable. Sivaji was but sixteen when he began to aspire to independent rule. Quick to discern his opportunity, he observed that the Bijapoor State, intent on conquest in the south, had neglected to garrison the majority of the unhealthy forts with Government troops, and had left them in the hands of local and hereditary feudatories. With the aid of his three earliest adherents, he induced the governor of Torna, a strongly situated castle south of Poona, to put him in possession of it (1646). He then sent agents to the king, with plausible tenders of zealous service, and a higher rent than the late ruler had paid; which, backed by bribes to influential persons, postponed strict inquiry into his proceedings. Meanwhile he put Torna into a better posture of defence; and finding there a considerable treasure, he piously or prudently ascribed the godsend to the favour of Bhowanee, and employed it in arming his followers, and rearing another strong fort, which he called Rajgurh.

On his father's behalf, his guardian remonstrated, but in vain; and the Brahmin becoming a convert to his designs, or anxious to turn them to account in favour of his countrymen and co-religionists, sanctioned them with his dying breath, charging the young adventurer "to protect Brahmins, kine, and cultivators; to preserve the temples of the Hindoos from violation; and to follow the fortune which lay before him." Sivaji did not forget the injunction; and the last words of his venerable preceptor contributed powerfully to raise him, both in his own estimation and in that of others, from a leader of bandits into a champion of Hindoo freedom, nationality, and religion.

He assumed the management of his father's district, and contrived to evade paying over the revenue, on the plausible ground of heavy current expenses. He next gained quiet possession of Chakun, an important fort north of Poona, and retained its commander in his own service, or nominally in that of his father, taking care that the people in the district should be well treated. Still more important was the acquisition of Kondaneh, where he bribed the commander, and which he now called Singurh—or the *lion's den.* His mother-in-law's brother, Baji Mohitey, was in office under Shahji at Sopa, and was little inclined to admit Sivaji's pretensions. In a night attack he was overpowered and taken prisoner with all his people: some of them entered their captor's service, the rest, with Mohitey himself, were sent off to join Shahji in the Carnatic. Poorundhur, another considerable fort, was suddenly deprived by death of its commander. Three sons contested the situation. Sivaji undertook to mediate between them; on specious grounds effected an entrance with some of his followers, and made prisoners of all the brothers. Then his persuasive tongue won them over to his cause; and they served him faithfully.

Not a drop of blood had been shed, in the course of these daring and crafty enterprises. The Maratha habitually prefers management to what he considers inartistic violence. Besides his civil jurisdiction, and the revenues which he drew on his father's account, he had now gained the military command of a large and strong district from Chakun to the Neera; and secure of a sound base of operations, and of an almost impregnable repository for his spoil, he prepared to descend into the plain, and try direct conclusions with the Bijapoor Government.

Having increased the number of his *Mawulees*, or foot soldiers, from the *Mawuls* or valleys of the Ghat Mahta, and formed a body of 300 troopers, whom he mounted on horses captured at Sopa, he fell upon a royal convoy escorting treasure; carried off the spoil to Rajgurh (1648); and seized in rapid succession no less than six forts on the Ghats, just north-west of Poona. Tala, Gossala, and the steep natural fastness of Rairee surrendered soon after; the Concan was invaded, and several wealthy places were sacked; lastly, one of his Brahmin followers took Kallian itself, and a number of forts dependent on it. Sivaji was in ecstacies. He gave the command of the district to the captor; established mild and popular regulations; and politely releasing the Governor of Kallian, allowed him to carry to Court the tidings of the now avowed revolution. Against the Seedee, the Abyssinian admiral of Bijapoor, who held the southern coast, he strengthened himself by erecting two new forts.

The king was violently incensed, and caused Shahji to be treacherously seized in the Carnatic by one of his own countrymen, Baji Ghorepuray, and sent to Bijapoor; where he was threatened with death if Sivaji should not submit (1649). But the son rescued the father, through the powerful mediation of the Emperor, whom as yet he had scrupulously refrained from provoking. For four years, however, Shahji was detained at Bijapoor, until the troubles in the Carnatic and Sivaji's quiet attitude induced the king to release him. He was bound over by oath to keep the peace towards his ensnarer; but entrusted the task of vengeance to his son, who at a later time repaid the debt with heavy interest. An attempt was made to entrap Sivaji himself. But, always well informed, he turned the tables on his assailants, and hunted them into the jungles. Shahji's liberation was the signal for renewed aggression on the part of his son. The Raja of Jowlee administered a large tract of country between the Warna and the Kistna. Like Sivaji he was a Maratha, and disposed to keep on friendly terms with the rebel, but neither to submit to him, nor himself to rise against Bijapoor. And he was powerful, valiant, the head of a warlike house, and well provided with soldiers. Sivaji had a grievance against him for having given passage to his pursuers. But he preferred to act covertly. Two of his influential envoys appeared at Chunder Rao's Court, and sought his daughter's hand for their master. Pending the negotiation, they proposed to assassinate the Raja. Sivaji approved the dark design, and moved stealthily up with his troops to take advantage of the consequent confusion. The Raja and his brother were slain; the assassins escaped; and the place, after an obstinate defence, was taken. Its dependencies were also occupied; but popular Hindoo sentiment strongly disapproved of this treacherous and cruel treatment of a Hindoo Princelet. Rohira, the chief place of a large district between the Neera and the Kistna was soon after scaled in the night, and its commander slain. The completion of this second great stage in his progress to dominion was commemorated by the erection of Pertabgurh, and the appointment of the first Peishwa Shamraje Punt.

Sivaji had hitherto invariably respected the Mogul boundary. He had even made overtures to enter the imperial service. And Aurungzib, who at this time represented Shah Jehan in the Dekkan, was very anxious to form a friendly league with one, who could lend him valuable assistance in his scheme of reducing both Bijapoor and Golconda. But Sivaji, coolly calculating the odds, though he gave fair words, concluded that more was to be gained at present by a rapid raid into the imperial territory, while the Prince with the bulk of his army was making war upon Bijapoor. He accordingly fell upon the large town of Joonere by night; carried off much money and other *loot,* including 200 horses: and followed up this bold step by the still bolder surprise of Ahmednuggur, whence he drove away 700 horses and four elephants (1657). Henceforth his warfare changed considerably. Though his *Mawulees* and other Maratha foot-soldiers continued as active and useful as ever, he organized a large body of cavalry; and shortly after, with much hesitation, consented to admit a proportion of Afghan or Pathan infantry, who, though less adapted to his earlier circumstances, were of importance as he advanced towards normal sovereignty, and began to make occasional stands against regular armies in the field.

For the moment, however, he had miscalculated. Aurungzib's arms and arts were so rapidly successful that Bijapoor was besieged, and seemed on the point of falling: and Sivaji began, in anticipation of the exasperated conqueror's vengeance, to humble himself abjectly, when the announcement that Shah Jehan was seriously ill, produced a sudden and momentous revolution in Indian politics. Aurungzib patched up a peace with Bijapoor; marched off to the north; by a remarkable combination of energy, bravery, duplicity, and cruelty, circumvented and ruined in turn all his brothers; deposed the aged Emperor; and seated himself upon the throne of the great Mogul. Meanwhile Sivaji had renewed his submission, promised fidelity, and plausibly represented that his increased numbers were designed to serve Aurungzib's purpose. In return he demanded the concession of certain beneficiary and revenue rights within the imperial territory, which he represented as traditional in his family; and hinted that he could govern the Concan much better than the Royal official stationed there. Aurungzib in the crisis of his own fate temporised; pardoned Sivaji; allowed him to wage war in the Concan; but stipulated for 500 cavalry—which were *not* sent, and promised to consider Sivaji's claims—which were *not* now pressed. Each of these consummate dissemblers was in fact playing with the other: they were well matched at such a game; but the serious contest between them was postponed.

Sivaji promptly sent the Peishwa with a large body of troops into the Concan. But the Seedee gained a bloody victory over them. Shamraje was recalled and deprived of his office; and this first check heralded a more serious crisis. Humbled by Aurungzib, torn by faction, and their king a mere boy, the Bijapoor Court yet felt the necessity of attempting to crush its aspiring rebel, before he should again be able to co-operate seriously with the Mogul. A select and finely-appointed army of 12,000 men was collected under an eminent noble, Afzool Khan, who, with Ney-like vaunting, promised soon to present Sivaji in chains before his sovereign's footstool. The Maratha saw that open resistance was out of the question, and fell back upon his favourite arts. He shut himself up in Pertabgurh, affected extreme terror, and professed his readiness to abandon all his possessions, could he but be assured of the powerful intercession of the renowned Afzool Khan. The vanity of the haughty Mussulman was touched; and he sent a Brahmin agent, Puntoji Gopinat, to negociate. After a formal public interview, Sivaji in the dead of night appeared alone before Puntoji; appealed expressly to his own divine mission from Bhowanee, and to the more unquestionable selfishness of his hearer, and gained him over completely to his own interest. For the good of the great cause it was resolved, that Afzool Khan should be made a memorable victim. He was by Puntoji's help lured to a private colloquy; a single attendant only stood near him; his troops were at a distance; the Marathas were secretly posted on all sides in the thick jungle. Sivaji meanwhile "having performed," says his historian, "his ablutions with much earnestness, laid his head at his mother's feet, and besought her blessing." Then he secreted under his clothes a coat of mail and a dagger; and his left hand concealed a *wagnuck*, a deadly instrument called from, and somewhat resembling, the claws of the tiger. Thus prepared, and crouching as in fear, he slowly approaches the unsuspecting and linen-clad general; and folding him in a ceremonious embrace, buries the *wagnuck* in his body, following up the blow by another with his dagger. His armour saves him from a sword-cut aimed at him by the dying man, whose head is carried off to Pertabgurh, and whose fall is the signal for a general onset on his troops, who are quickly destroyed, captured, or dispersed (1659). Afzool Khan's son and family were saved by a Maratha whom they had bribed. But Sivaji beheaded his follower for this venial act of insubordination; though he spared and treated well most of his prisoners, and released a fellow-tribesman of importance, who declined to desert Bijapoor and share his fortunes. Many Marathas, however, took service with him.

This perfidious and bloody deed was highly applauded in Maharashtra; and Sivaji at once gained by it 4,000 horses, besides elephants, camels, a well-filled military chest, guns, and stores. In the first shock of the tragic occurrence, moreover, the very important fortress of Panalla was also surrendered to him; Powan Gurh experienced the same fate; and

Sivaji lost no time in reducing Wussuntgurh and a number of other forts, and levying black mail along the Kistna. Next he routed another officer who had been sent against him, and dashing across the country almost to the gates of Bijapoor, spread general havoc and dismay; under cover of which he rushed down the Ghats, and while he was believed to be still on the table-land, Dabul and other places were seized, Rajapoor put to heavy ransom, and Rajgurh was enriched almost at once with the miscellaneous plunder of the upper and the lower country.

Indignant and terror-stricken at this most unexpected issue of the first serious attempt to subdue Sivaji in regular warfare, the distracted Government for a while suspended its disputes; and a second army, twice as numerous as Afzool Khan's, marched under a distinguished officer, Salabat Khan, to cooperate with the Seedee and the Sawunts of Waree, who were to conduct a joint attack from the Concan. Sivaji made prompt and careful dispositions to resist his enemies in each quarter. But he found too late that he had committed a great mistake, in undertaking to defend Panalla in person. Here he was blocked up for four months, unable to exert his usual vigilance and control over the operations of his troops. To hold out, and to escape, seemed equally impossible. He proposed to surrender; in a personal interview with Salabat arranged all matters of importance; and the next day was to open his gates. The besiegers, so near the term of their labours, slept securely; and woke to find that in the darkness Sivaji, with a picked band, had passed through the midst of them, and was far on his way to Rangna. A hot pursuit took place; and the fugitives were overtaken within six miles of their destination. Confiding the defence of a narrow pass to Baji Purvoe, once an enemy, now a devoted follower, Sivaji pushed on. Thrice the pursuers were gallantly repulsed by the little band in the pass; a fourth time they advanced under the avenger of blood, Fazil, the son of the murdered Afzool Khan. A desperate contest ensued. Half of the covering party, including their brave leader, fell; and the post was forced. But as the mist of death was gathering over the eyes of Sivaji's lieutenant, he learnt by a signal gun from Panalla, that his beloved master was safe; and the survivors made good their retreat, carrying off in the teeth of the enemy Baji Purvoe's body (1660).

The king, taking the field in person, re-captured Panalla, Powangurh, and many other of Sivaji's recent acquisitions; while *he* again assailed and plundered Rajapoor, and reduced Sringarpoor, the capital of a *Maratha* chieftain, who fell in the contest. This act also was condemned by Hindoo sentiment; and Sivaji, half by way of atonement, half apparently from deepening superstition, henceforth became more devoted than ever to religious rites, and built a temple to Bhowanee at Pertabgurh. Meanwhile he pressed his operations against the Seedee with various success. But he swooped presently upon a more tempting prey. Baji Ghorepuray, who had entrapped Shahji, and had been commended by him to Sivaji's vengeance, was now preparing to march against the irrepressible outlaw. Sivaji came upon him unawares in the bosom of his family, killed him and the bulk of his household, fired their place, and retired unopposed.

Disturbances in the Carnatic compelled the Government to recall the army destined to act against Sivaji, and thus he was enabled to conquer the Sawunts of Waree, and to retrieve most of his recent losses above the Ghats. He now occupied various ports, began to construct a navy, and procured artillery from Goa. At length Shahji seems to have brought about a reconciliation with Bijapoor (1662). The old man was enchanted at his son's punishment of Ghorepuray, and paid Sivaji a visit, who received him with graceful reverence.

"Sivaji," says the historian of the Marathas, "now possessed the whole of the continent of the Concan, from Kallian to Goa, a length of coast about four degrees of latitude; and the Concan Ghaut

Mahta, from the Beema to the Warna, a distance of about 160 English miles." He is said to have had at this time an army of 50,000 foot and 7,000 horse. And he now removed the seat of his government to Rairee, the name of which he changed to Raigurh, and which he fortified in a very elaborate manner. He then resumed operations against the Moguls. While one of his officers captured forts far to the north, another made a rapid excursion to the immediate neighbourhood of Aurungabad, laying the whole country under contribution, and exciting general dismay.

The Emperor ordered his lieutenant, Shaisteh Khan, to reduce the insolent *rebels*. Chakun was besieged, but held out for two months; and its brave defender, when compelled to surrender, declined to abandon Sivaji's service for that of the Emperor. Shaisteh Khan occupied Poona, and took up his own quarters in a house formerly inhabited by Sivaji and his mother. The towering steep of Singurh overlooked the city, which was unwalled. Sivaji betook himself to his eerie fastness; descended with a numerous party, most of whom he disposed along the road to Poona; stole with a chosen band into the town, and joining in a marriage procession, made his way to the familiar house in the dark; effected an entrance; dispatched most of the inmates; lopped off the Khan's finger as he was letting himself down, in undignified haste, through a window; retired safely with his companions:—and the Moguls could, by the light of his mocking torches, trace his triumphant re-ascent to his rocky den (1663).

Next morning, for the first time, the Maratha horsemen pursued and routed a prancing squadron of Mogul cavalry, which had advanced in bravado to the foot of the hill.

Shaisteh Khan was disheartened, and recalled. And before his successor could accomplish anything, Sivaji, extending the sphere of his evolutions, darted off with 4,000 cavalry to Surat; plundered it for six days of immense wealth (though the English resisted him), and returned to hear that Shahji was dead (1664). He now took the title of Raja, and coined money in his own name. While his vessels swept the sea, and seized and put to ransom the holy pilgrims bound to Arabia, he renewed his own depredations on land, penetrating close to Aurungabad itself, and plundering the town of Ahmednuggur.

Meanwhile, two Bijapoor generals had thought the occasion favourable for reconquering the Concan; but Sivaji overtook them, and defeated them with terrible slaughter. Then he returned to face the Moguls; and again, while he was still believed to be on the point of attacking their camp, he made his way to the coast, embarked, plundered Barcelore, one hundred and thirty miles south of Goa, and many other places; sent his troops back by land, and re-embarking, suffered much from storms and sea sickness, before with unwonted tardiness he could regain his capital. His superstitious countrymen discerned in this bad passage the displeasure of Bhowanee, at her *protégé's* adventuring on the forbidden waters. Nor did he repeat the unpropitious and uncomfortable experiment.

Aurungzib was too suspicious of his subordinates, too contemptuous of the *mountain rat,* as he called Sivaji, and too anxious to effect the reduction of the Dekkan in person, when his affairs in the North should admit of it, to take such steps as would have finished the war at a stroke. He had, however, now entrusted the command of a powerful army to two generals whom he disliked, but who might act as a check, both on Sivaji and on each other. One was the renowned Rajput chief, Raja Jey Sing; the other an Afghan, Dilere Khan. Possibly Sivaji and his people had scruples at contending against an unquestionable representative of the oldest and proudest race of whilom Hindoo sovereigns; while *he* was but an upstart Raja, and, at the most, but a partial scion of that sacred stock. Certain it seems to be that both he and his chiefs lost heart, though his soldiers gallantly defended Poorundhur against Jey Sing in person. While the place still held out, Sivaji having prepared the way by negotiation, and obtained Jey Sing's plighted word—which he knew he could trust—for his safety, pardon, and entertainment by the Emperor, made his way to the Rajput's camp, tendered his submission, and was kindly received. Dilere Khan was more implacable, but was propitiated by Sivaji's personally offering him the keys of Poorundhur. Terms were arranged, and the Maratha abandoned all his conquests from the Moguls, and consented to hold his remaining territory as a *fief* under the Emperor. His son was to receive an honorary military command; and Sivaji requested to be allowed to prosecute certain claims on Bijapoor. Aurungzib ratified the conditions, though without specifically sanctioning the claims in question, which were no less than the famous *chout* and *surdeshmookhee,* or a fourth and a tenth of the revenue; on the plea of exacting which, not only the Bijapoor territory, but all India, was afterwards convulsed and periodically plundered. Thus reconciled, and recognised as a legitimate ruler, though with curtailed dominion, Sivaji served with distinction in the imperial army against Bijapoor; and shortly after accepted the Emperor's invitation to visit Delhi, still under the safeguard of Jey Sing's plighted word.

He took strict precautions for the guidance of his own conduct at the Mogul Court, and for the safety and regulation of his own community during his absence. Then with 500 chosen horsemen, 1,000

Mawulees, and his young son Sambaji, he departed to seek his fortunes in a sphere altogether different from that in which he had hitherto distinguished himself. Aurungzib's reception was cold and disparaging. The hitherto successful adventurer was galled to the quick, probably all the more so, from being involuntarily dazzled by the unwonted display of imperial magnificence, and somewhat nonplussed by the suave and silky manners of the courtiers around him. He bluntly expressed his disgust; and received a polite hint, that the sight of him did not refresh the Great Mogul's eyes. A written petition, recapitulating the circumstances which had caused his appearance at Delhi, and intended to test Aurungzib's disposition towards him, rather widened the opening breach; and Sivaji soon found himself almost a prisoner, though at large. How should he quit this uncongenial scene, and at the head of his army hurl renewed defiance at the haughty and capricious tyrant? First he obtained ready permission for his soldiers to retire from what he represented as a climate unhealthy to them. But his durance became stricter. Still, relying on the connivance of Jey Sing's son (who respected his father's pledge), and free to consort with the nobles of the Court, he cultivated them, and made them frequent presents. Then, finding himself almost a close prisoner, he professed to fall ill; took medicine; and seemed reduced to a very weak state. But from his sick bed he still sent ample gifts of sweetmeats to his new friends, and to devotees at the mosques both inside and without the city. These were carried forth from his quarters at all hours in huge baskets. Late one day it was ascertained that the recumbent invalid was a changeling. A servant had occupied his master's place; while Sivaji and his son had vanished, each under his separate *bonbon* cover, and were already safe out of the Emperor's reach. Leaving Sambaji to the care of a Maratha Brahmin at Muttra, the fugitive rode for his life, and after an absence of nine months reappeared at Raigurh, unhurt, and with an important store of information as to the characters and views of Mogul politicians (1666). He immediately recommenced a war of aggression; and his "safe arrival in the Concan was announced by the recapture of a great portion of the province of Kallian." *

Mortified at Sivaji's escape and continued success, Aurungzib replaced Jey Sing and Dilere Khan by his son Prince Mauzum and Jeswunt Sing, another distinguished Rajput chief, whom Sivaji had courted at Delhi, and ascertained to be open to bribery, as well as tenderly disposed towards the asserter of Hindooism. And the Prince was much guided by the Rajput. How far from their friendly disposition

* Grant Duff.

aided by bribes, how far from Aurungzib's desire to lull his wily adversary into a treacherous security, and entrap him anew, is not very clear; but certain it is that amicable relations were restored (1667): the Emperor acknowledged the Rajaship of the Maratha, gave him a *jaghire* or fief in Berar; and raised the young Sambaji to the promised military post. The Poona, Chakun, and Sopa districts were also restored; but Singurh and Poorundhur were still garrisoned by imperial troops, as a check on the slippery tendencies of so uncertain a feudatory. Thus matters continued for two years; but at the end of that time a mandate arrived from Delhi to apprehend Sivaji and some of his chief officers. Again, however, Aurungzib counted without his host, who, duly informed, at once took his measures. Singurh was escaladed in the most gallant style at night; its terrible precipices were surmounted with the help of rope ladders; a terrific and doubtful combat ensued between the valiant Rajput garrison and the desperate *Mawulee* assailants; Tannaji Maloosray, Sivaji's oldest and staunchest companion, was slain in leading the attack, and his soldiers, appalled at his loss, were forced back to the edge of the declivity; but they were rallied and led on again by his brother; and after losing a third of their force, and slaying or driving over the precipice twice that number of their antagonists, they made themselves masters of the place; and a month later Poorundhur also was recovered (1670). Thus Sivaji's communications between his northern and southern territories above the Ghats were again open; and fresh successes crowned his efforts in all directions, though he failed to take Jinjeera, which was transferred to the Mogul.

Again, with 15,000 men he attacked and plundered Surat; and on quitting it left a formal demand of twelve *laks* annually, to avert a repetition of the visit. On his return he was intercepted by two Mogul armies near the Nassuck Pass. Dividing his men, he fell upon and kept in play the larger body, while a select band carried off his plunder. Then he routed the enemy in his rear, and promptly wheeled and defeated the main host, capturing and afterwards releasing and sending home a valiant Maratha lady, who had commanded a party of her countrymen in the Emperor's service.

The *chout* was shortly after levied for the first time in an imperial Province, that of Candeish (December, 1670). And the Moguls sustained the most severe defeat ever inflicted on them during Sivaji's lifetime; while an attempt to block up the passes, and confine the Marathas to their mountains, ended in more daring and systematic incursions than before.

At this time the King of Bijapoor died, and Sivaji at once took up arms against his successor. An unprecedented amount of plunder was realised; the imperial officers were apparently bribed into quiescence; and Satara, and many other places of consequence, annexed to his dominions. He now formally ascended the throne, and assumed the state for which his deeds, his actual power, and popular acclamation, had long proclaimed his fitness. But he never deviated, in personal conduct, from the energetic simplicity of his earlier years.

How he at length made peace both with the Imperialists and with Bijapoor; strengthened his frontier with a continuous line of forts; how, his hands thus free, and his territory better guarded than before, he marched with 70,000 men eastward (1677); duped the King of Golconda; made conquests at his expense; compelled his half-brother Vencaji to yield the legal portion of their father's inheritance in Carnata; made further conquests on his return march; interposed in favour of his old and now expiring enemy Bijapoor against the gathering hosts of the beleaguering Moguls; how he once more displayed, in assailing their rear, cutting off their supplies, evading their pursuit, matchless skill in his characteristic mode of warfare; how he died suddenly of fever (April, 1680) at the age of fifty-three, and left his throne to a degenerate successor, who soon fell a victim to Aurungzib's vengeance:—I have not space to do more than mention.

Such then was Sivaji: a man difficult to describe except by his actions, (which I have done my best to represent faithfully); and by his institutions, which deserve more attention than they are apt to receive. His good and bad qualities, the causes of his success, and the steps of his progress, I have tried to indicate in the course of the preceding sketch, and may forbear to recapitulate them.

The romantic character of his adventures, the momentous results of his career, and the fact that he is still the cherished idol and half-deified hero of Maharashtra, alike appear to justify an endeavour to interest Englishmen in his fortunes.

The recurrence in India at present of such a career as his, is, thank God! impossible, almost inconceivable. But is it not a little ominous that, while few Englishmen care to hear of him, or of so many other famous men who have left their mark indelibly upon the greatest and most critical dependency of the British Crown, he still occupies so prominent a place in the imagination and affections of his people?

The ghastly tragedy of Cawnpore, the vindictive work of one whom our Government had declined to recognise as the adopted son of the deposed Peishwa, has too recently attested the patient vitality of Maratha hatred.

While Russia is close on our Punjab borders, Amcrica not too friendly, our Indian Exchequer not too flourishing, and the sovereignty of England has been suddenly struck down in the person of her Viceroy, may no self-complacent ignorance, on our part, of the feelings of our fellow-subjects, no contemptuous disregard of their deep-rooted prejudices, no supine indifference to their fair claims, henceforth tempt them to brood more than is good either for them or for us over the olden tale,—how Marathas threw off the yoke of Bijapoor, destroyed the mighty Mogul Empire, and rose to ascendancy on its ruins!

The general causes of Sivaji's success have been implicitly indicated. But the peculiarity of his genius, and his careful adaptation of means to the great ends of his policy, will be better understood from a short account of his military institutions. Never did a historical community more strictly owe both its separate existence, and its permanent character, to the creative and moulding force of a master mind. With far more propriety than his contemporary Louis XIV. might Sivaji have exclaimed, "*L'Etat, c'est moi!*" The original conception, the later modifications, and the prolonged vitality of the Maratha polity are equally remarkable. But through all vicissitudes, the primary type was never lost. And as it seemed to involve, to a certain extent, a contradiction in terms, it is the more necessary to elucidate the apparent anomaly.

To reduce chaos to order in a turbulent age, has

been pronounced the great statesman's proper function. But Sivaji, at first sight, appears to have done more than this. He compelled chaotic and explosive forces to do prescribed task work; to operate with full intensity, but only in obedience to his will, and in the direction that suited his purpose. He opened the flood-gates of anarchy, and let in the full tide of cupidity and military license. Yet he was not overwhelmed, or even embarrassed by it; but calmly devoted this self-seeking and devouring force to the evolution of a new political order, and the secure vindication of regulated liberty. He fanned the glowing flame of ambition, alike in his soldiers and in their leaders: yet he seemed never even in danger of being consumed by it, or of forfeiting the ascendancy which he had grasped so cunningly and unscrupulously. He throve by fraud and treachery: yet he was never betrayed. Lawlessness was his very *raison d'être,* and that of his community: yet he was a strict legislator; and his laws were rarely infringed, and never with impunity. In short, he was at once the Lord of Misrule, involving the countries which he overran in a whirlwind of discord and confusion; and the mighty Spirit which could

"Ride in the whirlwind and direct the storm."

Such is the paradoxical impression which the mere story of Sivaji leaves on the mind of the English student. But a survey of his institutions will remove the apparent contradiction; and will explain, not only how a robber chieftain rose to be the founder of what was, for a century, the most formidable and wide-spread Power in India, but how, whatever his moral laxity in such an age and state of society, he deserved to succeed in his great and by no means simply selfish enterprise.

Some general observations will perhaps here be not out of place.

(1). The predatory occupation, and the treacherous, even murderous, practices of Sivaji and his followers were quite compatible with the co-existence of many virtues in the same men. Macaulay has argued, that a vice not condemned by public opinion does not sink the *average* man, at least, in his own estimation, and therefore does not so thoroughly corrupt and debase him, as one which the society in which he lives has distinctly and strongly reprobated. And those who remember that even the Great Duke, the incarnation of independently realised and manly duty, thought himself bound to fight a duel when Prime Minister of England, may be inclined to admit that there is much truth in Macaulay's distinction. Now, so completely did the point of honour with the Marathas consist in plundering successfully, that their standard expression for gaining a victory was—"to spoil the enemy."

Treachery, too, has always been esteemed among

them legitimate, and speaking generally laudable, in public affairs; though in private life I have found them conspicuously faithful and straightforward. How far assassination was considered venial, depended on circumstances. The murder of the Mussulman General, Afzool Khan, by Sivaji himself, was highly approved; that of a Hindoo Raja, at which he connived, was strongly condemned. But this leads to another remark.

(2). Sivaji and his people (as I have already said), even in their warfare, were by no means mere bandits. A halo of heroism, patriotism, and religious zeal invested their proceedings, and induced them to regard the son of Shahji as a predestined, divinely-favoured, indeed as an inspired deliverer.

Race, religion, and to a considerable extent geography, discriminated them from the Mahometans of Bijapur and Golconda. With such aliens, and still more with the invading Moguls and the persecuting Aurungzib, they had a complicated, irreconcilable, and righteous quarrel. The Gods of the mountains were not the Gods of the plain: the Maratha citizen, whether Rajput, Brahmin, Sudra, or of aboriginal lineage, justly apprehended himself to have been defrauded and displaced by the progress of Mahometan conquest in old time; and to be yet more seriously and grievously threatened by the advance of the Mogul arms and administrative system. And the pent-up mountaineer has constantly, in similar circumstances, made a sort of conscience of pressing upon the prosperous and luxurious denizens of the open country at his feet. On the whole, both Sivaji and his original followers might well hold, and did hold, that in waging war after their own fashion with the Mussulman, they were doing both God and man good service, covering themselves with glory, and gaining not only welcome, but creditably retributive spoils.

(3). Gibbon has, in the case of Timour, pointed out an apparent contradiction, very similar to that which we are now considering. The general spoiler and devastator of Asia was, at home in the heart of Tartary, and in relation to his own people, a beneficent legislator. So it was with Sivaji. Stern, grasping, vindictive, and treacherous towards the hostile Mussulman, he was, as far as the grim exigencies of his military system allowed, mild, just, forbearing, and faithful, in his dealings with his tribesmen, his followers generally, and with the inhabitants of districts which submitted to his rule. Not only was

"Parcere subjectis, et debellare superbos"

his maxim, but he shewed habitual and systematic consideration for vested interests, religious prejudices, traditional sentiments, stereotyped habits. Thus, destructive of Mahometan sway, he was conservative of Hindoo nationality; creative of a new, or (as his followers thought) restorative of a purer and more primeval form of native society than had been compatible with the political ascendancy even of their more tolerant Mahometan rulers. Hence he secured the willing obedience and enthusiastic attachment of all classes throughout his native glens; and from his post of vantage could without misgiving pour his forces upon the central plain, or even extend his ravages to the seaboard beyond.

(4). Still, it may be objected, a lawless life begets a general temper of lawlessness. And the sanction aud practice of habitual treachery are apt to recoil upon the patron and perpetrator of such practices. Sivaji was not unaware of these dangers; and the history of his descendants soon illustrated the reasonableness of such fears. But he secured himself for the time by what I may call the directness and centralising spirit of his rule. He had ministers, officers, and agents in abundance and of every description; but they were not such by original *status*, but by his own appointment: and it was part of his plan that their continuance in office should invariably depend on proved personal fitness and fidelity. He disapproved of *jaghires*, as tending to root their holders in the soil, and limit the spontaneous action of the Raja. Hereditary village and district authorities he did not deprive of their dues; but he levied those dues through officers of his own selection, and allowed no fenced villages or other strongholds in his country, except the forts garrisoned by his own trusty instruments and special bands.

And while, in earlier days, he was as careful in picking and inspecting his soldiers as Cromwell in enrolling his Ironsides; throughout his career he insisted on no man being admitted without the precaution of securing, from those already in the service, a kind of *bail* for the fidelity and good conduct of the recruit.

Thus he held himself the reins in the conduct of every department. And while, as regarded treachery, his own consummate cunning was more than a match for most plotters, his vigilance was equal to his sagacity. His eye was everywhere: and besides the service of recognised spies, he controlled every thing and every body by playing off one class, one race, and one profession against another; by checks and counterchecks; and by secret agency and latent and minute *espionage*, not less complicated or subtle than the famous and intricate machinery of Loyola and his successors.

I proceed to give an outline of his military arrangements in each department.

The student of military history would do well to notice the successive phases of Maratha warfare, from the days of Sivaji to those of Lord Lake,

Colonel Wellesley, and Dowlut Rao Sindia. From the few half-naked, undisciplined, and ill-armed mountain rovers, whose unsophisticated gallantry, agility in climbing, and devotion to their hardy and skilful companion in the chace, helped him to seize fortress after fortress on the borders of the Ghats, and to pounce upon and hide away the spoil of the Dekkan:—to the eighty artistically-drilled and well-appointed battalions of Dowlut Rao, officered by Frenchmen, supported by a magnificent park of artillery, and acting in concert with a vast host of showy, dashing, and terrible horsemen, who, in "wild Mahratta battle," threatened to overwhelm the hero of Assye, and to change the history of the world:—between these two extremes of military array the whole orbit of the tactical system seems to have been traversed.

But I confine myself, at present, to Sivaji's own ultimate arrangements. He naturally began with infantry alone, and those exclusively Hindoos, or of the earlier mountain refugee races. Later, after much hesitation, he enlisted Mussulmans—especially Afghans. Cavalry he adopted as soon as his operations in the Dekkan required them. Artillery he never used, except on his last great expedition into the Carnatic Plain, when he persuaded the King of Golconda to lend him a siege train.

Both infantry and cavalry were lightly clad.

Both used shields; but I believe that, at this period, neither ever had any other defensive armour. The infantry were divided into *Mawulees* and *Hetkurees*; the cavalry into *Bargeers* and *Sillidars*. The former terms were geographical, denoting the foot soldiers levied in the Ghats and in the Concan respectively. The *Bargeers* were horsemen mounted at Sivaji's expense, and in fact his soldiers, strictly so called, forming collectively the *Pagah*, or household troops. The *Sillidars*, like the Mogul *Ahdis*, were of a higher class socially; and were troopers, mounted at their own cost, and more nearly resembling our irregular native cavalry in modern times in India.

The foot were armed with swords and matchlocks, or in some cases, with the newly-invented firelock. But for stealthy service, as in night attacks and the capture of forts, each tenth man carried a bow and arrows. The *Hetkurees* were the better marksmen; the *Mawulees* the stouter in hand-to-hand combats with the sword. The horsemen carried swords, and some had matchlocks. But their characteristic and most efficient weapon, as in the case of the Cossacks whom they so much resembled, and whose name they adopted through the Moguls, was a long spear. The readers of Erckman-Chatrian's romances will be at no loss to conceive their celerity of movement, their dexterity, or the terror which their sudden apparition was wont to inspire.

On the fidelity of the infantry, Sivaji could confidently depend. The *Bargeers*, too, he could trust better than the *Sillidars*. To check the erratic tendencies of the irregular and too independent horsemen, he therefore, with characteristic prudence, habitually interspersed among them parties of the household cavalry.

In the infantry he had officers of ten, fifty, a hundred, a thousand, five thousand; the last being immediately subordinate to the *Surnobut*, or Commander-in-Chief. The organisation and supervision of the cavalry were more complicated. The smallest division, consisting of twenty-five, was commanded by a *Havildar*. Five such divisions formed a *Jooma*, with its corresponding military officer. Five of these again were massed under a *Soobedar*. Lastly, ten *Soobehs*, really mustering 6250 horsemen, but formally rated at 5000, were united under an officer, whose harsh name I am afraid to mention; and who was immediately subordinate to the Commander-in-Chief, or *Surnobut*. This last was distinct from the chief general of infantry.

But the accounts of the *Soobeh* were managed and audited by separate agents, civilians and either Brahmins or Purvoes, appointed by Sivaji, responsible directly to him, and designed doubtless to act as a check on the military chief. This was also the case with the commander of 5000. Each division also, except the smallest, had its staff of news-writers and professed spies; while secret emissaries (as I have said) pervaded every part of the army. The foot-soldiers' pay averaged *monthly* (?) from seven or eight shillings of our money to thrice that sum. That of the *Bargeer* was about double the foot-soldiers': while the *Sillidar* had from two to four guineas. Before the army took the field, a strict scrutiny of each soldier was instituted, and for a double purpose. His losses in the field were, if duly proved to have occurred in the public service, replaced. And whatever he brought back in addition to what he took with him, he was bound to produce; otherwise it was liable to forfeiture. For all spoil was, in the first instance, Sivaji's property. The captor on presenting it was partly rewarded on the spot, partly recorded for favourable treatment or promotion later. And if he preferred to redeem it, he was usually allowed to do so. Government settled annually all out-standing claims of the soldiers, either in ready money or by bills on the Raja's revenue collectors. Both to prevent the villagers being oppressed, and to guard against the growth of any power over which he had not complete control, Sivaji did not permit any charges in favour of individuals to be imposed on the revenues of villages. Nor did he suffer cows, women, or peasants to be carried off or ill-treated. The only prisoners he sanctioned were wealthy Mussulmans, or Hindoos in their service, who could afford to repurchase their liberty at a high price. He was fond however of ostentatiously liberating distinguished prisoners, and in this proceeding had no doubt a secret eye to diplomatic business, as well as to acquiring a reputation for generosity. The strictness of his discipline may be inferred, from his visiting with death the offence of taking the field accompanied by a *chère amie*. He was equally exact in reward and punishment.

Rent-free lands in perpetuity he granted to deserving soldiers, to temples, and to the guardians of his forts. He never confiscated sacred revenues, even if devoted to Mussulman rites, or to the memory of Mussulman saints.

His most peculiar military institution, and the nursery of his power, was his fort system. Each stronghold, besides any occasional Maratha force stationed there, had a large and permanent staff of inhabitants and defenders, minutely organised, carefully trained, and warmly interested in its maintenance. Of these, the Marathas proper were destined to fight; the Brahmins were charged with the victualling and other civil cares of the place; the Ramoosees and other primitive tribesmen were appointed to note and baffle the approach of an enemy, and stealthily impede his operations, when he could no longer be diverted from an attack. All these classes were paid by rent-free lands, which descended to their posterity. Sivaji, when campaigning, of course made war support war—and more. But while his cavalry were browsing in the enemy's country, his Brahmin storekeepers were carefully collecting, in the immediate neighbourhood of each fort, the crop of hay and grain, against the approach of the rainy season; when the horsemen and their beasts regularly returned to secure quarters in the hills. Each fort had its Commander-in-Chief, or *Havildar*; and his subordinates were multiplied according to the size and importance of the place.

"Orders," says Grant Duff, "in respect to ingress and egress, rounds, watches, and patrols, care of water, grain, stores, and ammunition, were most minute; and the officer of each department was furnished with distinct rules for his guidance, from which no deviation was permitted. A rigid economy characterised all Sivaji's institutions regarding expenditure."

It may be remarked in conclusion, as to his military arrangements, that there was little of barbarism in this barbarian's dispositions.

CHAPTER VI.

THE MARATHA WAR OF INDEPENDENCE.

THE sudden death of Sivaji was an event most critical to the Maratha community, of which his influence had been both the bond of union, and the animating principle. He had, indeed, not only excited the strongest passions, and appealed to the deepest and most abiding sentiments of his people; but he had founded institutions well calculated, in some respects, to endure both the lapse of time, and the stress even of imperial antagonism. But what is apt to become of newly-created institutions among a rude people, even in the West, without the presiding spirit of their founder? His territory, indeed, was ample; the original district which formed his military base was naturally almost impregnable, and had been carefully strengthened by a complicated chain-work of forts; his army was numerous and in fine condition; his revenue was elastic, and he had accumulated an immense treasure; the terror of his name was widely diffused, and he had formed a school of officers whose talents had been developed under the stimulus of his suggestive example, keen criticism, and stern discipline. Yet, to keep in order the formidable warlike engine which he had constructed, and worked with such remarkable success, was a task which had taxed to the utmost the activity of his master-mind. To sustain the strange paradox of a State stable and harmonious within, yet forming in fact but a vast entrenched camp of marauders, and seeking its very principle of existence in the continuous practice of military license, might well exceed the powers of any but one, whom a unique genius and a singular variety of favourable circumstances had combined to befriend in an undertaking essentially transitory.

In the East the death of the leader is the constant signal for the dissolution of the army. Would it now be otherwise with the Marathas? Would not internal dissension, the ambition of chiefs, the cupidity of followers, fatally interfere with Sivaji's wise arrangements, and leave the community (in Gibbon's phrase—"at once in a state of childhood and caducity,") a prey to the implacable vengeance of the mighty Monarch whose authority it had so long disputed?

Such misgivings could not in any case fail to

occur to a thoughtful and patriotic Maratha. And Sivaji's family circumstances gave additional weight to them.

His eldest son was Sambaji, whose mother was dead, and whose own insubordinate and licentious conduct had caused his strict father to place him in easy confinement within the fortress of Panalla. But the deceased hero had left also a younger son, Raja Ram, at this time ten years old. To him an ambitious mother attempted, by a *coup d'état*, to transfer the Rajaship; and with the connivance of some of the Maratha leaders the boy was actually installed. But Sambaji made his escape from Panalla, and acting with much energy, soon recovered his ground, gained over some of the conspirators, imprisoned others, and obtained quiet possession of the throne (June, 1680). On this occasion he showed much address; he had inherited all his father's courage, and his natural capacity seems to have been by no means despicable. In spite of the late plot many of the chiefs were disposed to give him cordial support; and the eldest son of Sivaji could not appeal in vain to the Maratha people for co-operation in his great father's work. Some advantages were in fact gained; and the partial incursions of the Moguls were more than once repelled with loss and ignominy to the invaders.

But from the first it was too clear that Sambaji was quite unequal to the task of replacing his heroic parent, and that the interests of the new commonwealth must incur much peril from his mismanagement and vices. He was sluggish, sensual, extravagant, vindictive, and reckless both of the feelings and the welfare of his subjects. The unusual and brutal severity with which he punished the conspirators whom he had baffled, produced a most unfavourable impression; encouraged the announcement of evil omens on his installation; sowed the seeds of further sedition; led some chiefs to desert his service for that of his enemies; and thus weakened his authority and impaired his resources. A new plot to liberate one of his victims resulted in the execution, on mere suspicion, of one of Sivaji's oldest and most distinguished companions, who was also a Brahmin. What was to be expected from one who thus lightly severed the connexion both with the military glories of Maharashtra, and with the religious scruples which Sivaji had so profitably cherished? The administration was relaxed; the close and minute attention which the father had bestowed on his singular institutions was abandoned; the best and most tried officers were slighted, if not discarded; and an incompetent favourite, Kuloosha, a stranger from Northern India, a man of cultivation, indeed, and learning, but of no practical ability either civil or military, became the all-powerful Sejanus of the secluded and infatuated Raja.

In vain did Sivaji's spiritual teacher, on his death-bed, endeavour to arouse Sambaji by earnestly delineating the views, the character, the deeds of his renowned father. Only a momentary reformation resulted from the still more outspoken protest of a powerful and venerable Maratha statesman, who travelled from the eastern coast expressly to urge upon his degenerate sovereign the obligations of his position. The influence of the favourite seemed irresistible, and was popularly ascribed to magic. Under such auspices it may well be believed that the public interest did not prosper. The internal decay which hence threatened the Maratha Power is described by Colonel Grant Duff in the subjoined passage :*—

* "The system, which Sivajee introduced, soon fell into decay, wherever the efficiency of the establishments depended upon the vigilance or care of the executive authority. This was first perceivable in the army where the discipline and strict orders of Sivajee were neglected. When the horse took the field, stragglers were allowed to join, plunder was secreted, women followers, who had been prohibited on pain of death, were not only permitted, but women were brought off from the enemy's country as an established article of plunder, and either retained as concubines, or sold as slaves.

"The small returns brought back by the commanders of the horse, were insufficient for the pay of the troops; they took the field in arrears, and permission to keep a portion of their plunder was an ample and desirable compensation for the regular pay allowed by Sivajee.

"Sumbhajee was prodigal in his expenses, and as he considered his father's treasure inexhaustible, even the favourite minister was unwilling to rouse his dangerous temper by touching on that theme.

But the freebooting commonwealth so ingeniously organized by its founder, so recklessly disordered by his successor, was not to be allowed the option of internal dissolution. It had several enemies. Above all, the crafty and powerful Aurungzib was on the watch, and was preparing to make a mighty effort for the general conquest and pacification of the Dekkan. The impolicy of Sambaji was in this respect remarkable, almost incredible. He was warlike and ambitious, but he had the soul of a Sudra; and in local efforts against his piratical neighbours, the Abyssinians of Jinjeera, and against the Portuguese, he forgot or disregarded the Continental and anti-imperial warfare, to which his station and the antecedents of his people pledged him. He had not even the prudence to follow his father's example, and ally himself with Bijapoor and Golconda against the

No revenue was received from the Carnatic after the death of Rugonath Punt; the districts in that quarter maintained themselves, but as loss rather than advantage was now the result of most of the expeditions, by which, in the time of Sivajee, so much was amassed, Kuloosha conceived he had discovered an easy mode of replenishing the treasury, by raising the land-rent, through the addition of various assessments; but when he came to collect the revenue, he found that the receipts were as much diminished from what they had been in the time of Sivajee, as the assessments were nominally increased.

"The managers of districts were in consequence removed, for what appeared to him, evident peculation. The revenue was farmed, many of the ryots fled from their villages, and speedy ruin threatened the territory of Sumbhajee."

common enemy. Much less had he the wisdom to co-operate with the warlike Rajputs, whose religious and political sympathies were with him; whose chiefs had befriended his father; who were now in rebellion against the Emperor; and who had instigated Prince Acber also to rebel. That Prince's movement was indeed foiled by his father's astuteness, but he had escaped and joined Sambaji; and the latter, had he inherited any share of his father's political genius, would have turned such an opportunity to good account, and effected a powerful tripartite union between himself, the insurgent Rajputs, and the disaffected subjects of the Emperor elsewhere, represented and headed by the young Prince.

Thus, even before Aurungzib commenced the long war in which he was destined to wear out the remainder of his strenuous life, the Maratha prospects were most gloomy, and the disastrous fate of the Raja is said to have been anticipated and openly predicted.

Before the Emperor himself appeared on the scene, he sent forward two of his sons, each at the head of a considerable army, to hem in the Marathas and give them occupation at home, by reducing the Concan and the country around the Northern Ghats (1684). But the difficulty of such an undertaking at once became apparent. The strong fortress of Salheir was indeed betrayed to Sultan Azim; but here his success ended, and he soon threw up the command in disgust; while two other generals were successively foiled in repeated efforts to reduce Ramseje. The former of these officers was Shabodeen Khan, afterwards styled Ghazi-ud-deen, the father of the famous Nizam-ul-Mulk. Meanwhile Sultan Mauzum had penetrated into the Concan. But here his troops were beset in the usual Maratha fashion; Sambaji issued orders to "stop the roads, cut off supplies, harrass them by desultory attacks, and destroy the foragers and stragglers." Thus they were reduced to great extremities; and an attempt to relieve them by sea ended in the capture of the ships by the indefatigable enemy, who had now quite overcome the Hindoo prejudice against sailing on the Ocean. Ghazi-ud-deen at length defeated the Raja in person, and extricated the Prince from his perilous position; but the misfortunes of the Concan army did not end here. After capturing some places in the Bala Ghat, it was so much reduced by famine, pestilence, and the arts of its vigilant opponents, that it is described on its return to Ahmednuggur as a mere "wreck." Nor was this all. The Marathas, not content to stand on the defensive, or rather rightly judging that aggressive measures were their best mode of defence, prosecuted their ravages far to the north, plundering successively Burhanpoor, which the Emperor had only recently quitted, and Baroach, on the confines of Hindostan Proper, and firing the whole country as they went. In vain the imperial general toiled after them: their Parthian flight always mocked his efforts, and left him far behind.

Aurungzib however had now advanced in person with the grand army, and took up his station at Sholapoor. The amount of his force does not seem to be well ascertained, though it must have been very great. But the proverbial magnificence of the Mogul Court, a magnificence then at its acmé, was exhibited in the imperial appointments, and reflected in those of the Omrahs and other officers in the field, in conspicuous and instructive contrast to the homely and business-like arrangements of the Marathas. The subjoined fine passage, though long, is not only so picturesque, but so illustrative of the fortunes of the impending strife, that I make no apology for reproducing it entire.*

* "Besides foreigners, his cavalry, assembled from Cabul, Candahar, Mooltan, Lahore, Rajpootana, and the extended Provinces of his vast Empire, was the flower of his army, and presented an array of gigantic men and horses completely armed and accoutred, whom it might be imagined, the more slender and lighter-armed natives of the Deccan could hardly venture to oppose. His infantry was also numerous, and was composed of musketeers, matchlockmen, and archers, well equipped; besides bodies of hardy Boondelas and Mewattees accustomed to predatory contests among the mountains, and the better able to cope with the Mahratta Mawulees. To these were afterwards added many thousands of infantry, raised

It was not, however, against the Marathas that the Emperor's first operations were directed. After Sultan Azim had been sent forward to attack Bijapoor; had been involved in difficulties similar to those experienced by his brother in the Concan; and had been similarly relieved by Ghazi-ud-deen; Aurungzib closely invested the capital, breached the walls, then allowed famine to do its work, and at last compelled a surrender (1686). The territory was reduced to a

in the Carnatic. Besides a number of field-pieces, which accompanied the royal tents, there were several hundred pieces of cannon manned by natives of Hindoostan, and directed by European gunners; and a great number of miners were attached to the park of artillery, with artisans of every description. A long train of war-elephants was followed by a number of the same animals as the Emperor's private establishment, employed to carry the ladies of his seraglio, or to convey such of his tents as were too large to be borne on camels. Numerous led horses, magnificently caparisoned, formed a stud for the Emperor's riding; a menagerie accompanied the camp, from which the rarest animals in the world were frequently brought forth, and exhibited by their keepers before the Emperor and his Court; while hawks, hounds, hunting-tigers, trained elephants, and every accompaniment used for field sport, swelled the pomp of this prodigious retinue. The canvas-walls, which encompassed the royal tents, formed a circumference of 1,200 yards, and contained every description of apartment to be found in the most spacious palace. Halls of audience for public assemblies and privy councils, with all the courts and cabinets attached to them, each hall magnificently adorned, and having within it a raised seat or throne for the Emperor, surrounded by gilded pillars with canopies of velvet, richly fringed, and superbly embroidered; separate tents, as mosques and oratories; baths and galleries for archery and gymnastic exercises; a seraglio as remarkable for luxury and privacy as that of Delhi; Persian carpets, damasks, *subeh*, or Province; the King was imprisoned, and most probably poisoned; the chief men were admitted into the imperial service; and the capital, still retaining monumental vestiges of its former greatness, sank first into a provincial town, and then became almost a city of the dead. Golconda shortly after shared the same fate (1687); its sovereign, though intrigued against and deceived by the cunning Emperor, and deserted by the bulk of his own followers, resisting

and tapestries; European velvets, satins and broad-cloths; Chinese silks of every description; and Indian muslins and cloth of gold, were employed in all the tents with the utmost profusion and effect. Gilded balls and cupolas surmounted the tops of the royal tents; the outside of which, and the canvas walls, were of a variety of lively colours, disposed in a manner which heightened the general splendour. The entrance into the royal enclosure was through a spacious portal, flanked by two elegant pavilions, from which extended, on each side, rows of cannon, forming an avenue, at the extremity of which was an immense tent containing the great State drums, and imperial band;—a little farther in front was the post of the grand guard on duty, commanded by a nobleman, who mounted with it daily. On the other sides, surrounding the great enclosure just mentioned, were separate tents, for the Emperor's armoury, harness, &c.; a tent for water, kept cool with saltpetre, another for fruit, a third for sweetmeats, a fourth for betel, and so on, with numerous kitchens, stables, &c., &c. Such luxury in a camp is scarcely to be conceived; but besides what has been described, every tent had its exact duplicate, which was sent on in advance to be prepared against the Emperor's arrival. His march was a procession, and when he entered his pavilions, a salvo from fifty or sixty pieces of ordnance announced the event; and he assumed and maintained every form and ceremony observed at the established residences of the Imperial Court."

bravely, until treason consigned him to the same gloomy and inaccessible stronghold, whither his former rival, the King of Bijapoor, had preceded him. Hyderabad, however, as the capital of Ghazi-ud-deen's descendants, has revived to a certain extent the traditional glories of the city, whose fort formerly gave name to the kingdom. The territory was made a sixth imperial Dekkan Province.

Sultan Mauzum, for the benevolent offence of interceding to mitigate the lot of the unfortunate king, was imprisoned for six years by his imperious and jealous father.

Meanwhile the degenerate son of Sivaji had done little to arrest the progress of the invader, and the fate which with sure and swift steps was advancing against himself. Distracted by local jealousies, petty disputes, and feeble intrigues among the western coast Powers, enervated by vicious indulgence, and neutralising, through the paramount influence conceded to the arrogant and imbecile Kuloosha, the spontaneous activity of his abler and more energetic followers, he threw away more than one grand opportunity for bringing the united power of Southern India to bear against the Moguls. Had Sivaji been at the head of affairs, there seems little doubt that he would have succeeded in effecting at the eleventh hour at least a temporary league between his own people, the threatened Afghan Monarchies, the English and Portuguese, who already began not only to dread, but to experience the insolence and tyranny of the Emperor, the Seedee, whose interests lay in the same direction, the enterprising Hindoo Raja of Mysore, Chick Deo, who was now rising into importance, and even the primitive and almost independent Poligars, in the wilder parts of the country, one of whom many years afterwards long baffled all the assaults of the imperial army, headed by the Emperor in person.

It may be objected, that at this period the English were mere timid traders, and would not have ventured on war with Aurungzib. But this point seems to me by no means so certain as it is generally assumed to be. In fact, they did actually, on more than one occasion, and on both sides of India, contend single handed on the sea with the Emperor's servants.

But Sambaji was obviously unequal to either the conception or the development of such an extensive and intricate combination. And though he attempted a feeble diversion on the Carnatic seaboard, it ended in failure and disgrace. Even the trump card that was already in his hand he threw away. Prince Acber, who had exerted himself energetically against his father's and brother's armies, and had on many occasions given useful advice, and whose presence lent a certain amount of moral support to the Maratha cause, was wearied out by Sambaji's inactivity, and obtained leave to retire from his Court (1688), whence he proceeded to Persia, and died there shortly before his father.

Sivaji's political and military machinery became more and more disorganised, until, except in the retention of the forts, it could hardly be said to exist. The Maratha open country was reduced, and at length the forts themselves were threatened, and some of them actually occupied; and in their fall the doom of the depressed and fast dissolving community would be sealed.

It may seem strange that a high-spirited and lawless people did not take the remedy into their own hands, and act on the principle—" It is expedient that one man should die for the people." But no design of the kind is hinted at. To slay, or even to depose, the Raja, who was at the same time a son of Sivaji, would have cruelly shocked the feelings and prejudices of his Hindoo clansmen. But the Mogul at length effected precisely what was wanted to liberate the spirit of his dangerous enemies, and launch them on a career of desperate enterprise, steady progress, and final triumph.

Yeatikad Khan, an active officer employed in the Western Bala Ghat, having ascertained the place where Sambaji, like Tiberius at Capreæ, was grovelling in a constant round of low pleasures, explored the mountain tracks that led thither; and making a rapid dash across the hills with a select body of troops, he came unexpectedly upon the Raja's retreat; captured both him and his favourite; escorted them to the imperial camp bound on the backs of camels, amidst insult, mockery, and the exulting cries of a huge multitude of their enemies. Aurungzib seemed at first disposed to spare the life of the degraded Prince, on condition of the immediate surrender of the forts. But the extremity of his position, and the aspect of his hereditary foe, aroused in the unhappy man the spirit of his father, and he concentrated into one short sentence the expression of his despair, his hatred, and his determination to provoke an immediate deliverance from a plight worse than death. "Tell the Emperor that if he will give me his daughter, I will become a Mussulman." And then he cursed Mahomet.

He was not disappointed. The bolt had struck home. The pride, the bigotry, and the vindictive wrath of the Emperor led him to forget all ideas of policy; and found vent in an instant order for the execution of the prisoner with circumstances of peculiar barbarity. He was blinded; his tongue was cut out; and he was then beheaded (1689).

Such was the end of Sambaji, an end, however tragical, perhaps indispensable for the timely recovery of his people from the fatal lethargy in which he had steeped both himself and them. Kuloosha perished with him.

Sambaji's death, in fact, gave new life to his community. That fate which his own people would have shuddered to inflict upon him, they bitterly resented at the hands of the Moguls, and it quickened their resolve to resist *à l'outrance.* A council of chiefs was held, presided over by Jessoo Bhye, his widow, and attended by Raja Ram, the brother whom it had formerly been attempted to set up against him, and who had since spent his life in prison: and it was unanimously determined that Sivaji, the son of the late Raja, being too young to undertake the government at such a crisis, his uncle Ram Raja should be made Regent, and the whole energies of the public should be devoted to avenge the insult which it had suffered in the cruel execution of the sovereign, and to recover what had been lost during his fatuous reign. The measures now concerted were admirably calculated to secure these objects. The desperate condition of affairs was calmly surveyed, and appropriate remedies were devised. The treasury was empty: [the military system had degenerated into mere predatory license; the remaining fortresses were ill-appointed and ill-supplied: the open territory was occupied by the enemy: the original subjects of the Raja had lost the *prestige* of success; and neither the Maratha chiefs who had lately served

Bijapoor, and might be expected to sympathise with men of their own religion and race, nor the mere soldiers of fortune to whom all sides that paid were alike, were inclined to throw in their lot with a beaten and decaying mass of disorderly bandits. But the judicious, comprehensive, and far-sighted arrangements now adopted met all the requirements of the situation, and rapidly turned the ever wavering scale of fortune.

To garrison and provision the forts, and to collect and store up in them grain and hay, was the first care of the Government. To restore the strictness of Sivaji's discipline, and to replace illicit and self-maintained plunderers by salaried soldiers, was, in the exhausted state of the exchequer, a slower and more difficult task; which, however, the exertions of a capable finance minister, and the assistance of public spirited individuals facilitated. Another minister, whose influence with the roving Sillidars was great, undertook to engage them, and dispersing them quietly over the face of the country, to keep them well informed, and available for sudden emergencies. The enthusiasm and gallantry of other leaders, which had been repressed under the late disastrous reign, now burst forth anew, and proved infectious with their followers.

The Marathas in the imperial service were tampered with, and when not prepared to commit themselves openly, already began to meditate a patriotic desertion. The Regent, like a more modern military dictator in a national uprising against invasion, flew about the country, organising the defence, inspecting each focus of resistance, and communicating to his people his own indomitable spirit.

His brother's widow, with her young son, took refuge in the strong fortress of Raigurh, formerly the nucleus of Sivaji's military power, and the receptacle of his spoil. To be prepared for all contingencies, it was resolved from the first, that if Ram Raja should be unable to hold his own in the upper country, he should transfer the seat of government to the Carnatic plain land, with which his family had a hereditary connexion, much of which his father had reduced, and where the Regent had secured the possession of the stupendous treble-crested and fortified rock of Gingee, in later days the advanced base of the French throughout their wars with the English.

The monsoon had afforded the Marathas some respite, and leisure to prepare their plan of defence. But on the return of the dry season the contest began in earnest. The exterior *cordon* of forts, the construction of which had been one of Sivaji's latest cares, had already been pierced. Raigurh, around which clustered so many associations of successful raids and hair breadth escapes, achieved by the adventurer whose genius and energy had created a nation, and where his grandson and namesake was deposited under the care of Jessoo Bhye, was first assailed, and fell through treachery (1690).

The capture of the young Sivaji and his mother seems in no way to have discouraged either the leaders or their followers. But it did not fail to affect materially, in the sequel, both the fortunes of the Marathas, and the character of their government. The Emperor's daughter took a warm interest in the prisoners, who were well treated in the courtly camp, though strictly secluded from intercourse with those even of their countrymen who still followed Aurungzib's standard.

Under the same officer who had seized Sambaji and gained Raigurh, Yeatikad, henceforth called Zoolfikar Khan, the Moguls pushed on and took Merich and Panalla.

Raja Ram now thought it time to secure the free action of his government and armies, and to cause at the same time an important diversion, by betaking himself to the Carnatic *Payen Ghat*. After carefully assigning their respective functions to the officers who were to represent him in Maharashtra, and making a final tour of inspection and encouragement throughout the fortified district that still held out; and after an adventurous flight to the coast, closely pursued, and narrowly escaping capture by the imperial officers, the Regent and a party of the ablest and most enterprising chiefs entered Gingee safely. Here the formal installation of the Raja, or (as his nephew's party afterwards maintained) of the *provisional* Raja took place: a Court was established; official titles were conferred; honorary dresses and other decorations were issued; and grants were made —even of lands not only in the hands of the Moguls at the time, but which had never yet belonged to the Marathas. By these and other means the vitality of the Government, and its confidence in the reality and permanence of its mission, were signified; and confidence was diffused among those who might have augured ill from the disappearance of the head of the administration. Sympathisers continued to flock to the national banner in the upland, and to seek at Gingee employment in a service, which appealed at once to many of the higher and lower impulses of human nature.

But the Emperor, while diligently tracking the robbers in their native mountains, had no intention of allowing them to gather to a head elsewhere.

Again Zoolfikar Khan was called to take the command; and while detached bodies of Marathas boldly overspread the Dekkan, and alternately alarmed various places that were supposed to have been delivered for ever from their ravages, that active general marched eastward, and prepared to besiege Gingee (1691). But the strength of the place disconcerted him: he found or conceived his force inadequate to its complete investment; and he preferred, for the present, to levy requisitions in the rich districts of Tanjore and Trichinopoly, and to apply for a reinforcement from the Dekkan.

This, however, in spite of the immense resources of the Emperor, was more easily asked than given. The tide of resistance was rising higher daily; and the new system worked wonders, such as Sivaji himself had hardly achieved. The primitive Poligars now engaged in a contest so congenial to their tastes and circumstances; and the imperial forces were successfully opposed by the Beder chieftain already referred to, and who ultimately occupied the final efforts of Aurungzib himself. The Mogul Foujdar of Waee was taken, with his whole force, and replaced by a Maratha governor (1692). Raigurh and Panalla were recovered; and the imperial commander of Merich shared the fate of the Foujdar of Waee. The Maratha *chout* again began to be regularly and deliberately levied, and other exactions, such as *ghasdana*, or forage allowance, were added, to encourage and reward the enterprise of the leaders. Their services were cordially acknowledged by the Raja; and honorary presents were secretly transmitted from Gingee, to stimulate them to renewed exertions. Emboldened by success, they now began to attack the Mogul convoys from Hindostan; cut off several of them; and thrice defeated and captured the commanders sent to avert this formidable danger.

At length a large force was despatched to the assistance of Zoolfikar Khan. But jealousy and dissension broke out in the Mogul camp; it contained also many Marathas, the old servants of the Bijapoor State; and both these circumstances were carefully improved by the crafty Brahmins who surrounded Ram Raja. Zoolfikar was indignant that the Prince Kam Buksh should have been sent to supersede him in the chief command. He, therefore, began to play into the hands of Ram Raja, and paralysed the energies of the attack (1694).

Five years had elapsed, and Gingee remained untaken. But a more degrading reverse before its walls was reserved for the imperial arms. Santaji Ghorepuray, the most distinguished and enterprising Maratha commander in the Dekkan, approached to raise the siege (1696). He was preceded by a flying force under Dhunnaji, another daring and accomplished officer, who came upon the scattered besiegers unawares, and inflicted heavy loss upon them before they could offer any effectual resistance.

Santaji followed up this success by another greater and more complete victory.

At Covrepauk, a place since memorable as the scene of one of Clive's brilliant engagements, he encountered Ali Murdan, the imperial Governor of the

Province; defeated his army; took his baggage, his camp, and eventually the flying Governor himself.

He then proceeded to hem in the besiegers in the way so well known to Marathas; spread a report that Aurungzib was no more; and offered to support the claims of Prince Kam Buksh to the vacant throne. This was a cunning and telling stroke. Zoolfikar and his father, the Prime Minister, who was also in camp, on the true or alleged ground that the Prince had listened to these overtures, placed him in arrest. His troops thereupon became mutinous: Santaji seized the opportunity which he had prepared; redoubled his attacks on the disunited foe; compelled them to raise the siege; and blockaded them in turn. From this predicament they were extricated by an ignoble truce, which allowed them to retire. Aurungzib recalled the Prince and the Minister, and left the undivided command to Zoolfikar.

But instead of resuming the siege, he again marched southward, and allowed his opponent, with whom he was probably in collusion, to gain another important advantage. Kasim Khan, a distinguished officer, and the Governor of a neighbouring Province, advanced with a large army to check Santaji's depredations. But he was intercepted; harrassed incessantly; beaten in detail; compelled to seek refuge outside a town into which the inhabitants refused to admit him;

starved out; and forced to surrender with all his army. So deep was the humiliation that the circumvented General took poison; and the Emperor publicly disgraced his subordinate officers. Shortly afterwards Santaji enticed another army into an ambuscade; routed it, and took its baggage. The Emperor insisting on the reduction of Gingee, Zoolfikar at last took it by assault (1698). But Ram Raja and his family were allowed to escape, and returned to Maharashtra.

Besides the loss of this great fortress, two other circumstances threatened the rising fortunes of the Marathas. Jealousy had sprung up between Santaji and his lieutenant Dhunnaji, who had led his advanced guard to victory on the march to Gingee. The former, who had achieved so much for the cause, and had been for seven years the terror of the Moguls, was basely murdered, not (it was thought) without the connivance of the Raja. His family withdrew from the service of their ungrateful sovereign. But they continued to fight against the common enemy on their own account.

On the other hand, the Emperor, convinced by long and bitter experience that he had to deal with a far more formidable and complicated problem than he had at first imagined, and that he was making little way towards the complete conquest of the Marathas, devised a new plan of operations. A systematic division of labour was adopted. The armies were distributed into a flying field force under Zoolfikar's direction, and a besieging force, which was to be commanded by the Emperor in person, and devoted to the exclusive task of reducing the forts. Great exertions were made to stimulate the flagging energies of the imperialists; and the aged Emperor was indefatigable and constant as ever in a design of which all around him were heartily tired. To the disgust of his luxurious officers he broke up the great camp, and prepared to encounter the hardships and perils of a campaign in the wild hill country.

Meanwhile the Raja had celebrated his return to the Dekkan by the largest military muster, and the most systematic and wide ranging exaction of tribute, that had hitherto taken place. As with Sivaji,

"Parcere subjectis, et debellare superbos"

was his literal plan of action; and where he could not raise ready money, reversing the late Prussian system of requisition, he took promissory notes for future payment, thus establishing a precedent which, in Maratha interpretation, laid the sure foundation of a right. But on his return from the neighbourhood of the Nerbudda, he was vigorously attacked and pursued by Zoolfikar with his new-modelled army; and suffered so much from his exertions during the long and harrassing retreat, that he fell ill, and at the end of a month died (1700).

He had done much to retrieve the fame of his father's house. His one crime had been his alleged privity to the murder of Santaji. But this is hardly proved. The Moguls rejoiced at his death. But, at the time, they gained little by it; though later the disputed succession, which his removal perhaps tended to promote, was of some advantage to them.

Tara Bhye, Ram Raja's widow, became Regent, in the minority of her son, another Sivaji; and being a woman of ability, ambition, and masculine vigour, moved from place to place, distracting the pursuit of her enemies, and animating the exertions of her friends.

Besides some smaller successes, gained by the imperialists, they reduced what may be called the royal fortress of Satara, after a long and obstinate defence. But a reverse soon followed. As in the case of Owen Glendower, the elements were said to fight on the side of the Marathas in their native glens. As in that case, the invaders really suffered heavily from want of experience and preparation for the peculiar dangers of mountain warfare in a tempestuous season.

Year after year the weary war dragged on. Aurungzib continued to take fort after fort. But again and again these were recovered. On the other hand, the open country was everywhere exposed to the incursions and requisitions of the insurgents. The imperialists were again and again defeated, until they dreaded to meet the enemy, and fled before those whom they had formerly held in supreme contempt. Treachery was added to discouragement, cowardice, and military demoralization. The Mogul generals and local officers compounded for exemption from hostilities with their irrepressible opponents; and even began privately to share the spoil, and thus find their account in the continuance of the war. The Marathas in the imperial service deserted to their tribesmen, or gave them secret assistance.

The Emperor could not realise the resources of the country which he had nominally conquered, nor provide for the safe arrival of the convoys from Hindostan, which, while they exhausted his original territories, had become more and more indispensable in his present position. The whole imperial system was out of gear; and the end was as disastrous and ignominious, as the effort to accomplish impossibilities had been stubborn and prolonged.

Aurungzib humbled himself, and proposed to make peace, release Sambaji's son, and formally concede a portion of the Maratha claims to tribute from the imperial Provinces (1705). But this treaty was broken off, only to be succeeded by an equally impotent attempt to work upon the feelings of the

Hindoos by issuing a proclamation in the name of their imprisoned Raja, calling upon them to lay down their arms. The Beder chief's petty fortified town of Wakinkerah long detained and baffled the Great Mogul. And, finally, he was pursued, and very nearly taken prisoner, by his indefatigable and emboldened enemies.

This last trial was too much alike for the mind and the body of the proud and aged Emperor. A generation ago he had pronounced Sivaji a "mountain rat." And after devoting the whole interval, and the whole resources of the Empire to the extermination of this political vermin, the thronging followers of the mountain rat had hunted him in the plain, and tracked him to his doom! Twenty-one years before he had left Ahmednuggur in the magnificent array which has been described. Thither he now returned, and confessed himself unequal to the prosecution of the task in which he had then engaged so confidently. He seems to have felt that his life had been, after all his subtlety, activity, glory, and power, on the whole, a *carrière manquée*; and with an expression of fatalistic resignation to the results of the irrevocable past, he breathed out his soul at the age of eighty-eight (1707); and with him may be said to have departed the integrity and greatness of the Mogul Empire, for which he had so long striven, "not wisely, but too well."

The causes of the signal and momentous failure which I have endeavoured to sketch faithfully in each of its stages, are not far to seek. Aurungzib's renowned kingcraft was altogether at fault on occasion of a crisis so peculiar. His love of annexation betrayed him into a fatal error. While the elements of disorder were rife among the Marathas, and while it remained to be seen how far the imperial armies, which had failed to crush the power of Sivaji in its earlier forms, would be able to exterminate a people mature in the art of ravaging, enriched by long-continued and distant expeditions, inflamed with national animosity, religious zeal, and the memory of great achievements, and capable of rapid concentration in a most difficult country, studded and begirt with innumerable fortresses; Aurungzib had decreed the simultaneous destruction of the kingdoms of Bijapoor and Golconda, or in other words, the annihilation of the only institutions, which at that time maintained in the South Mahometan ascendancy, and the cause of regular government. To destroy is in India, even more than elsewhere, much easier than to re-create. And the old order of political society once dissolved, it by no means followed that either the Hindoo subjects, especially the Maratha *mansubdars* of those States, or the lawless classes generally, who had been hitherto restrained or employed by the waning, but still respectable Afghan monarchies, would not gravitate with fatal force towards the humble but resolute *jungle wallahs,* the Hindoo representatives of independence and license. This, in the end, was precisely what happened; as in similar circumstances a similar phenomenon has been so often exhibited in Europe.

Nor was this the only way in which, in spite of his cunning, local knowledge, activity, and perseverance, the Emperor's faults of temper and policy embarrassed his proceedings, and contributed ultimately to defeat his designs. As with his contemporary, Louis XIV., whom to a certain extent he strikingly resembled, both in character and in historical position, his pride, his bigotry, his love of pomp, and his fathlessness, gave his enemies a great advantage against him, and combined to sap the immense power by which, at the outset, he overawed the Eastern World. His pride led him to underrate his irregular and rustic opponents, and to neglect the problem of adapting his warfare to their special character and circumstances. Again, studious to appear as the rigid champion of the faith, to reproach the Gallio spirit of the Afghan kings of the Dekkan, and perhaps to promote conversion by the alternative infliction of a mulct on infidels, he was imprudent enough to commence operations by decreeing in anticipation the *jezia* throughout the whole region south of the Nerbudda.

Moreover, the magnificent array in which he moved onward to encounter the wild Cossacks of the far East, might dazzle the imagination, and tempt the treacherous instincts of the effeminate courtier of Bijapoor or Golconda; but while its maintenance exhausted the ample but finite resources of the Empire, it simply stimulated the cupidity and the overreaching invention of the matter-of-fact and greedy Maratha. Thus, however ill-commanded for a time, however often defeated in pitched battles, and deprived of particular strongholds, the "rebels" not only continued unsubdued, not only repeatedly enriched themselves with the intercepted stores, treasures, and luxurious appliances of the imperial armies; but at length, in concert with their countrymen still actually in those armies, they mockingly drank long life to the glorious Alumgeer—the purveyor of so much wealth to themselves! Lastly, though treachery towards enemies might be condoned, if not esteemed a virtue, especially when, as in Sivaji's case, it was accompanied by strict fidelity to friends, and a temper though severe yet genial; the cold haughty cynicism and universal suspicion of Aurungzib, while it multiplied his precautions against perfidy towards himself, repelled all attachment, demoralized his servants, and as his fortunes declined, resulted in general jobbery, and treasonable compromise with the enemy.

CHAPTER VII.

THE RAJA, THE NIZAM, AND THE PEISHWA.

The death of Aurungzib not only changed the whole aspect of affairs all over India, but entirely and permanently altered the relations of the Marathas with the Empire. At first allies of the Mogul in a common attack upon the kingdom of Bijapoor; then restless and troublesome neighbours to the imperial Provinces; at a later time desperate and successful maintainers of their national and religious independence against the ever advancing tide of Mussulman domination; finally, exultingly triumphant over an expiring but still haughty foe :—they now enjoyed the spectacle of a fierce contest between the sons of their persevering enemy; they were brought thenceforth into more or less friendly connexion with one or other of the pretenders to empire; they were never again exposed to the danger, or even the design, of a general subjection; and they seemed to have a fair opportunity for consolidating their own power, and reaping the fruits of their protracted and gallant exertions against the collective force of the Empire.

However abnormal and rapacious their system of warfare, and however strongly inclined they might be, from the mere force of habit, to continue the practice when the necessity for its exercise had ceased, they had certainly been hitherto making an honest and gallant stand for rights which, equally prized but not always so strenuously maintained by more scrupulous men, may well command our sympathy, and lead us to approve the successful conclusion of the war of independence. Henceforth, though the predatory disposition is unchecked, and its range, in fact, gradually extended, until the whole of India is pervaded by its action; yet in other respects the political position, character, and relations of the community are entirely changed.

1. For his own purposes, Azim Shah, on his way northward to contest the throne with his brother, releases the long imprisoned son of Sambaji, the Raja Shao, in whose name Raja Ram had at first at least professed to govern. Shao, the *protégé* of Aurungzib's daughter, and a favourite of the Emperor himself, had become to a great extent imperialised. The silken cords of courtly luxury had encircled the young heart of Sivaji's grandson; and the memory of

a secure, peaceful, and kindly life in the Zenana had disposed him both to acquiesce when liberated in the condition of a Prince dependent on the Emperor, and *more Orientali* to leave the administration to others, rather than resume his ancestor's personal vigilance and activity; in a word, to reign as a Mogul feudatory, rather than rule as an independent military chieftain.

2. Hence, while his power is established, his authority extended, and his revenue realised, not in antagonism as hitherto to the Mogul sovereignty, but under imperial auspices; he sinks gradually towards, though he hardly, like his successor, quite reaches the level of a *Roi Fainéant;* and, as usual, the reins of empire which his faltering grasp tends to let drop are promptly seized and skilfully handled by his energetic, ambitious, and far-sighted ministers. Thus it is that the Raja becomes, after a short interval, a figure more or less shadowy, and subordinate to that most peculiar incarnation of the later Maratha spirit, the Peishwa.

3. But the release of Shao produced two other important changes among the Marathas. This step had been recommended to Aurungzib for the purpose of sowing dissension among "the rebels," and facilitating the progress of intrigues against their leaders. This effect it actually produced. Tara Bhye, the widow of Raja Ram, and Regent on behalf of her

son, refused to acknowledge Shao's authority, affected even to doubt his being the genuine son of Sambaji, and a schism took place, many important men adhering to her cause. Satara, which Shao had recovered (1708), became his capital. But the anti-Raja ruled at Kolapoor. Nor did the evil end here. As in feudal Europe in similar circumstances, and notably under Stephen in England, the disputed succession not only made each claimant more dependent on his supporters, and compelled him to allow them a licence which was most injurious both to his own and to the public interests; but under pretext of partisanship with one or other of the *soi-disant* true representatives of Sivaji, many turbulent, fierce, and rapacious chieftains waged a cruel and indiscriminate warfare on their own account, inflicted endless misery on the people, and reduced the country to a state of anarchy and destitution which, but for the village system, must have been almost hopeless. Meanwhile the Moguls looked on, not displeased, no doubt, to see their old enemies thus turning their weapons against each other, and leaving the imperial Provinces beyond the scene of the strife comparatively free from incursion.

4. Another circumstance must be mentioned in connexion with Shao's release, and the new aspect of Maratha affairs, which, while it was characteristic of the change that had come over the relations of

the rival nationalities and political systems of the Dekkan, was not without its influence on the later arrangements of the same district. It has been mentioned that Shao became virtually a dependent Prince. But he did not acknowledge the imperial supremacy without an equivalent. He may almost be said to have been bribed into a vassal relation, or rather, a sort of *concordat* established the point, that the Raja should enjoy the *chout*, or fourth of the revenue from the six imperial Provinces in the Dekkan, with the important condition, that the Subahdar, or general Viceroy of those provinces, should levy and pay it over to the Maratha (1709). Thus the pretext for invasion and spoliation was removed; the Raja acquired a fixed revenue of considerable amount; he entered regularly, so to speak, into the imperial system; but, at the same time, the way being closed against the pursuit of the irregular and illicit plunder which had been wont to support the hosts of the insurgent people and their miscellaneous following, the internal anarchy and devastation of what may be called their home district, were indefinitely aggravated.

The anomalous, confused, and anarchic state of the Dekkan was characteristic of the times, and in keeping with the general condition of India. Everywhere the Empire had been shaken to its foundations, and was breaking up. The administrative system had been disarranged; revolutions at Court, and wars of succession followed each other with accelerated rapidity; the Emperor had become a puppet in the hands of his ministers, and feebly endeavoured to buy off hostility by concession, and to guard against rebellion by promoting divisions among his nominal servants. Wild tribes and adventurous chieftains were preying on the vitals of the State, and draining its resources by their depredations. Soon it was to become a question with each ambitious Satrap, whether he should not withdraw altogether his allegiance to so effete an authority, and constitute himself an avowedly independent potentate.

Thus, to recapitulate the political aspect of the South in the early days of Shao's reign, there was an imperial Viceroy, the valiant Zoolfikar Khan, but he was non-resident, and left the conduct of affairs to Daood Khan, his deputy, who concluded the formal grant of the *chout* already mentioned. Shao called himself at once King of the Hindoos, and Zumeendar or Arch-Collector of the Emperor. The Anti-Raja was now another Sambaji, the son of a second wife of Raja Ram; and his fortunes were sustained by Ramchunder Punt, a vigorous minister, who had, on the death of her son, imprisoned Tara Bhye. The leading chieftains were apt to transfer their adhesion from one to the other on trivial grounds, and especially on supposed slights and personal quarrels, though Shao had the ablest and more numerous followers. Many partisans meanwhile hung loose on society, and made the prospect of a settled and strong government each day less hopeful. The engagement, too, between Shao and Daood Khan was a personal one; and the removal of the latter might at any moment render the confusion worse confounded.

But another great change was at hand. This political and social medley was destined ere long to give place to the prominent and well-defined antagonism of two remarkable men, whose disputes hushed, or gathered up into themselves, all other disturbances; whose conspicuous and contrasted figures dominated, if they did not occupy the whole scene; and who represented in themselves the several principles, powers, and methods, that had so long and so hotly contended for existence or supremacy in the Dekkan.

It is not necessary here to dwell in detail either on the domestic conflicts of the Marathas, or on the vicissitudes of the imperial dynasty; but it is desirable to mention briefly the circumstances and events which brought Baji-Rao and Nizam-ul-Mulk face to face in the Dekkan, and involved them in inevitable conflict.

The office of Peishwa was, it will be remembered, as old as the time of Sivaji. It had been held by several distinguished men. But the founder of the hereditary Peishwaship, or Mayoralty of the Palace to the Satara Raja, was Balaji Wishwanath, the father of Nizam-ul-Mulk's great rival. This man, a Brahmin from the Concan, combined all the subtlety and insinuating ways of his caste with an amount of enterprise and vigour in action, that more rarely distinguish the members of his order; but that were possessed in an equal or even greater degree by his posterity. To the influence of his early home among the rough and almost trackless spurs of the Ghats we must, perhaps, ascribe the fact that, unlike most Maratha leaders, he was a bad—indeed, a very clumsy horseman. Contemporary MS. attest this point, and even add, that when compelled to flee hastily from his enemies, he required a man on each side to hold him on his horse! But mountaineers, like sailors, may be excused a defect which is due to their training, and which is not incompatible with good service in the field, as well as in the Cabinet.

Wishwanath's talents and exertions gradually raised him above the jealous competition of his rivals, and gained the complete confidence of the Raja, who appointed him Peishwa, and rather imprudently made over to him the strong fortress of Poorundhur, and the country around; and eventually entrusted him with the task of re-arranging the Maratha revenue system. This was effected on an altogether new plan, which bore the impress of the contriver's extraordinary ingenuity, and contributed essentially to promote the collective power of his people, and more indirectly the ultimate ascendancy of the Peishwa.

He first exerted himself to put an end to the confusion in Maharashtra and on the Western Coast, and in this he succeeded. He studied meanwhile to improve his own districts round Poorundhur, and the city of Poona, the capital of his successors. "He immediately suppressed a banditti which infested it; gave his attention to restoring order in the villages; discontinued all farming of revenue; and encouraged cultivation, by the usual means of very low and gradually increasing assessments." *

His revenue scheme was the result of a new compact with the Moguls, in the person of Hoosein-Ally-Khan (1717), who visited the Dekkan as Subahdar, under circumstances which will be mentioned below. The details, both of the concession and of the mode of realising and extending it, are far too complicated to be here given; but their general character and object must be mentioned as intimately connected, both with the history of this strange people throughout, and with the career of the Peishwa's son.

A large part of the territory, possessed at the time of his death by Sivaji, was ceded outright to his suc-

* Grant Duff.

cessor. Moreover, the *chout*, or one-fourth of the revenue; and the *surdeshmookhee*, or an additional tenth of the six Mogul Regulation Provinces (as we should call them); and of the tributary States of Tanjore, Trichinopoly, and Mysore, were alienated for an equivalent, which may be summed up in the obligation to pay a fixed annual cess to the Imperial Treasury, to maintain order in the country, and to provide a specified force—nominally for the Emperor's, really for Hoosein Ally's service.

The Marathas were now again free to collect their own dues. And they were not the men to neglect the opportunity of levying them stringently, and gradually increasing them, To facilitate this object was one of Balaji Wishwanath's aims. He took care to assess the *chout* on an estimate of the revenue which, in the impoverished state of the country, was altogether ideal in amount. Thus, taking what they could get *on account*, the unscrupulous yet pedantic claimants always contrived to exact a variety of indefinite contributions, under the plausible pretext of arrears. To give the greater chiefs a keener interest in pushing the virtual conquest in particular districts, their respective rights were to a certain extent localized. But to check the tendency to isolation and consequent dismemberment, and to promote unity of action through a general sense of community of interest, the original assessments were ingeniously and minutely divided and sub-divided, and the fractions assigned to particular leaders; so that the same district engaged the attention of several chiefs and their respective followers. Moreover, with a similar object, and to gratify the family feeling of the Raja's clannish supporters, single villages or particular districts within the limits of one leader's general area were granted, either in *jaghire* or in *enam*, or as we should say, either as benefices or allodially, to other favoured persons. Thus ample and artful provision was made for the general and constant advance of the Maratha fiscal pretensions; while the illiterate character of the people, and even of the chiefs, would render so complex a system more and more a means of strengthening the influence of the wily Brahmin accountant of each chief, and ultimately that of the political head of the order, the Brahmin Peishwa himself.

Such appears to have been the main drift of these intricate arrangements, which are said by Mr. Grant Duff to have exhibited the greatest effort of Brahmin subtlety, unconnected with religion.

While Balaji was maturing this cunning plan for appropriating the revenues of the Dekkan among his tribesmen, Nizam-ul-Mulk was preparing to enter a counter claim to the same rich inheritance. He was the son of that Ghazi-ud-deen who had twice entitled himself to Aurungzib's gratitude, by rescuing the

Emperor's sons from their perilous position in the Concan and before Bijapoor. After the fall of that monarchy, the young Chin-Kilich-Khan (as he was at that period called) served well in the Maratha war; and became Foujdar, or Governor of the Bijapoor Province. In the civil war that followed the death of Aurungzib, Sultan Mauzum triumphed over the other sons of that Emperor (1707), and appointed the gallant Zoolfikar Khan Subahdar of the Dekkan. But Daood Khan (as already stated) ruled there as Zoolfikar's deputy, and continued to do so until, on the death of Sultan Mauzum (or Shah Alum the First) a new dynastic struggle placed on the throne Ferokshere, a grandson of the late Emperor, and led to the judicial murder of Zoolfikar (1712-13). The leading spirits of this enterprise were two Syuds, or reputed descendants of the Prophet, Abdullah and Hoosein, with whom for the present Chin-Kilich-Khan acted, and who rewarded him with the splendid appointment of his old rival, and removed Daood Khan, the deputy, to Guzerat. During a short administration, the Subahdar felt his way in the labyrinth of Dekkan politics, and anticipated his later course by coquetting with the Kolapoor Raja, and endeavouring to undermine Shao's authority. He entertained malcontents from the Satara Court, sent an army to interfere with the exactions of Shao's officers, defeated them, and occupied some of their districts. But terms were after a time arranged; the Raja was honoured by the new Emperor with the nominal rank of commander of 10,000 horse; and the Subahdar was still busily engaged in watching over and pacifying the country, when he was suddenly supplanted by the overbearing Hoosein Ally, who, leaving his brother to manage the weak Emperor, assumed the southern Vice Royalty, and concluded after a time the arrangement with Balaji that has been already described. His predecessor retired sulkily to the government of Malwa, and henceforth bore his former allies, the Syuds, a heavy grudge. The Emperor, equally fickle, cowardly, and treacherous, sought to deliver himself from the bondage of the brothers, by inciting Daood Khan to attack Hoosein Ally. Hoosein however prevailed, and his opponent fell (1716). But the danger that he had sustained from this royal plot, the consciousness that the powerful and subtle Chin-Kilich-Khan was his enemy, and the experience of more than one defeat at the hands of the Marathas, disposed him to secure their friendship and their co-operation in an attempt which he meditated against his sovereign. With Balaji Wishwanath and a large Maratha contingent in his army, he marched to Delhi; deposed, imprisoned, and murdered the miserable Ferokshere (1718); and three phantom Emperors were set up in succession within a few months, under the jealous auspices of the imperious Syuds; the last being Mahomed Shah (1719), destined to a prolonged though most inglorious and unhappy reign.

At this crisis two other memorable events occurred. The Peishwa who had done so much for his sovereign, his own family, and his people generally, died on his return southwards, and left his place to be occupied, and his policy developed, by a yet more remarkable man, his son Baji Rao. While Chin Kilich-Khan, smarting under both personal and public wrongs sustained from the Syuds, crossed the Nerbudda, determined to make the Dekkan a vantage ground for a decisive contest with the obnoxious usurpers of supreme power.

The convulsed and semi-chaotic condition of the moribund Empire, and the nature of the Maratha Power, combine to impart a bewildering complexity to the events of the period on which we are entering. But while much of the detail may be safely, and indeed profitably, neglected by those who would rise to a comprehensive view of the general tendencies and permanent lessons of the time; a considerable approach to unity, and even dramatic interest, is afforded by following the fortunes of the two singular men, who are at once the most prominent and influential characters at the moment, and the founders of two of the greatest Houses that flourished in India long after their own careers had been run.

In many respects the circumstances and characters of Nizam-ul-Mulk and Baji Rao were very similar.

Alike the sons of fathers who were, comparatively if not strictly speaking, *novi homines*, but who securely prepared the way for their sons' exaltation; alike familiar in early life with the localities and the intricate politics of the Dekkan, with the mysteries of the corrupt and tricky Imperial Court, and with the peculiarities of Maratha warfare; alike accustomed to regard the Southern Provinces, not to say the whole Empire, as a vast debateable land, and its revenues as the natural prey of daring or insidious aggression, and legalised spoilation; alike trained to consider their respective Sovereigns as august in pretension, venerable in popular estimation, useful as fountains of honour, and ratifiers of bad titles, but as equally inevitable puppets in the hands of skilful and determined ministers; alike conscious of being constantly exposed to hereditary enmities, and official and personal jealousies, which made wary walking at all times absolutely necessary:—they resembled each other also in unbounded ambition, farsightedness, tenacity of purpose, resolution in the battle-field, and freedom from the darker shades of cruelty which stained the characters of so many of their eminent contemporaries. Both seem to have been simple in personal tastes and habits, though both knew well the value of pompous titles and conventional display. Each had learned to desiderate and embrace much that belonged properly to the other's sphere. Nizam-ul-Mulk resorted very successfully on many occasions to the Maratha tactics, and made a great point of securing Maratha alliances and contingents: Baji Rao coveted and obtained imperial grants and offices, and even in adjusting the relations of his tribesmen among themselves adopted Mussulman designations.

Yet there was a great contrast between the two men; and singularly enough the national temper of the Brahmin and the Tooranee Mogul seemed reversed. Baji Rao, though a skilful politician and a profound statesman, was at the same time a comparatively straightforward, plain-spoken soldier, prompt to act—a man for a word and a blow. Nizam-ul-Mulk, though especially in early life bold as a lion when his passions were roused, and swift and terrible as fate when he deemed the time for action come, was habitually cautious, calculating, given to a variety of expedients, fond of entangling his adversaries in a network of diplomacy, and of reducing their strength by cunningly fomenting dissensions among their followers. This lesson he had no doubt learned in the bad school of Aurungzib. As usual, the tendency grew upon him; and, in the end, the practice of deferring too long the decisive effort cost him dear, as we shall see.

The original contrast of disposition in these two remarkable men was increased by the circumstances in which they found themselves placed, or into which they naturally drifted. Though (as I have said) Baji Rao had jealous rivals, his father had bequeathed to him a decided pre-eminence in the Court and counsels of Satara, which the son's abilities were quite adequate to sustain and confirm. Nizam-ul-Mulk, on the other hand, though introduced and promoted under Ghazi-ud-deen's auspices, was but one of a crowd of ambitious and able public men, many of whom had originally much higher claims than himself to the Emperor's favour. He was, in fact, far more than his rival, the architect of his own fortunes. And consummate art was requisite to construct, out of the slippery and crumbling materials within his reach, an edifice that should bear the formidable assaults sure to be directed against it.

Again; the Raja was a mild, trustful, and acquiescent master: while the Emperor was fickle, jealous, and equally incapable of firmly asserting his own authority, and of steadily supporting that of a minister. The perpetual slave of volatile courtiers and low favourites, he was ever, at their instigation, intriguing to undermine the power of those, who might otherwise have served him faithfully, but who were thus reduced, almost in self-defence, to a distrustful, tortuous and antagonistic line. Baji Rao's attitude was simple, loyal, and at the same time popular: in extending his own conquests he deferred habitually to the Raja's authority, and, through his father's wise arrangements, promoted the interest of the whole community. That, in so doing, he should gradually supplant his master in effective influence, and establish, on behalf of his own family, what amounted to a federal hegemony if not a sovereignty, was natural, but did not involve a daily practice of crafty devices, or the studious many-sidedness inevitable from Nizam-ul-Mulk's ambiguous position. Lastly, the latter depended mostly on himself. The former, besides the sympathy and occasional assistance of a Rajput Prince, was throughout zealously aided both in the field and in the Cabinet by a like-minded brother, Chimnaji Appa.

Nizam-ul-Mulk's measures, when once he had resolved to try the fortune of war against the Syuds, were equally prompt, skilful, and decisive. He passed the Nerbudda with 12,000 men; effected a junction with a Maratha force, partly headed by malcontents from Satara, partly consisting of Sambaji's adherents, and soon made himself master of Candeish. He was in much danger of being taken between a cross fire. For while Alum Ally, the deputy and nephew of Hoosein, lay with one large army at Aurungabad, Dilawar Ally with another pushed on rapidly from Malwa against the invader. But taking advantage of Dilawar's impetuosity, and of his own experience in Maratha tactics, Nizam-ul-Mulk broke the force of the first attack with a part of his army; enticed his enemy into an ambuscade, defeated, and slew him. He then advanced against the deputy, who was supported by a large contingent of Shao's troops. Thus Marathas encountered each other, and skirmished in their peculiar fashion. But after a time Alum Ally, unwarned by the fate of Dilawar, was involved in a similar catastrophe, utterly routed, and killed (1720).

The Emperor was overjoyed at this successful stand against the power of his domineering ministers. They, too, deemed the crisis so serious, that Hoosein prepared to march in person against the victorious rebel, taking the Emperor with him. But on the eve of his departure, he fell a victim to a conspiracy, in which many interests were united against him and his brother. Sadut Khan, the ancestor of the future rulers of Oude, emerges into notice as one of these conspirators. Abdullah, the surviving Syud, made a determined effort to retain his ascendancy, but was defeated and imprisoned. The Emperor, the Court, and the city were in ecstacies; and magnificent festivities celebrated the release of the degenerate Mogul from a bondage, which he had lacked the fortitude himself to discard. Nizam-ul-Mulk, as the indirect cause of this revolution, was in high favour with His Majesty, who, among other appointments, ratified his tenure of the Dekkan

Viceroyalty; allowed him to retain Malwa in addition; and created him Vizier of the Empire.

But, through the weakness and mismanagement of the Sovereign, the political horizon was soon again overclouded. Ajit Sing, the Raja of Joudpoor, rebelled, and was privately pardoned, to the disgust of one friendly and zealous minister, who had been sent to reduce him; and of another, who was deprived of Agra, which was given to the reconciled rebel.

Nizam-ul-Mulk, meanwhile, continued in the Dekkan, busily engaged with the Marathas. As during his former administration there, he showed a strong disposition to play off the rival Rajas against each other; and by favouring the weaker, to evade the claims of the stronger. But already Wishwanath's policy had given such unity and force to the party of Shao, that the Subahdar found himself, for the present, compelled to retire with a good grace from the attempt, and sheltered his retreat under the pretext of an imperial ratification of the Satara claims. Shao and his people were gratified by the peaceable concession of half the revenues of the Dekkan; and the Emperor had the treble satisfaction of reflecting, that his too powerful subject had thus crippled his own resources, set an edifying example of prompt obedience, and promoted such a balance of power in the South, as was most favourable to the tranquillity of the imperial rule.

The anomalous position and the tortuous policy of the Nizam are thus described by the historian of the Marathas:—

"On a general view, his plans were calculated to preserve his rank at court, and his power in the Deccan; to keep alive the old, and to create new dissensions among the Mahrattas; to preserve a connection with that nation, in case it should ultimately be useful to direct their attacks from his own to the imperial territories; and, however inconsistent some of those designs may seem, in this system of political artifice, through the remainder of a long life, Nizam-Ool-Mulk, not only persevered, but generally prospered."*

Soon after this period, he made his appearance as Vizier at Delhi (1722). But he found himself as much out of his element at Mahomed Shah's Court, as the old-fashioned and testy Clarendon at that of Charles the Second. Not less stern, haughty, and archaic in his general demeanour in society, than he was, when he thought fit, pliant and insinuating in his political course, the grim and sober veteran was equally hateful to the perfumed courtiers whom he snubbed, and to the volatile and licentious Emperor, whom he endeavoured to reclaim.

Between them they cast about for an expedient to get rid of him; and devised one worthy of its

* Grant Duff.

authors. The Governor of Guzerat had been insubordinate; he was now goaded into rebellion by threats of severe punishment at the hands of the Vizier, who on the other hand was, by similar arts, exasperated against the rebel, and sent in this mood to chastise him, in the hope that Hyder-Kooli-Khan, being a stout soldier at the head of a fine army, would give long occupation—if not a permanent *quietus*—to the formidable Minister.

But Hyder was soon worsted, more by the arts than the arms of his opponent; and, on his flight, Nizam-ul-Mulk assumed the governorship of the Province, assigned to himself certain *jaghire* districts within it, appointed his uncle, Hamed Khan, his deputy; made an alliance with a Maratha chief there, the ancestor of the Guikwar, and returned in triumph to Delhi.

His reappearance under such circumstances was so unwelcome, that a new coolness, and a more serious alienation than before, ensued between him and his Sovereign, which ended in a compromise. He abandoned all idea of life at Court; resigned the Viziership; received instead the high-sounding, but empty title of "Supreme Deputy in the Empire;" and, his plans thus simplified, returned for the third time to the Dekkan, with a full determination to establish there a practically independent power (1723). In terms he continued a subject of the

Emperor: in reality, he was the rival of the Peishwa for the sovereignty of the South.

His first contest, however, was not with the Marathas. From what has been already said of Mahomed Shah's character and habitual policy, it might be inferred, that however much he might be relieved for the moment by the departure of the ex-Vizier from his Court, he would be little disposed to acquiesce quietly in the too obvious designs of one whom he at once feared and hated. Nor could any sovereign, in such a case, have contemplated with complacency the prospect of such an extension of command and consolidation of territory in the hands of an ambitious, not to say a domineering subject. If to Malwa and Guzerat, which already obeyed him, Nizam-ul-Mulk was now to add the resources of the Dekkan, the Empire would be dismembered, and the aspiring Deputy would be virtually the supreme master of nearly a third of the Mogul dominions. It was resolved to stir up a distinct competitor against him, and if possible to supplant him, in each quarter. Thus one *firman*, or royal decree, deprived him of the government of Malwa, which he had long held by imperial authority, and of Guzerat, which he had recently assumed by right of conquest, on the flight of the late rebellious Governor; and authorised Raja Geerdhur Bahadur to reduce and rule the former, and Surbulund-Khan the latter Province.

A second and more secret commission enjoined Mubariz Khan, the Subahdar of Hyderabad, to oppose and dethrone the self-constituted Viceroy of the Dekkan, and, in the event of success, transferred to Mubariz himself the splendid prize.

The plan was well laid; Malwa was already drained of troops for the prosecution of the southern enterprise; and Raja Geerdhur entered quietly into possession. Greater difficulty was experienced in Guzerat. For there Hamed Khan, the Nizam's uncle, made an obstinate resistance to Surbulund's deputy, Shujaet, whom he defeated and slew, and followed up this success by inflicting a similar fate on a brother of the deputy, who had endeavoured to avenge him and reassert the imperial authority.

In these operations Hamed was assisted by two Maratha chiefs, Peelaji and Kantaji, ancestors of the Guikwar, whose power was now creeping into existence in those parts, partly through regular delegation from Satara, the reward of spirited services in partisan warfare; partly through a good understanding, and, indeed, a close league with the robber tribes of the hills, the Bheels and Coolies, who were then and long afterwards the terror of the country around, and who have been reclaimed to civilised life and useful occupations by Outram and others in our own day. The jealousy of the two Maratha leaders gave Hamed much trouble, and their quarrels weakened the common cause. Still, when Surbulund himself, at the Emperor's urgent request, appeared with a powerful force, he was so far disconcerted by the imposing attitude of his enemies that he began to entrench himself. Then the Maratha spirit, prompt to rise on any symptom of fear on the part of its antagonists, hastened an engagement, in which Surbulund was defeated. But their heavy loss disinclined the Marathas to continue the contest; and henceforth Hamed's power melted away, and he became himself a mere partisan and plunderer. Even irregular warfare was suspended during the monsoon; Surbulund ruled undisputed; and the second part of the imperial programme seemed accomplished. It was, however, only a lull in Guzerat; while very different had been the fortune of the strife on the principal theatre of the war.

There Nizam-ul-Mulk had put forth all his strength, both as a diplomatist and as a general. After spending months in sowing sedition among his antagonist's troops, and fooling Mubariz with fallacious schemes of pacification, he at length brought him to action; in a desperate battle defeated and slew him; and with cruel and insulting irony sent his head to the Emperor, congratulating the baffled sovereign, in the tone of a devoted subject, on the happy suppression of a dangerous and wicked rebellion (1724).

Mahomed Shah was caught in his own snare.

And the furtive attempt to confound the Nizam, by raising a storm in the Dekkan, ended only in clearing the political atmosphere there, strengthening Nizam-ul-Mullk's position, and leaving him free to consider and adjust his relations with the formidable and encroaching Marathas. His knowledge of their character and circumstances was intimate; he was on friendly terms with many of their leading men; he relied much, not only on his own skill, but on the jealousies which, as he was well aware, prevailed among them; and his first plans were favoured by the absence of the young Peishwa, who, in the pursuance of a bold and ambitious policy, was pushing his own and his people's fortunes in the North. Baji Rao's principal rival at the Court of Satara was Sreeput Rao, a Brahmin from the upper country; while the Peishwa, as I have said, came from the Concan. Sreeput had strongly advocated the policy of at once consolidating the Raja's dominion in Maharashtra, of reducing the Anti-Raja of Kolapoor, and of recovering the territory in the Carnatic Plain, of which Sivaji had, in his later days, made himself master; but which had since fallen away, partly to the Moguls, partly to the family of Sivaji's brother.

But the Peishwa well understood that such a force as his master's was ill adapted to thrive quietly, or even to hold together at all in a settled condition of the country; that to keep it constantly employed in exploring new regions, and levying contributions from the hitherto untouched provinces of the Empire, would both best meet the wishes of the community, and best enhance the power of the successful leader who should conduct these extended incursions. He therefore advocated a continuous scheme of distant operations, whereby the sovereignty of the Raja was to be nominally promoted, the public exchequer was to be replenished by regular levies of tribute from Province after Province, the troops were to be kept in good humour, and thus tranquillity at home was to be secured, and the great plan of vengeance against their former oppressors was to be developed, until the Empire itself should lie prostrate, and drained of its life's blood, at the feet of the robber horsemen whom it had so long endeavoured to exterminate.

He concluded an eloquent speech with the enthusiastic appeal to his master :—"Now is our time to drive strangers from the land of Hindoos, and to acquire immortal renown. By directing our efforts to Hindostan the Mahratta flag in your reign shall fly from the Kistna to the Attok." "You shall plant it on the Himalaya," exclaimed the Raja; "You are, indeed, a noble son of a worthy father."*

Thus Baji Rao carried the day in the council chamber. His progress in the field will be de-

* Grant Duff.

scribed below. Meanwhile his absence left the coast clear for the manœuvres of the wily Nizam.

The latter's first move was important, and completely successful, at least for the time. He had already been compelled (as has been said) to acquiesce in the Maratha pretension to a substantive half of the Dekkan revenues, and this pretension had also the imperial sanction. His immediate object was to commute these claims over a considerable district around Hyderabad, his intended capital, and thus to relieve himself from the perpetual presence and domiciliary visits of the Marathas, and to establish a compact and independent nucleus for his future dominions. This, by a system of exchanges, and by personal gratifications, both to the Raja and to Sreeput, he effected. The Peishwa, on his return, condemned the arrangement; and while it was still under eager and angry discussion at Satara, learned that the veteran intriguer had gone a step further, and repeated a device which he had formerly practised with good effect. Encouraged by his late success, by the disputes and heart-burnings to which it had given rise, and by the chronic split with Kolapoor, Nizam-ul-Mulk now withheld all tribute; removed the Satara Raja's collectors, and affected to arbitrate as Viceroy, and in the tone of a superior, between the claimants to the Rajaship. Shao, usually so mild, was transported with fury at this wholesale sequestration of his revenue, and challenge of his title, and was with difficulty dissuaded from leading in person the national army against the venomous Mogul. But the Peishwa eventually obtained the command of the expedition; his influence and character mustered around him the full strength of the people, and numbers of the wavering and independent soldiers of fortune; and the conduct of the ensuing campaign went far to transfer to him "the virtual supremacy" of the Maratha nation.

True to his favourite policy, Nizam-ul-Mulk, before committing himself to actual hostilities, tried the effect of negotiation. He professed to have acted in the interest of Shao himself, and with a view to deliver him from the ascendancy of the Peishwa and his tools. Those who had been removed were to be replaced (he urged) by more obedient and faithful subjects of the Raja. But here the Nizam's cunning was at fault. The offence was certain and exasperating: the excuse not very credible, as well as too naked a statement of an ominous and not flattering fact. In other circumstances the Raja's jealousy might have been aroused against his powerful minister. But Shao's wrath was already directed elsewhere; and the Peishwa's persuasive tongue and deferential tone prevailed, and placed him at the head of the avenging army.

The monsoon was spent by both parties in energetic

preparation. On the return of the fine weather, the Peishwa struck the first blow; withstood for a time the onset of the Nizam's vanguard; suddenly retired, manœuvring to perplex his opponent, and threatening Aurungabad; spread a report that he intended to destroy Burhanpoor, and thus drew his enemy northwards to protect it. With a part of his force he then made a feint, while he darted off with the bulk of his army to Guzerat, which he plundered; and, in the sudden panic which he inspired, was suspected to be covertly in league with his pursuer. Nizam-ul-Mulk meanwhile, abandoning the fruitless chase of his flying foe, returned southwards, bent on attacking Poona. But the Peishwa, leaving behind him a track of desolation as he sped to the rescue of his own domain, came swiftly up with his rival, whose operations were retarded by the inefficiency and mutual jealousies and distrust of the Maratha allies, on whose help he had much counted. Thus disappointed, he was soon reduced to great straits. His artillery, indeed, did good service; but the relief thus afforded was only temporary. His army was presently completely blocked up in rugged ground, destitute of water. Still he struggled on, and made his way good to a better position. But here he was finally brought to bay, and forced to admit once more the claims which he had repudiated. He refused, indeed, point blank to give up Sambaji, his

Kolapoor ally. But he pledged himself to make good all arrears of tribute, and to surrender several strong places, as security for the future payment of the revenues in question (1729).

Thus ended the earliest encounter between these two typical men, who, on the conclusion of hostilities, met for the first time face to face, and exchanged presents of ceremony. A proud and auspicious day must that have been for the young and gallant Brahmin, who had thus triumphed, at the outset of his career, over the veteran arms and redoubted artifices of Aurungzib's old lieutenant, the conqueror in so many fields, and but lately apparently almost Dictator of the Empire! And the triumph was destined to be repeated over the same formidable antagonist. Personal pride, too, was reinforced by family considerations and dynastic hopes. Shao's acquiescence in Baji Rao's guidance and generalship on such an occasion, and with such an issue, could not fail to advance the Peishwa far on the road to supreme power. A profitable arrangement, which he shortly after concluded with the Mogul Governor in Guzerat, and which will be explained elsewhere, increased his influence, and tended to confirm his brilliant prospects.

But Nizam-ul-Mulk was not disposed to give him leisure to mature his ambitious schemes. A man of infinite expedients, though he had been worsted for the moment, his arts soon raised up against the Peishwa a fresh and very dangerous opponent.

Trimbuk Rao Dhabaray, a Maratha chief of consequence, who had been engaged in Guzerat, considered himself aggrieved by the terms concluded between the imperial Governor of that Province, and the Peishwa. He entered into a close league with the Nizam: gathered many other chiefs around him; assembled an army of 35,000 men, and prepared to march into the Dekkan, avowedly to emancipate the Raja from the control of Baji Rao and the Brahmins. With this force the Nizam was to co-operate in his own neighbourhood. The Peishwa learned the state of affairs with his usual promptitude and accuracy; and resolved by taking the initiative, to prevent the junction of two such formidable enemies. Though Trimbuk's army was twice as numerous as his own, he had with him a choice body of the *pagah* or household troops, and other good soldiers. Once more he marched to Guzerat, determined

"To beard the lion in his den;"

But imitating the Nizam's preliminary attempts at negotiation. His van was attacked and routed near the Nerbudda. But, undeterred by this mishap, and feeling that it could only be retrieved by a bold stroke, he made a sudden and furious attack on the main army. The superior quality of his men made amends for their fewness, and a partial rout of his enemy soon took place. But Trimbuk, resolved to conquer or die, chained the legs of his elephant, to give confidence to his supporters, by seeing the determination of their chief. The fight was stubbornly contested, Baji Rao on horseback emulating the bravery and vigilance of his antagonist. But the latter at length fell, killed by a chance shot (1731); and his fall not only decided the day in favour of the Peishwa, but left him "all but nominal control of the Mahratta sovereignty."*

Thus the Nizam's arts had again recoiled against himself; and he had now to settle accounts with the victor.

* Grant Duff.

CHAPTER VIII.

THE EMPIRE IN EXTREMIS.

It will be remembered that, when the Emperor undertook to reduce the overgrown and threatening power of Nizam-ul-Mulk, Surbulund Khan was sent to supplant him in Guzerat, and Raja Geerdhur in Malwa; and that each of these officers had, for the moment, obtained undisputed authority in his Province. But the expulsion of the dangerous Mogul only facilitated the encroachment of the not less dangerous Marathas, who were ever watching the opportunity of worming their way into countries which they had already more than once overrun, and in the former of which the Guikwar had already gained a footing, and strengthened himself by the alliance of the primitive Bheels and Coolies, who inhabited the wilder, and plundered the more settled country around.

The Peishwa's triumph over Nizam-ul-Mulk, and the persevering and troublesome depredations of the Marathas and of their rude confederates, hastened an arrangement, whereby Surbulund Khan, finding his frequent and urgent applications for help from the imperial Court in vain, made large concessions, which mark another stage in the onward march of the Marathas to empire (1729). These, technically the grants of the *chout* and *surdeshmookee*, amounted in fact to thirty-five per cent. of the land revenue and customs duties. To save appearances, he professed to base this liberal donation on "the progress of improvement, the increasing population, and the general tranquillity in the Dekkan." Some peculiar conditions are annexed to the grant of the *chout* :—"Two thousand five hundred horse are constantly to be kept up [by the Raja?]; the fourth part of the actual collections only, to be paid; no more than two or three persons to be placed in each district, as collectors, on the part of the Mahrattas; no extra demands whatever to be made on the ryots; and every assistance to be afforded in maintaining the imperial authority."*

But the clause which had the most important bearing on the immediate future was one which bound Baji Rao, on the Raja's behalf, in return for these concessions, to forbear "supporting disaffected Zumeendars, and *other disturbers of the public peace*"

* Grant Duff.

—of the Province. For this stipulation was adverse to the interests of the Guikwar, on account of his allies the Bheels and Coolies, who lived by plunder; and the Guikwar was but, at this period, the agent of Trimbuk Rao Dhabaray, whose jealousy and iudignation were thus kindled at the lofty assumption of the Peishwa to be the enforcer of peace against him and his friends. *Hinc illæ lacrymæ!* This it was that threw him into the arms of Nizam-ul-Mulk, and led him to proclaim the revolutionary expedition to Poona, which was to remove the Peishwa from Shao's counsels and armies; but which, through Baji Rao's promptitude and boldness, ended in the overthrow and destruction of Trimbuk and many other powerful chiefs.

We left the Nizam in a state of perplexity at the failure of this new scheme against his rival. His own position was now somewhat critical. But he extricated himself in a manner most characteristic of the man and of the times. After an elaborate and mysterious negotiation with the Peishwa, he succeeded in warding off harm from himself, and propitiating Baji Rao by a compact, which diverted the Maratha arms against the Emperor, and thus left Nizam-ul-Mulk free to pursue his scheme of establishing an independent sovereignty in the Dekkan, while his two most formidable opponents were engaged in hostilities in Hindostan (1731).

Under these altered circumstances, the Peishwa's first care was to allay, as far as he could, the ill feeling that had arisen out of the late civil war. His charities, in continuation of those formerly maintained by Trimbuk, were ample and ostentatious. The son of that ill-fated noble was raised to his father's position of *Senaputtee*; and the minor surviving chiefs of the same party were pardoned and entrusted with appointments. Thus, for the present at least, a dangerous split in the Maratha camp was avoided.

Meanwhile the Emperor, having done nothing to support Surbulund in time, had yet indignantly refused to ratify the grant, which his destitution had constrained that officer to make. And Abhee Sing, Raja of Joudpoor, was sent to supersede Surbulund, who had suffered similar indignities on former occasions. Whereupon Nizam-ul-Mulk, ever ready to make political capital in any quarter, and already foreseeing that it might be useful to secure a new ally against the growing power of the Peishwa, affected much virtuous indignation at the unworthy treatment of the man, who had, in fact, entered Guzerat to wrest that Province from himself; but who had now given place to a Rajput, the suspected friend and secret confederate of Baji Rao.

I need not at present follow further the course of events in Guzerat; but may state generally, that except in the capital, where the imperial authority still lingered, the Marathas and their rude allies appropriated between them the whole country, and maintained their independence; until in happier days, the might of England prevailed in this region; settled and improved it; maintained the subordinate and friendly authority of the Guikwar; and eventually reclaimed the savage hill tribes, whom the Mussulmans had never been able to subdue.

In Malwa also Raja Geerdhur's triumph had been short lived. The Peishwa's agents, Holkar, Sindia, and Powar, had levied contributions there; encountered and slain both Geerdhur, and a relation who endeavoured to replace and avenge him. A new Viceroy entered the Province. But Baji Rao had now assumed the command, after concluding his bargain with the Nizam; and he lost no time in shutting up the Viceroy in a fort, and clearing the country of the imperial troops. Another change of governors was made by a Court ever ready to "meddle and muddle," and to punish the ill success which it had itself too often brought about. This time another Rajput, Baji Rao's ally, Jey Sing, was nominated; and after some struggle between the dictates of private friendship and official duty, he quietly handed over the government to the Peishwa (1734); and, for the time, the Emperor was fain to acquiesce tacitly in this transfer.

In the course of the late operations against the

Viceroy of Malwa, the Marathas had also pushed on into Bundlekund, where a petty Rajput Prince whom the Peishwa had assisted, adopted the latter as his son, and dying soon after, left him a third of his territory, the rest devolving on two actual sons. Thus the Maratha frontier was again advanced, far into the heart of Hindostan.

And now the end of the distracted, enervated, and tottering Empire seemed at hand. At the opening of his career, the daring son of Wishwanath had explicitly announced the programme which he was now prepared to carry out. "Let us strike" he had exclaimed with enthusiasm, "at the trunk of the withering tree, the branches must fall of themselves!" * Well had he laid his plans, and taken his measures, for the execution of this great enterprise. Peace had, some years before, been concluded with the Raja of Kolapoor. Nizam-ul-Mulk had agreed to give free scope to Maratha ambition in the North, provided he were left to prosecute his design of local sovereignty, a design whlch now occupied his whole energies, though not his exclusive attention. The Peishwa had humbled the enemies of his master on the western coast, in the interval of his more remote campaigns. Guzerat, Malwa, Bnndlekund, were swept almost clear of imperial functionaries, and their revenues now went far to defray the growing cost of

* Grant Duff.

Baji Rao's large armaments. The Rajputs, both of Ajmir and of Bundlekund, were friendly; and a new outpost of Maratha power had been established in the occupation of Berar by a chief of the Bonslay family, the founder of the Maharajaship of Nagpore.

This chief indeed proved, in the end, unfriendly to the Peishwa's ambition; but that was both natural, and quite compatible with active co-operation against the Mogul. Sindia and Holkar were zealous and useful instruments, and were entirely devoted to the interests of their immediate patron. On the whole, Baji Rao felt that his time was come for measuring his strength against the Emperor himself.

Holkar preluded by a raid into the Agra Province (1736). This at once alarmed the Vizier, Khan Dowran; who, however, instead of taking active measures, made imposing preparations which ended in nothing, and ineffectually sought to procure the assistance of the Nizam. Holkar hardly intermitted his levying of requisitions to throw a few rockets into the splendid but unserviceable camp of the imperialists, and to cut them up with his flying cavalry.

The Peishwa's return to the army was announced by urgent demands on the Emperor, to ratify formally the grants of the Guzerat and Malwa revenues, which circumstances had already conferred on the Marathas. A party at Court opposed all concession. But Mahomed Shah and the Vizier were inclined to a liberal compromise; and deeds were privately prepared to that effect. The Peishwa's agent discovered the important secret: and the Peishwa himself thereupon became elated and rose in his demands. These were resisted, but at last a grant was made—at the expense of Nizam-ul-Mulk! This was no doubt done with a view not only of buying off the hostility of the Peishwa, but of rousing the Nizam to become the champion of oppressed imperialism, a character which the minister had been for some time trying to force upon him. The last object, as we shall shortly see, was attained; the former altogether failed. Baji Rao, undeterred by the pending negotiation, or by the assembling of a large and magnificently appointed army near Delhi, advanced remorselessly; levied contributions in a country hitherto free from Maratha incursions; approached within a day's march of Agra; and sent forward his lieutenants to devastate the Doab, where, however, they were held in check by the advance of Sadut Khan from Oude. But, on exaggerated accounts of this check being circulated in and around Delhi, the Peishwa resolved, in his own words,—"to prove that he was still in Hindostan, and to show [the Emperor] flames and Mahrattas at the gates of his capital." *

Thither, therefore, he rapidly proceeded, and encamped in the suburbs, abstaining from general

* Grant Duff.

plunder, but giving one or two significant specimens of his ability to inflict unlimited harm (1737). He then coolly entered into a correspondence with the Emperor and one of his Rajput nobles; but with no result. After a time he removed further from the city, politely intimating that he feared his troops might otherwise injure it. This retrograde step gave some heart to the imperial forces, which for the first time since his approach to the capital now ventured to look his men in the face; but were speedily beaten back again in confusion, and with some loss. The Peishwa then retired; and after exacting a promise of the formal grant of the Malwa Viceroyalty, and thirteen *lacs* in money, he returned to the Dekkan, flushed with success hitherto unexampled in the history of his people, but not free from anxiety as to the policy that would now be adopted by the Nizam. Nor was this anxiety uncalled for. The feeble Emperor, always hating most the powerful subject whom he had last seen, and by whom he had been humiliated last, had now veered round, and in his distress implored the assistance of the man, whom he had so grievously affronted and persecuted. The Nizam, too, felt that the political balance required redressing, and that every effort ought to be made to prevent the upstart Hindoo from becoming the Dictator of the Mogul monarchy.

The *entente cordiale* between the old rivals was

thus exchanged for a mutual determination to bring on an issue decisive both of their own relative strength, and of the fate of the Empire. The Nizam's forces, including those of several Rajput chiefs who still adhered to Mahomed Shah, amounted to 35,000 men, with a fine train of artillery. The Peishwa's army was more than twice as numerous, though several contingents on which he had counted failed to attend. The old renown of Asof Jah had not been obliterated by his failure in his former encounter with Baji Bao. The Rajputs were known to be formidable warriors; and the imperial name still had its terrors. Above all, the cannon were an object of fear to the light-armed Marathas, who had no skill in that description of warfare.

They advanced with some hesitation, but were quickly reassured and elated by observing that their enemy had entrenched himself in a strong position. This sign of fear—as they interpreted it—encouraged them to make an attack, which, though indecisive, led to more serious results. Nizam-ul-Mulk was at once oppressed by a sense of responsibility, and enfeebled by age. He showed no spirit in guarding himself against a reverse by boldly taking the aggressive. He could not now avail himself of his old practice of setting Marathas to encounter their countrymen. A force which was coming up to his support was cut off, and this mishap stimulated his opponents, and damped the ardour of his own men. It seemed to their superstitious minds prophetic of the end. The Viceroy of Oude failed to make his appearance, and finally retreated, thus again discouraging the Nizam's army.

After a time an almost exact counterpart of the former passage between the same antagonists was presented. The Peishwa contrived to hem in the Mogul army; inflicted upon it much suffering; and increased that suffering by refusing to receive deserters who would fain have crowded into his own camp. Each party then used every effort to incline the scale in his own favour by reinforcements. But in this each was disappointed. The Bonslay would not move to swell the triumph of the Peishwa; and Baji Rao's own brother was too busily engaged in pressing the decisive siege of the Portuguese settlement at Bassein to quit his prey on the eve of capture. On the other hand, Nazir Jung, the Nizam's second son (the eldest was at Court), failed to bring up in time a relieving army from the Dekkan.

Driven in and crowded—Sedan-like—upon the small city of Bhopal, the Nizam struggled desperately to extricate himself; and at length, by the aid of his cannon, made good a retreat for some distance, at the dismally slow rate of three miles a day. But at length, as on the former occasion, he was brought to bay, and the champion and avenger of the Emperor was "compelled to sign a convention, promising, in his own handwriting, to grant to Baji Rao the whole of Malwa, and the complete sovereignty of the territory between the Nerbudda and the Chumbul, to obtain a confirmation of it from the Emperor, and to use every endeavour to procure the payment of a subsidy of fifty lacs of rupees to defray the Peishwa's expenses."*

The rivals then parted, to meet no more, though another hostile encounter was to take place between Baji Rao and the aged Nizam's son; in which the Maratha, over-tasking his strength, and aiming at the complete conquest of the Dekkan, and the extinction of the Power which he had alternately abetted and opposed, was in turn worsted, and compelled to retrace his steps with something like ignominy. But between his present renewed triumph over his life-long rival and that later humiliation, occurred an event so appalling and extraordinary, that it stilled for awhile all other commotions. Hardly had the convention just described been concluded (1738) before Nadir Shah burst into India, and advanced rapidly against Delhi, instigated (many thought, though it would appear erroneously) by Nizam-ul-Mulk himself.

The rise of this extraordinary man dates from one of the most disastrous periods of his country's annals.

* Grant Duff.

He was a Persian of low birth, a native of Khorasan; and his earliest exploits, as in the case of Sivaji, were those of a freebooter. But his energy, valour, and military abilities soon enabled him to assume the position of a general, a patriot, and a national deliverer; and thus to win his way, step by step, to the throne itself.

The degeneracy of the Suffavean sovereigns, and the consequent weakness of the kingdom, had tempted the Western Afghans to invade Persia. Under Mahmood, a brave and artful chief, they had penetrated to the heart of the country; besieged and taken Ispahan; captured Hussein, the Shah, along with his capital, and placed their own leader upon the throne (1722). They then endeavoured, with various fortune, to reduce the rest of the kingdom. But their original numbers were inadequate to the undertaking: and they were too slenderly reinforced by their countrymen, who were attached to their native hills, and were further deterred by unfavourable reports of the character and bearing of Mahmood in his new sphere of authority. His jealous and sanguinary temper had alienated several of his chief supporters; while his first attempts to conciliate the conquered by mildness soon gave place, under the influence of distrust, and a sense of the increasing difficulties of his position, to a systematic and desperate policy of terrorism and wholesale assassination. Within three years of his accession he became deranged, and expired in what were not unnaturally deemed retributive torments (1724). He was succeeded by his relative Ashraff, a man of great reputation both as a soldier and a statesman. But, meanwhile, Russia, under Peter the Great, and the Sublime Porte, had taken advantage of the anarchy attending the Afghan enterprise; had invaded the northern provinces, and actually concluded a partition treaty, which would have gone far to complete the dismemberment of the kingdom. But for Nadir Shah, Persia would probably have shared the fate of Poland.

The Prince Tamasp, indeed, the son of the imprisoned Hussein, had escaped, and taking refuge in the unsubdued north-eastern region, had assumed the title of Shah. After a time he succeeded in procuring the doubtful assistance of both Russia and Turkey, stipulating in return the cession of the provinces which those Powers had seized. Peter was now no more. But the Turks marched against Ashraff. They were checked, however, both by the arms of the Afghan, and by the scandal of aiding a *Shia* against a *Soonee* Prince. Tamasp, too, was a man of weak character; his resources were small, his efforts desultory; and his rival despised rather than feared him: when the acquisition of one determined and able follower suddenly changed the aspect of affairs (1727), and procured the refugee Pretender a brief and delusive restoration to the throne of his ancestors.

Nadir Cooli—such was the original name of the future sovereign of Persia, and dominator of the Mogul Empire—belonged to a Turkish tribe. His father is said to have lived by making coats and caps of sheepskins. Nadir's early life was adventurous. At seventeen he was made prisoner by the Usbeks in one of their periodical incursions. Escaping after four years, he entered the service of a small chief in Khorasan, whom he murdered, and whose daughter he carried off and married. He next figured as a bandit chief; and his bold attacks on his old enemies, the Usbeks, procured him employment under the Governor of Khorasan, who, however, presently bastinadoed and dismissed him for insubordination. He then joined his uncle, who held the fort of Kelat; but *he*, too, was soon glad to get rid of so troublesome a follower.

Now, however, the course of public events had opened to this untameable but profoundly able man a career of better omen, and of undeviating success, until the crown itself was within his grasp.

The Afghan invasion took place; and in the unsettled state of the country the bold and skilful partisan soon rose to the command of a small army. Three thousand men followed his lead, and made war support war in his native province. Again his uncle, impressed by his achievements, invited him to repair to Kelat, and assist their distressed sovereign. Nadir accepted the offer; procured an easy pardon for past misdeeds; and added to them a yet darker one by treacherously murdering his uncle, and seizing the fort. From this point of vantage he then assailed the Afghan governor of Khorasan, and was once more pardoned by Shah Tamasp, whose depressed fortunes he now undertook to retrieve.

Hitherto, there is little in the doings of such a man to interest the European reader, though it has seemed desirable to trace from its source the turbid stream of ambition, that was hereafter to expand into such vast proportions, and to overwhelm with such sudden ruin the tottering House of Timour. But rarely have equally remarkable military and political feats been performed, with such startling rapidity, as those now to be achieved by the low born, uneducated, and unprincipled, but eminently sagacious and commanding soldier of fortune.

To arouse the prostrate spirit of his degenerate countrymen; to teach them enterprise, fortitude, and discipline; to lead them on from victory to victory, until the capital was recovered, the sovereign restored, the Afghan intruders driven headlong out of the land, cut up in their flight, or destroyed on the sea coast or in the inhospitable desert (1730): to check the advance of Russia along the Caspian, and conclude a secure peace with that encroaching Power; to curb the Arab in the West, and repel the Sultan of Roum in the North, defeating the boasted janizzaries, and regaining province after province, that had been lost in the late evil times; to retrieve with marvellous celerity an almost overwhelming reverse (1733) sustained in the course of the same arduous war, and prosecute the desperate contest to a completely successful issue, wihch re-extended Persia to her ancient limits (1735); to sweep away the Suffavean dynasty, and to suppress in a day the distinctive religion of the country, and thus prepare the way for the more facile subjection of foreign Mahometans, by compelling the Persians as one man suddenly to turn *Soonees* (1736); to retaliate upon the Afghans the evils of invasion (1737), and yet so to treat them as to secure their allegiance and devoted fidelity to himself; to descend like a thunderbolt upon the plains of India (1738); rout hopelessly in a single battle the army of the Great Mogul, and constrain the trembling sovereign to resort a suppliant to the victor's camp (1739); to enter the proud capital without further resistance; rifle its far-famed treasury; levy severe contributions from its inhabitants, "benevolences" from the nobles, taxes from far-off provinces; to destroy for ever the reputation and almost the existence of the Empire; yet to refrain with deliberate policy from "breaking the bruised reed," or dismembering the quivering form (except by the resumption of the trans-Indus districts), and to reinstate and guarantee obedience to the fallen monarch, with patronising imperiousness; to convey safely through the tremendous mountain passes booty to the amount of upwards of £30,000,000 sterling; to coerce the wild tribes of the North, and extend the terror of his name in Upper Asia; to give the loose to new passions and unfounded suspicions, by blinding the heir to the throne (1743), and thereby (in the unhappy victim's memorable words) "putting out the eyes of Persia;" to repent at leisure, but with no salutary sorrow, and to testify his ireful remorse by the execrable and almost incredible cruelties of a conscience-stricken maniac; to plunge the country, which he had saved and restored to greatness and prosperity, into the worst miseries attendant on the excesses of unbridled and sanguinary despotism; and to perish abruptly by assassination (1747)—the inevitable penalty of his frantic crimes and growing hostility to his subjects:—such was, in outline, the marvellous, but lurid and meteoric course of one, who appeared to his contemporaries, not less than Attila or Timour, a *Scourge of God;* who might justly have been described, not less than the Emperor Frederick the Second, as a veritable *Stupor Mundi!* *

* Not the least curious among the many circumstances illustrative of the impression produced in Europe by Nadir's character and career is a story, endeavouring to establish the fact, that he was in reality a native of Brabant. It occurs in a French work, now little known.

Nadir's quarrel with the Court of Delhi was grounded chiefly on the refuge afforded in the imperial territories to his Afghan enemies. His advance beyond the Indus excited general astonishment, and profound terror. But a hasty attempt was made to arrest his course, which ended as such attempts have so often done, in speedy and irretrievable failure. The conqueror's proceedings previous to his entry into Delhi are recorded in a letter from himself to his eldest son and future victim, the most important parts of which will be found in the subjoined note.*

* "*We, whose wishes were for such a day, after appointing guards for our camp, and invoking the support of an all-powerful Creator, mounted, and advanced to the charge. For two complete hours the action raged with violence, and a heavy fire from cannon and musquetry was kept up. After that, by the aid of the Almighty, our lion-hunting heroes broke the enemy's line, and chased them from the field of battle, dispersing them in every direction. This battle lasted two hours; and for two hours and a half more were our conquering soldiers engaged in pursuit. When one hour of the day remained, the field was entirely cleared of the enemy; and as the entrenchments of their camp were strong, and the fortifications formidable, we would not permit our army to assault it.*

"*An immense treasure, a number of elephants, part of the artillery of the emperor, and rich spoils of every description, were the reward of our victory. Upwards of 20,000 of the enemy were slain on the field of battle, and a much greater number were made prisoners. Immediately after the action was over, we surrounded the emperor's army, and took measures to prevent all communication with the adjacent country; preparing at the same time our cannon and mortars to level with the ground the fortifications which had been erected.*

"*As the utmost confusion reigned in the imperial camp, and all*

Nadir, on entering Delhi, though prepared to assert very fully the rights of conquest in the way

discipline was abandoned, the emperor, compelled by irresistible necessity, after the lapse of one day, sent Nizam-ul-mulk, on Thursday, the seventeenth Zilkadeh, to our royal camp; and the day following, Mahomed Shah himself, attended by his nobles, came to our heaven-like presence, in an afflicted state.

"When the Emperor was approaching, as we are ourselves of a Turkoman family, and Mahomed Shah is a Turkoman, and the lineal descendant of the noble House of Gurgan, we sent our dear son, Nasser Aly Khan, beyond the bounds of our camp to meet him. The emperor entered our tents, and we delivered over to him the signet of our empire. He remained that day a guest in our royal tent. Considering our affinity as Turkomans, and also reflecting on the honours that befitted the majesty of a king of kings; we bestowed such upon the emperor, and ordered his royal pavilions, his family, and his nobles, to be preserved; and we have established him in a manner equal to his great dignity.

"At this time, the emperor, with his family, and all the lords of Hindostan, who marched from camp, are arrived at Delhi: and on Thursday, the twenty-ninth of Zilkadeh, we moved our glorious standard towards that capital.

"It is our royal intention, from the consideration of the high birth of Mahomed Shah, of his descent from the House of Gurgan, and of his affinity to us as a Turkoman, to fix him on the throne of the empire, and to place the crown of royalty upon his head. Praise be to God, glory to the Most High, who has granted us the power to perform such an action! For this great grace which we have received from the Almighty, we must ever remain grateful.

"God has made the seven great seas like unto the vapour of the desert, beneath our glorious and conquering footsteps, and those of our faithful and victorious heroes. He has made, in our royal mind, the thrones of kings, and the deep ocean of earthly glory, more despicable than the light bubble that floats upon the surface of the wave; and no doubt his extraordinary mercy, which he has now shown, will be evident to all mankind."—(Quoted in Malcolm's *History of Persia* from the translation in the *Asiatic Researches*).

of regular exaction, showed every disposition to protect the lives and persons of the terrified inhabitants, and to restrain unauthorised plunder. Taking up his own quarters in one of the imperial palaces, he distributed troops throughout the city to maintain order, and denounced the penalty of mutilation against any soldier who should insult an Indian. The strictness of his discipline was notorious, and the terror which he inspired began to subside into sullen resentment. Quiet reigned for the space of two days, while the work of graduated spoliation proceeded. "Nadir claimed," says Sir John Malcolm, "as a prize which he had won, the wealth of the emperor, and a great proportion of that of his richest nobles and subjects. The whole of the jewels that had been collected by a long race of sovereigns, and all the contents of the imperial treasury, were made over by Mahomed Shah to the conqueror. The principal nobles, imitating the example of their monarch, gave up all the money and valuables which they possessed. After these voluntary gifts (as they were termed) had been received, arrears of revenue were demanded from distant provinces, and heavy impositions were laid upon the richest of the inhabitants of Delhi."

Moreover, the collection was farmed to native agents, who, with incredible heartlessness, took the opportunity of enriching themselves out of the misfortunes of their countrymen, by exacting four or five times the sums paid into the Shah's coffers.

Many proud or money-loving men, some of very high rank, sought relief from their misery in suicide; and the despondency of the population deepened; until, in the course of the third night, a fatal report of Nadir's sudden death led to an outbreak, which consummated the horrors of the occupation. The mob rose; murdered in all directions the soldiers who had been posted to protect them; the base and craven nobles abandoning them to the rage of the insurgents. In vain Nadir sent messengers to appease the tumult; they also were slain. In vain, as the day broke, he rode out to exert his personal influence with the misguided and frantic people. His own life was attempted; and, provoked at length beyond endurance, he gave orders for an indiscriminate massacre. The miserable rabble instantly recoiled, and cowered before the justly exasperated soldiers. But too late: a frightful slaughter took place; and fire added its ravages, until a great part of the city was in flames.

The stern conqueror, in the interval, had betaken himself to a mosque, and "remained there," says Sir John Malcolm, "in a deep and silent gloom that none dared to disturb. At last the unhappy Mahomed Shah, attended by two of his ministers, rushed into his presence, exclaiming, 'Spare my people!' Nadir replied, 'The Emperor of India must never ask in vain:' and he instantly commanded that the massacre should cease." The command was at once obeyed, and proved the extraordinary ascendancy of this dread general over his troops, even in their wildest mood.

The number of those who perished on this terrific morning it is impossible to estimate. But it was undoubtedly very great. It was not until noon that the avenging sword was sheathed. And several hundred persons were executed more deliberately afterwards, as instigators or participators of the rising.

To how low a moral level the worthless cockneys of Delhi had sunk may be best understood from the fact, that they could shortly after the departure of the Persians, enjoy "a ludicrous representation of their own disgrace, and the fierce looks and savage pride of their conquerors, which had been so late their dread, became, in these imitations, one of their chief sources of entertainment."*

After marrying his second son to a prince of the imperial house, and remaining at Delhi for two months, Nadir evacuated the city, and commenced his march homewards. He is said to have given much good advice to Mahomed Shah. He certainly exhorted that monarch's subjects to obey their sovereign faithfully henceforth, on pain of another exterminating visit from himself. His circular-letter to this effect ends with the significant threat:—

* Malcolm's *History of Persia*.

"May God forbid! but if accounts of your rebelling against your emperor should reach our ears, we will blot you out of the pages of the book of creation."

He never had leisure, even if he had the inclination, to execute the threat. And his example, and the effects of his crushing visitation, were more potent in hastening, than his sententious exhortations and formidable menaces in retarding, the irretrievable downfall of the dynasty, which he had so grievously humiliated and despoiled.

Nadir Shah's defeat of the Emperor and terrible dealings with the capital were soon followed, in the natural course of Oriental polities, by the permanent separation from the Empire of the three finest Provinces of Hindostan. Bengal, Behar, and Orissa, became a practically independent kingdom under a new and remarkable adventurer, Mahummud Ali, or as he was ultimately called, Aliverdy Khan. His father, Meerza Mahummud, originally an adherent of Azim Shah, had after that prince's overthrow entered the service of Shuja-ud-Dowla, who was then Deputy-Governor of Orissa. Meerza provided in the same service for his two sons, Mahummud and Hajee Ahmud, and they obtained high appointments and much influence with Shuja. The latter, on his death (1738), was succeeded by a son, Serferaz Khan, with whom he had been on bad terms: and the brothers, Mahummud and Ahmud, partly, perhaps, sharing their original patron's grudge, partly conceiving themselves to be too lightly esteemed by the new Viceroy, conspired against and overthrew him (1739). How far this was an unprovoked act of treachery; how far the conduct of Serferaz or his confidants gave occasion to it, it would not be easy to determine in a few words, and perhaps is hardly worth attempting to determine now at all. It is more certain that Mahummud Ali's career from this time until near the close of his agitated reign is most characteristic of the troubled state of the times, of the complication of political interests that were at work in destroying the old and evolving the new order of things, and of the astonishing and continuous energy displayed by the denizens of a clime, which (it is so often assumed) tends almost irresistibly to languor, self-indulgence, and inertness. Without a summary sketch of Aliverdy's adventures the picture of imperial disintegration would be most incomplete; and the slippery foundation of Suraja Dowla's power, the subversion of which led to the establishment of the English rule in Bengal, will be thus better understood.

Aliverdy had held the government of Behar under Serferaz. The destruction of that unfortunate ruler, and the tender of a large part of his treasure to the venal and trembling Court at Delhi, had given the conqueror the actual possession of Bengal, and the titular Viceroyalty of the three Provinces. But Orissa was in the hands of a brother-in-law of Serferaz, Moorshud Koollee Khan, whose relatives induced him to reject Aliverdy's pacific offers, and to risk the fortune of war. Moorshud was defeated, but escaped, and thenceforth declined to resume the contest. But hostilities were soon renewed in Cuttak, where Aliverdy's deputy, Sowlut Jung, a son of Ahmud, mismanaged the country and the army, and was made prisoner in a popular tumult, and handed over to Baukir Khan, one of Serferaz' relations. Aliverdy, contrary to the wishes of Sowlut's parents, who, to obtain their son's release, would fain have ceded Orissa to Baukir, marched against that officer; routed him at once; recovered the captive from the jaws of death; and, having put the government into better hands, was returning at leisure and in triumph to his capital, when he suddenly learned that the Marathas were upon his track, bent upon their usual course of extortion and rapine (1742).

This was the first attempt of Rugoji Bonslay, of Berar, to extend his operations to Hindostan, under his general, Baskir Pundit, at the head of 40,000 cavalry. Aliverdy had hardly reached Burdwan, intending to deposit there his heavy baggage, when the enemy arrived, and began to plunder and devastate the suburbs. A series of skirmishes ended in an offer on the part of the Maratha to retire, on payment of ten *lacs*, which was refused; and Aliverdy prepared to push his way to Moorshedabad, his capital. But with an effective force reduced to 5000, and encumbered by a vast mass of camp followers, who, terrified at the invasion, had, contrary to his orders, persisted in accompanying him, he experienced a disastrous retreat, losing all his baggage, guns, and tents, but steadfastly declining the severe terms which his distress encouraged Baskir to propose. In four days he reached Cutwa, and was reinforced by his nephew, whom he had himself so lately rescued. Thereupon a detachment of Marathas, under Meer Hubeeb, an officer who had deserted the Viceroy's service for that of the Bonslay, made a dash at Moorshedabad. But Aliverdy, by a forced march, saved the city from plunder, though not before his friend, the great banker, Juggut Seet, had been despoiled of property to the amount of £3,000,000 sterling. The enemy then overspread the country so effectually that, "except Moorshedabad and its environs, nothing remained to the navob westward of the Ganges in Bengal." * This was during the monsoon. But Aliverdy had made such good use of the interval that, before the rivers were fordable, he crossed the Hadji on a bridge of boats, with an army in high spirits, and put the panic-struck Marathas to a hasty flight, capturing in turn their baggage and tents, and chasing them into the

* Scott.

thick jungles. After a time, however, the invaders rallied, invaded Cuttak, and once more engaged Aliverdy, only to be again routed, when they fled out of his dominions. The feeble Emperor, Mahomed Shah, recognised this public service by conferring titles on the Viceroy, his nephews, and his principal officers, and sending to his nominal representative a robe of honour, a jewelled dagger, and other marks of favour. He had also, on Aliverdy's application for assistance, directed Suffder Jung, Nawab of Oude, to co-operate against the invaders. But the victor, having saved himself, made haste to get rid of an ally, who was shrewdly suspected of an intention to turn to his own account the difficulties of his neighbour.

The ill success of the lieutenant aroused the wrath and activity of the principal; and Rugoji himself now made a formidable incursion. But the new Peishwa, Balaji, the son of the great Baji Rao, under circumstances which will be explained later, acted on this occasion with Aliverdy, against his own countryman; and, out-marching the Moguls, pursued his rival with such expedition, that he soon drove him out of the Province (1743).

The next year, however, Baskir again appeared at the head of a large army, offering peace at the price of a heavy contribution. Aliverdy now changed his tactics. Preparing his plans with much care and cunning, he lured the general and his chief officers to an interview, on pretence of adjusting the terms of the arrangement, and murdered them all. He then fell suddenly upon the Maratha army, and routed it; though a division left at the camp under the charge of a member of the Guikwar family, who had suspected treachery, escaped (1744). But this perfidious triumph only heralded new and more serious disturbances from another quarter.

Aliverdy in this instance, and towards enemies whom he regarded, no doubt, much in the light of irreclaimable beasts of prey, exhibited the gross perfidy so characteristic of the political atmosphere in which he flourished. He however was naturally generous, and by policy bountiful to those who were the instruments of his own aggrandisement, and who had a strong claim to their full share of the great fortune which they had helped to create. But in his recent straits he seems to have been too profuse of promises; and now found it inconvenient or dangerous to fulfil them. Hence serious dissatisfaction: and his refusal to commit the important Province of Behar to the command of his most powerful supporter, Mustapha Khan, brought matters to a crisis. Probably he too well remembered the precedent which he had himself set, when entrusted by his predecessor with the rule of that Province. Mustapha, indeed, is explicitly accused of a design to imitate his master's doings. However that may have been, the Nawab and his general became more and more estranged. Mutual suspicions of treacherous intentions were excited: and an ugly-looking incident at the Durbar presently gave Mustapha a pretext for abandoning a service in which he implied that his life was no longer safe. Aliverdy readily accepted his resignation, and paid up his arrears; but ordered him to quit his dominions without delay. After a vain attempt to enlist several Afghan chiefs in his rebellious schemes, the discarded general marched off with 8000 horse and a large body of infantry, setting fire to his cantonments on his departure; and openly entered on his plan of seizing Behar by force.

There Hybut Jung, Aliverdy's nephew, was in command; and the Nawab recommended that no battle should be fought until his own arrival. But Hybut rashly encountered the veteran leader of a veteran army with a force of raw troops, very inferior in number; and was saved from utter ruin only by Mustapha's elephant-driver being killed, and the animal turning restive, and compelling the general to dismount. Hence the usual panic set in, and in the confusion, each army in fact fled from the other. After a week's distant cannonading on both sides, Mustapha again assailed Hybut's lines. But again fortune favoured the inferior force. The rebel lost two of his best officers, and was himself wounded in the eye early in the battle; and Aliverdy's rumoured advance induced him to retire. He was vigorously pursued by the united armies of the uncle and nephew, and driven over the Oude frontier. Returning thence after a time, he once more met his old antagonist, Hybut, and was defeated and slain; though his followers still haunted the country in force.

Aliverdy meanwhile, had been compelled to confront a new invasion of the Marathas, under Rugoji in person. Indignant at the murder of his lieutenant and nineteen other officers, and relying on internal disorders, the Bonslay proceeded to make extravagant demands. But his antagonist kept him in play for two months, negotiating and making polite speeches, alternating with gasconading defiance; until a fit season for action came, when he threw off the mask, and resumed the offensive. He was out-marched at first, but defeated Rugoji in several battles, in one of which the Maratha narrowly escaped being taken prisoner. Again the invaders made a dash at Moorshedabad; and again Aliverdy's activity saved his capital from the fate that at this time overtook so many proud cities. This failure, a fresh defeat near Cutwa, and disorders in his own army, led Rugoji to retire (1745), still however retaining his hold over Cuttak, through Meer Hubeeb, with a mixed force of Afghans and Marathas.

For the moment all open war had ceased in Aliverdy's dominions; and he could celebrate with impressive pomp the marriage of his grandson, the stripling soon to become the notorious Suraja Dowla. But even now, during the single and brief period, until towards the close of his troubled reign, when the temple of Janus was closed, the successful soldier's mind was ill at ease. Cuttak was in hostile hands; and the escape of the Bonslay was confidently attributed to the treacherous connivance of two of the Nawab's Afghan officers. Other circumstances confirmed the suspicion of their unfaithfulness; and he discharged them and their followers; but with extreme and unaccountable imprudence he allowed them to settle, to the number of more than six thousand licentious and seasoned soldiers, in Behar. The fatal results of this plan were too soon to be disclosed.

Meanwhile, he brought to an end the short season of tranquillity by an attempt to recover Cuttak. Some successes were gained there, but were more than counterbalanced by the insubordinate and treasonable conduct of two of his generals, Meer Jaffier (the future English Subahdar) and Atta Oolla, both of whom he was compelled to remove, and sequester at Moorshedabad. He again foiled an attempt by Janoji (who now commanded the Marathas) to penetrate to that city; and was resting from his labours during the monsoon, when the most terrible tempest of his storm-tossed life broke suddenly upon him.

The discarded Afghan officers, Sirdar Khan and Shumsheer Khan, were settled, as I have mentioned, in Behar, with their numerous train of lawless and disaffected followers. Hybut Jung, Aliverdy's nephew, was still ruler of the Province; and from motives which appear very questionable, solicited his uncle to be allowed to re-engage them in the public service, reporting them to be sincerely anxious to retrieve their past misconduct. Aliverdy reluctantly consented, and preliminary interviews took place; Hybut, to allay in the minds of the turbulent chiefs suspicions of vindictive designs on his own part, rashly dispensing with the attendance of his troops, and even of his body-guard. The too familiar consequence followed. The revengeful and perfidious Shumsheer (Sirdar's complicity before the fact is doubtful) seeing his advantage, took occasion to murder the confiding Governor with his own hand; and, being supported by his numerous attendants, and promptly joined by the whole force of the late malcontents, placed Patna (the scene of the crime) under a reign of terror. In the commotion attending the assassination, resistance was out of the question; Hajee Ahmud, father of Hybut, and the Nawab's brother, who had, after taking part in the overthrow of Serferaz, quarrelled with Aliverdy, and retired into private life, devoting himself to pleasure and the amassing of wealth, was seized, tortured cruelly for many days, and expired without revealing the secret of his hoarded treasure. But it was discovered, and applied to raise new levies; heavy exactions on the terrified inhabitants were similarly employed; and Aliverdy's daughter, Hybut's princess, was carried off by the insurgents, who already contemplated the invasion of Bengal (1748).

This formidable insurrection, while the Marathas were in arms in the neighbourhood; the murder of his brother and nephew, and the abduction of his daughter, together with the general distrust of his remaining supporters, two of whom he had so recently been compelled to degrade for disaffection, drove the hitherto sanguine and energetic Viceroy almost to despair. But he hastened to make an earnest and pathetic appeal to his chief officers, handsomely acknowledging his great obligations to them; and tendering equally handsome promises of reward to those who might enable him to retrieve his affairs. At the same time, he artfully disclaimed all wish to retain the unwilling under his banners; and the result was a general and enthusiastic declaration of adherence to his cause.

Having thus secured the active support of the majority, and prudently winking at the lukewarmness of several important men, he adopted the bold policy of restoring Meer Jaffier to high office, and entrusting his capital to Atta Oolla, in concert with another nephew; and made prompt and vigorous preparations to march against the rebels. The wealthier non-combatants, at his suggestion, retired from Moorshedabad across the Ganges, out of the way of the Marathas; a proclamation frankly announcing that, for the moment, the city must be prepared to await the attack of those freebooters; and, with an army of 40,000 men, and an ample convoy of provisions, in a flotilla which was to attend his march up the river, he started in quest of the domestic enemy. His numbers swelled as he proceeded; and the chief rebel, by a new act of perfidy, played into his hands.

The insurgents, to the number of 50,000, had agreed to take service under the Maratha: but Shumsheer, to secure a material guarantee for the fulfilment of his large demands, seized Meer Hubeeb, who had come to arrange terms. A disturbance ensued, which ended in the Marathas standing idle, while the fortune of the field was contested between their treacherous allies and Aliverdy. The very next day the Viceroy came upon his rebellious subjects. Sirdar Khan was killed; and, his death causing a panic, Aliverdy gained a decisive and almost bloodless victory, captured the camp of the insurgents, and recovered his daughter. The Marathas absconded without striking a blow, and soon after retired from the victor's dominions, leaving only the usual force of occupation in Cuttak.

Aliverdy then did his best to heal the wounds which this internecine strife had caused. He was profuse in acknowledgment of the Divine mercy; bountiful to the religious classes and the poor, as well as to those who had stood by him in his extremity: and, with politic generosity, he sent safely and honourably away to their surviving friends the captured families of the chief rebels, and even sought in vain by a similar proceeding to conciliate Meer Hubeeb, the traitor of long standing and conspicuous achievements in the service of the Bonslay.

The following season saw him again in the field, pursuing the Marathas from place to place, as usual with little effect, though priding himself on keeping them out of Bengal. In the midst of this familiar occupation he was distracted by a new form of trouble. His peevish and worthless grandson, though the destined successor to his dominions, engaged in a rebellion which caused his doting ancestor more anxiety on the lad's account than on his own. But it was subdued with little difficulty, and (a momentous circumstance in the after fortunes of India) with no injury to the rebel, who was quickly restored to favour, and abused it in a manner which prepared his own premature and ignominious downfall.

After further hostilities with the Marathas, a definitive compromise was at length effected: Cuttak was ceded to them, and the *chout* of Bengal was commuted for an annual payment of twelve *lacs* (1751).

Thus Aliverdy, in spite of his indisputable superiority in the field, his indefatigable vigour (he was now seventy-eight years old), and his successful resistance to such a succession of enemies, was reduced to follow, at last, the example of his contemporary, the Subahdar of the Dekkan, and bow his neck, or at least open his purse-strings, and give a settlement in his territories, to the pertinacious and all-engrossing Hindoos.

Henceforth he reigned in peace and prosperity, though by no means free from anxiety for the future. His grandson's character he too well understood; but advanced in years, and deprived, by death, of his worthier relatives, he seems to have lacked the resolution to set him aside, or to have feared a new war of succession if he attempted to do so. He distinctly predicted the progress of the Europeans in India; but refused to expel the English, though he had his disagreements with them.

His civil government appears to have been admirable; and, with the exception of the disputable character of his proceedings at his accession, and his unquestionably gross treachery in the massacre of Baskir and his officers, his conduct seems to have been upright, humane, liberal, and conciliatory.

There is a curious account of his character and mode of life, given by his contemporary biographer, which may not be too long to quote, as conveying a singular picture of one of the most remarkable men of a remarkable age.

"Mahabut Jung from his early youth was not addicted to idle pleasures, as wine, or opiates, music, or the company of courtezans. He was regular in his devotions, and assiduously abstained from all things forbidden by the Divine law. He generally rose two hours before day, and, after ablution and prayer, drank coffee with his select companions. At daybreak he gave public audience, when the commanders of his army, the civil officers, and persons of all ranks who had any applications to make, were admitted without reserve to set forth their business, and received satisfaction from his bounty. At the expiration of two hours he retired to a private apartment, where such only as were invited came. These were generally his nephews, Shawamut Jung and Sowlut Jung; his grandson, Seraujc-ad-Dowlah, and particular friends. Pieces of poetry were now recited, or history or anecdotes read to him; and sometimes he even amused himself with giving directions to his cooks, who prepared victuals before him according to his palate. The officers of different departments, if necessary, also came for orders. He then sat down to eat with his friends, and many shared the bounties of his table. When the meal was over the company retired to repose. At this time a story-teller always attended to relate some amusing narrative. He generally rose about an hour after mid-day, performed his devotions, and read in the Koraun till near four. After saying the prayers for that time, and drinking a draught of water, cooled with ice or saltpetre, he received several learned men, in whose company he daily spent an hour, hearing them discuss points of divinity and law for his information. When they retired, the officers of the revenue, with Juggutt Seet, his banker, were admitted, and gave him the intelligence received from Dhely, and every province of the Empire; also of each district of his own government, when he issued his orders to them as affairs required. An hour passed in this manner, and sometimes his near relations were allowed to be present. By this time night set in, lights were brought, and with them certain jesters and buffoons, who entertained him with their repartees on each other for a short time. He then retired to prayers; after which he sat in privacy with his own Begum, to receive the visits of near female relations, till nine o'clock. The women then departed, and men were admitted who had business with him, till he retired to sleep, generally early, and without eating. In this manner he passed his time, having stated hours for every employment. He was unequalled in his benevolence to his relations, friends, and former acquaintance in his lower fortunes, particularly to those who had shown him the smallest kindness when he was distressed at Dhely in his youth, sending for them or their children to his Court, and conferring favours upon them beyond their expectation. The people at large during his life experienced such care and satisfaction from his gentle administration as could not be exceeded by the indulgence of a parent; while, at the same time, the lowest of his officers grew rich in his service. He was intelligent in all affairs, and encouraged the deserving of every profession. Affable in manners, wise in state affairs, courageous as a general, he possessed also every noble quality."—(From Scott's *Dekkan, &c.*, vol. ii. pp. 356-7.)

CHAPTER IX.

DEVELOPMENT OF THE MARATHA CONFEDERACY.

We have followed the rising fortunes of the Marathas to the death of the great Peishwa, Baji Rao the First. Henceforth the character of the history again greatly changes. For twenty more eventful years (1740-60), indeed, Sivaji's community continues to prosper, and to extend the area of its operations and dominion, until the Nizam's territory is almost entirely lost, either to his Hindoo enemies, or to the French allies whom he is fain to employ against them; and until Baji Rao's nephew storms the imperial city, affects to dispose of the imperial title, and even meditates transferring it to his own house.

But a new set of actors now appear upon the stage. The relations of the Maratha chiefs among themselves are entirely different from what they have hitherto been; the germs of jealousy and dissension, which Wishwanath's subtle contrivances for imparting to the confederacy a community of interest had failed to eradicate, now develop into perilous activity; and though the new Peishwa holds his own, he does so only by frequent and obstinate struggles, politic compromises, and cunning manœuvres, more in harmony with the conventional Brahmin character, than with the frank and bold bearing of his father and immediate predecessor.

But while a new generation arises among the native leaders, the whole circumstances of the case are still more changed and complicated, by the intervention of the Europeans on the Eastern coast; by the arts of Dupleix, the co-operation of Bussy with the Nizam, and the tardily aroused, but stubborn, and ultimately successful efforts of the English. Lastly, a new and terrible invader from Afghanistan, a pupil of Nadir Shah, the Abdali King of Cabul, repeats too faithfully his master's lessons; gathers to a head the Mahomedan forces of the North; and commits them in a crucial encounter with the major part of the Maratha name: and after an awful pause befitting the greatness of the issue depending on that day's strife, reverses in a few hours the current of predatory history for a century; overthrows and almost annihilates the vast Maratha army; and deals the Hydra a blow from which, though it rallies in its separate heads, it never as a whole recovers, nor is again in a condition to maintain the tone of general dictation which it had of late assumed.

Shortly before his death (April, 1740) Baji Rao sanctioned an expedition which, though at the moment apparently only an adoption of his rival Sreeput Rao's former counsel—to reduce and utilize the resources of the Carnatic Plain; yet in its consequences changed the whole political game, by bringing the French, and through them the English, to the front. Anxious, at present, to unravel the tangled skein of Maratha political encroachment, I shall touch very slightly on the course of this memorable expedition. But attention must be directed to certain circumstances, without a clear perception of which, Orme's classical narrative would be both incomplete and misleading.

That he nearly doubles the probable numbers of the invading army is not unnatural, and arises, doubtless, as in so many other cases, from the loose use of round numbers, and the phrase "a *lac* of men," among the natives. But it is more material, that he represents the campaign to have been undertaken with the permission, not to say at the command, of Nizam-ul-Mulk. This is not the only instance in which this admirable historian's tone implies, or is calculated to convey, an altogether erroneous idea of the political condition of the Dekkan, and the relations of the rival authorities there. As the English, hard pressed by Dupleix's claim to legitimate pro-viceregal power, by delegation from the contentious Subahdar of the Dekkan; and perplexed by the anomalous political attitude which the Coast War eventually compelled them to assume, endeavoured to found their rights on a similar basis, especially after they had succeeded to the alliance with the Nizam; it suited their line to ignore the fact, that (as I have taken some pains to show) Nizam-ul-Mulk was not only himself much of a usurper, as against the Mogul, but was on the other hand so far from being the lord, actually a tributary, almost a subject of the Marathas.

Orme's language, indeed, is singularly ill-timed as regards the Carnatic raid. For that raid took place in 1740, two years after Baji Rao had so deeply humiliated the Nizam in the North; a few months after he had planned, and but for Nazir Jung's unwonted display of energy, was in a fair way to accomplish, the complete conquest of his rival's territories; and at a moment when that rival, so far from being in a condition to hold the Maratha in the leash, was anxiously awaiting the rebellion of the very son, who had just rescued him from the threatening arms and arts of Baji Rao.

Again, since the base murder of Santaji Ghorepuray, Ram Raja's heroic lieutenant in the war of independence, his family had kept aloof from all connexion with the Satara Government. But now, for the first time, Moorar Rao, Santaji's great-nephew, recognized the authority of Shao, and joined in the expedition, of which he ultimately reaped the chief fruits. He claimed indeed, by hereditary right, the command-in-chief, but commuted the claim to some districts near the Toombudra.

The actual Generalissimo was Rugoji Bonslay, whose ambition the Peishwa thus sought to divert from disturbing his own designs in the upper country. But the venture was a thoroughly national one, and well illustrated the sort of co-operative society for fiscal appropriation, into which the measures of Wishwanath had a tendency to combine the various chiefs. Thus among the soldiers, the respective retainers of the Raja, the Peishwa, and the Bonslay, as well as numerous other less important leaders, were represented.

The events of the campaign were striking and decisive; but the *rationale* of their occurrence is not quite clear. The stout old Nawab of Arcot, Dost Ally, was overpowered and slain; his Minister, Meer Assud captured, and his territory laid under contribution. But his son, Sufder Jung, escaped; and his clever and enterprising son-in-law, Chunda Sahib, held out in Trichinopoly, which he had lately occupied by treachery. The Marathas retired; then returned, and resumed the siege of Trichinopoly, which was at last reduced by famine (1741); and its gallant defender became *Rugoji's* prisoner; and so continued until Dupleix, seven years later, obtained his enlargement, and employed him as an instrument of his own ambition.

Moorar Rao was left Governor of Trichinopoly, the garrison consisting partly of the Peishwa's troops, in the pay, however, of the Raja; and a part of the tribute of the Province being settled on Baji Rao's son and successor. These arrangements further illustrate the partnership character of the enterprise.

That this new triumph of the Marathas over the Moguls was facilitated by the mutual jealousies and want of concert among the latter, is evident. Dost Ally, all admit, was taken by surprise, but fought earnestly. But while some authorities assert that Chunda Sahib was hastening loyally to his support, others maintain that that wily statesman, for his own purposes, kept at a safe distance from the fray. Moreover, while there seems little or no doubt that Sufder, through the agency of Meer Assud, made his peace with the enemy, by directing their arms against Trichinopoly and his ambitious brother-in-law; some writers have gone so far as to declare or insinuate, that the whole incursion was instigated by the Nawab's son, for the purpose of getting rid of an obnoxious and overweening connexion, against whom Dost Ally himself was unwilling or afraid to proceed. The exact history of this intrigue is of no great importance in itself. But the momentous events to which it gave occasion later, seem to justify thus much allusion to it.

While the Carnatic expedition was in progress, the Peishwa died, leaving a son, Balaji Baji Rao, or Nana Sahib, as he was commonly called among his countrymen, who succeeded his father, though not without opposition.

The ascendancy of the Brahmin Peishwas had always been looked upon with an evil eye by most of the other Maratha chiefs of different lineage. Sindia and Holkar, indeed, were staunch adherents, at this period, of the family whose head had brought them into notice and importance. But the faction of the deceased Trimbuk Dhabaray still subsisted, and remained dissatisfied with the arbitrament of arms in which that leader had perished. Sreeput Rao, who bore a title signifying "The Express Image of the Raja," had been Baji Rao's constant rival. The older leading houses found themselves, under the new system of Brahmin supremacy, gradually sinking into insignificance. The Guikwar, from this time down to the very latest days of the Maratha Confederacy, had a standing difficulty with the Peishwa, as to their respective rights in Guzerat. And the most ambitious, powerful, and restless chief of all, Rugoji Bonslay, had shown a frequent disposition to dispute Baji Rao's right to the first place in the Satara administration. He had shirked supporting the last great effort of that warrior-statesman to crush Nizam-ul-Mulk in the North. His ambiguous attitude had probably contributed not a little to bring about the Peishwa's still later miscarriage, when he was foiled by Nazir Jung, in attempting to conquer the Nizam's home provinces. And though bribed into neutrality by the appointment of Commander-in-Chief of the Carnatic expedition, no sooner was he aware that Baji Rao was dead, than he left the army, hastened back to Satara, and brought forward an opposition candidate for the Peishwaship, cunningly selecting as his tool Bappoji Naik, a wealthy man to whom Baji Rao had been heavily indebted.

Thus he hoped to place the son in an awkward predicament. The creditor, duly tutored for the purpose, pressed urgently for an instant settlement of accounts, which the code of native honour made it disreputable to repudiate, which it was specially out of the question to think of avoiding on such an occasion, and yet which Balaji was in no condition to effect. A large sum was also offered to the Raja, on condition of his rejecting the hereditary claim of Baji Rao's son.

But Sreeput Rao was more jealous of Rugoji than of that son of his old rival: Chimnaji Appa, the late Peishwa's able brother, exerted himself vigorously on his nephew's behalf: Balaji found means, through his Dewan, of raising a considerable sum at once; and his own abilities and reputation, the renown and services of his father and grandfather, and the inveterate tendency to hereditary succession in the East, carried the day; and thus the new Peishwa's *first* great danger of being superseded was surmounted. But still more formidable opposition was in store for him: nor did he emerge from his later trials with such clean hands as in the present instance.

With Nizam-ul-Mulk, indeed, he maintained very friendly terms; assisting him against Nazir Jung. whose dangerous rebellion was promptly subdued (1741). In return, the Nizam backed the Peishwa's application to the Emperor for the government of Malwa. Shortly after that application had been forwarded, Chimnaji Appa, who had been a party to it, died—a double misfortune. For his support had been of the greatest consequence to his nephew; and Appa's young son, Sedasheo Rao, at this time but ten years of age, was thus left to develop, unchastened by parental care, the reckless and presumptuous character, which proved, in the end, so fatal to himself, his cousin Balaji, and his people.

The singular character, various aspects, and conflicting elements of the Maratha Power were curiously and copiously illustrated in the course of the next few years. At first sight that Power was simply an instrument of coercive requisition, and armed occupation. Province after Province was squeezed or taken possession of as opportunity offered; and the goal of the day was the vantage ground of the morrow. But this was the case not locally only. The fact was soon conveniently confused with the right; and the precarious black mail of one season was successively interpreted into the expected, the customary, and ere long the legitimate tribute of the following years. Still, the artful and litigious Maratha, like the artful and litigious Norman of old, never rested till he had established his connexion with the previous political system, and decorated his free lance with the pennon of imperial sanction. Thus, as Sivaji had demanded of Aurungzib the right to levy the *chout* in certain districts,—basing that right on his father's original real or alleged claims under the still older Afghan dynasty;—and had gladly ceded much of his actual territory, and many of his cherished fortresses, in return for a formal recognition of his Rajaship over the remainder; so his successors continually acted. And the Peishwa now, after arresting Rugoji's career in Bengal, procured from the Emperor the long coveted formal cession of the government of Malwa; though, to save appearances, he was appointed nominally the Deputy of Prince Ahmed, the Emperor's son (1743). The chief conditions of this grant were, that he was to keep order in the district; to refrain from sequestrating the rent-free lands and *jaghires,* devoted to charitable or religious objects; to prevent every other Maratha officer from crossing the Nerbudda; and to supply a considerable force for the imperial service. To promote more than one of these objects, Balaji was now reconciled to the Puar Chief of Dhar, who had sided with Trimbuk against the Peishwa's father; and who might serve to a certain extent, as a barrier between the Guikwar on the West, and Rugoji in the East.

A still more important, and to the fallen Mogul, more humiliating concession was the general grant of the *chout* in all the remaining imperial Provinces, which had not suffered more than occasional incursions (1742). General in two senses; for it seems not to have been reduced to writing in the shape of an explicit *sunnud;* and the promise appears to have been rather a comprehensive ratification of the Maratha practice, than a localised donation.

But the complication and anomaly of the Maratha claims proceeded yet further. Though the Raja now exercised little influence on the actual conduct of affairs, yet his sovereignty over the Maratha community, and even his right to dispose of the Mogul territories and revenues were freely recognised, and superstitiously maintained. The Peishwa annually, after each campaign, presented his accounts, and prepared a detailed balance-sheet. And whenever, as in his disputes with Rugoji, he was at a loss to arrange the terms of his connexion, or the limits of his jurisdiction and taxable districts, the convenient fiction of a grant from the Raja, embodying the compromise at which the contending parties had eventually arrived, was freely resorted to, and tended alternately to settle and to embarrass the position of the parties. Lastly, private agreements between Maratha chieftains, or between one such chieftain and a Mogul, a Rajput, or some other powerful representative of the many nationalities that were embraced within the wide limits of the Empire, still further modified, perplexed, and often embroiled, the political and social relations of this remarkable people during the era of imperial dissolution.

Thus though, when Rugoji invaded Bengal, the Peishwa first earned the imperial gratitude, as well as that of Aliverdy Khan, by vigorously opposing and defeating the invader; yet he shortly afterwards, in order to disarm a renewed conspiracy against himself at Satara, headed by the Bonslay, came to an agreement with the latter, to cede his own rights north of the Nerbudda and Mahanuddy, as far as Aliverdy's dominions were concerned, and thus left Rugoji to follow out undisturbed his plans in that direction (1744).

This was, in reality, a private compact, very similar to that formerly entered into between Nizam-ul-

Mulk and the late Peishwa with a similar object—*mutatis mutandis*—on either side. But, in the present case, the Raja's authority was called in to give formal shape to the agreement. While Balaji, for his private ends, was thus led to shuffle out of his stipulation with the Emperor, to keep all other Maratha chiefs away from the North; and thereby violated an express and capital condition on which his formal appointment to Malwa rested.

It has been already mentioned, that the *personnel* of the political drama was almost entirely changed soon after the death of Baji Rao. That event took place in 1740; and his brother, Chimnaji, expired in the following year. Chimnaji's young son, Sedasheo Rao, began about the period which we have now reached to take an active part in public affairs; and in 1746 was appointed by the Raja second in command of the national forces under his cousin, the new Peishwa. But while Sedasheo distinguished himself, both in military and civil duties in the Dekkan, Balaji's brother, Rugonath Rao, (or Ragoba, as the English generally called him,) commenced in Hindostan his career of fitful hopes, rash adventures, and disastrous reverses. In 1747 died Sreeput Rao, Baji Rao's competitor. But the year 1748 was above all memorable as the end of the old, and the beginning of the new age of public men. Then took place the first invasion of India by the Afghan King of Cabul, Ahmed Shah Abdali. Invited by the Vizier's nephew, he advanced into the Punjab, but was repulsed by the Emperor's son, his own namesake, Prince Ahmed. The Prince returned to find his father dead; and almost immediately after he had himself mounted the throne, the veteran statesman and warrior, Nizam-ul-Mulk, breathed his last. How many new characters thereupon appeared on the scene, both in the Carnatic Plain and in the Dekkan, I need not now specify. But it may be mentioned, that among others Hyder Ally was in the Mysore contingent which accompanied the unfortunate Nazir Jung to the Carnatic, and materially improved his then slender means, by securing two camels laden with treasure, when the army dispersed in panic on the murder of that Prince. Lastly, in the year 1749, the long reign of Shao, the Maratha Raja, the grandson of Sivaji, the prisoner and *protégé* of Aurungzib, the patron of three generations of Brahmin Peishwas, came to an end; and while Delhi was still tremblingly awaiting the return of the baffled, but formidable Abdali, and a general *imbroglio* was proceeding in the Carnatic Plain, a curious and complicated domestic struggle was waged at the Court of Satara.

Shao had no son to succeed him. He was inclined to adopt his relative and old antagonist, the Raja of Kolapoor. But neither had the latter any issue.

The strong family feeling of the Marathas was then shown in the attempt to substitute a descendant of so remote an ancestor as Wittoji, the great uncle of the hero Sivaji. But before any fit person from this distant branch could be found, and while Sukwar Bhye, Shao's wife, was loth to abandon a project which would make her, as the adoptive mother of a minor Raja, nominally, if not effectively, Regent of the Maratha Empire, a mysterious cross light was thrown on the scene by an alleged revelation of a great secret of State. Tara Bhye, the aged but still vigorous and ambitious widow of Ram Raja, Sivaji's son, now declared, that after the death of *her* son, the second Sivaji, and the first Raja of Kolapoor, she had concealed a posthumous son of the latter prince, consequently a grandson of her own. This alleged grandson she now produced, and demanded that he should be recognised as Ram Raja II., and prospective Sovereign of the Marathas, on the death of Shao.

It remains to this day a question whether her story was true or false. That through this new claimant she meant to acquire the virtual supremacy for herself, is evident enough. Shao's wife, of course, was proportionately disappointed and indignant, and formed a conspiracy to maintain her own contemplated power, through a contemplated adoption.

Thus Balaji, on his arrival with a large force at

Satara, was perplexed by a double feminine plot against his own authority. The strong popular sentiment in favour of the race of Sivaji, and the widespread antipathy to Brahmin ascendancy, forbade him to do what he seems at one time to have meditated—namely, to abolish the Rajaship altogether, and make himself avowed Head of the State.

Tara Bhye he misdoubted; and the other lady was resolved to push matters to extremities, both against him and against Tara. But, to conceal her ambitious designs, she dropped hints of an intention to become *suttee* on her husband's death. Balaji was a thorough Brahmin, in the *bad* sense, that is a man of consummate craft, little restrained by moral scruples, or even by prudential considerations that did not affect the attainment of his immediate object. He chose his line, and played his part with admirable skill, but with what the not too sensitive native mind pronounced most reprehensible artifice. Sukwar Bhye he knew was ready for action, and had influential men and an armed force at her command. His first care accordingly was to make himself master of the military situation, and to be prepared, on the Raja's death, to anticipate and counteract all the motions of the conspirators in the interest of Shao's widow. This was thoroughly done, and when the critical moment came, they dared not strike a blow. Balaji's next care had been to soothe Tara Bhye's haughty and suspicious temper, and at the same time to prepare the way for circumventing her, by professing a belief in her story. For this course enabled him, not only to make common cause with her against the Raja's wife, but to obtain from the Raja himself an important sanction for his own intended retention of the reins of power, the purport of which will be mentioned presently. While, for his own purposes, he took good care not to repress reports which were widely circulated, and which implied that the whole of Tara's tale was an invention, and the lad an impostor.

Thus far the Peishwa had hardly exceeded the lax limits of conventional native statecraft. But his master-stroke, whereby he determined to rid himself at once and for ever of his younger, and on that account at least, more formidable rival, remained to be delivered. And herein lies the peculiar infamy of his conduct, in the eyes even of Marathas. Trading upon Sukwar Bhye's rash hints of an intention to burn with her husband's body, he sent taunting and ironical messages, requesting her *not* to trouble herself to carry out her intention! He was well aware that such a message from such a quarter, and at such a crisis, could hardly fail to drive the unhappy Princess not only to suicide, but to suicide of a very melancholy kind. It would not be a case of genuine *suttee*—of voluntary and affectionate religious martyrdom, for her husband's sake; but the victim would be idly sacrificed to a point of honour, and compelled, for very shame, to act upon words never meant to be fulfilled! But, to make all sure, Balaji, moreover, tampered with the brother of Sukwar Bhye, and by alternate appeals to his family pride and his cupidity, persuaded him to throw his influence also into the scale in favour of the *suttee* offering. Thus, beset on all hands, and taken in her own toils, Shao's wife, lately so formidable, now so forlorn, succumbed to the superstitious rite, and removed from his path one obstacle to the complete ascendancy of her cold-blooded murderer.

Though the Peishwa's conduct was severely condemned, he contrived to bribe the other chiefs into acquiescence, by causing the Raja to confirm and enlarge their territorial possessions and fiscal rights. And Tara Bhye, who already began to turn restive in his hands, he appeased by the promise of an effective share in the government. But he had little intention of performing this promise, and had taken precautions to give a legal colouring to his proposed sole assumption of political power, by a deed which he had found means of extorting from the dying Raja. He had not indeed ventured, during Shao's last illness, to brave the consequences of removing Sukwar Bhye and her friends from his Sovereign's presence. But he had obtained a private interview, in which he procured the document in question. This empowered him "to manage the whole government of the Mahratta Empire, on condition of his perpetuating the Raja's name, and keeping up the dignity of the house of Sivajee, through the grandson of Tara Bhye and his descendants."* Special clauses in this deed gave a large, indeed an indefinite extent to the powers which were thereby vested in the grantee.

The prompt military measures which the possession of this document emboldened him to take; the summary manner in which he disposed of the Raja's wife; his causing the other chiefs to find their immediate account in compliance with his wishes; his careful management of Tara Bhye; and the doubt that hung over her story, and which Balaji was at no pains to dispel;—all contributed to assist his usurpation—if usurpation it is to be called—and to bring into prominence what had been hitherto a tendency only, though a marked tendency, in the Maratha State—the definitive supremacy of the Peishwa. Thus henceforth Poona became the real military and political capital: Satara sank to little more than the prison of the *roi fainéant*—the *doubly* discredited representative of Sivaji—as being at once a degenerate, and a doubtful scion of the heroic stock. Thus, too, as another symptom of the same revolution,

* Grant Duff.

whereas Shao had instituted an office, the holder of which was entrusted with the collection, or the auditing, of the *surdeshmookee* for the six Mogul Dekkan Provinces; the office was now retained, but turned into a sinecure, and paid by the proceeds of certain *jaghire* lands.

By the measures now adopted (1750), the Maratha Power was in fact converted into a Confederacy of chiefs, permanently and confessedly presided over by the Peishwa, as an almost sovereign Prince; loosely and grudgingly obeyed, indeed, but far more distinctly recognised as supreme on his own account than he had ever yet been. While, like the Deity in the Gnostic system, the Raja retires into unapproachable and inactive isolation and mystery.

But Tara Bhye by no means approved of such an arrangement, and jealously watched her opportunity for subverting it.

All India was now electrified by a series of rapid and startling surprises in the conduct of the Carnatic struggle, and the brilliant triumph of Dupleix's policy. A very brief summary of these events will enable the reader to appreciate their bearing upon the new period of Maratha history marked by the accession of Balaji to the enlarged functions just described.

Five years before his death, Nizam-ul-Mulk had descended with a large army into the Carnatic Plain;

had procured the evacuation of Trichinopoly and the whole Province by Moorar Rao and his soldiers, on condition of confirming Moorar as chief of Gooty; and had left at the time as Regent, and supported afterwards as actual Nawab of Arcot, Anwar-ud-deen —one of his own officers, while Chunda Sahib continued a prisoner at Poona. Anwar-ud-deen was the father of Mahomet Ally, whom the English afterwards supported.

On Nizam-ul-Mulk's death, Chunda Sahib was released through Dupleix's machinations; and then followed the tug of war which Orme has so fully and faithfully chronicled. Nazir Jung, at his father's death, was absent in the North; his eldest brother was at Delhi; and their nephew Mirzapha was in command in the Dekkan.

"While the English are making unprovoked war on the King of Tanjore, a tripartite alliance has been concluded between three daring adventurers, Mirzapha Jung, a young claimant of the Dekkan throne, Chunda Sahib, a veteran warrior and intriguer, who aspires to supplant the ruler of the Carnatic, and the French Governor-General, whose aims, if less definite, are certainly not less extensive than those of his confederates. French gallantry and skill again decide the day; and the Nawab of Arcot is slain. But a more formidable enemy of the allies is at hand. The nephew has sought to supplant the uncle in the Dekkan. But that uncle, Nazir Jung, appears with a countless host; the English join him; and, at the most critical moment, the French officers basely desert their post; and Dupleix's contingent, the flower of the allied army, is compelled to retreat in haste to Pondicherry. With it goes the Pretender to the Nawabship of Arcot; but the inexperienced claimant of the Dekkan Viceroyalty is deluded into throwing himself upon his uncle's mercy, and is instantly and perfidiously put in fetters.

The triumph of Nazir Jung is however short.

The French recover from their disorder, and seize the strongest fortress in the Carnatic. Their enemy's nobles are discontented. Dupleix, anticipating Clive in Bengal, intrigues with them and inflames their discontent. They conspire against their master; and while the French are contending against the faithful part of his army, he is murdered by one of the conspirators. Then his imprisoned rival is produced; saluted as Viceroy; proceeds to Pondicherry; is entertained there with Oriental pomp; constitutes Dupleix his Deputy for all the wide region south of the river Kistna; showers upon him favour, distinctions, and territorial cessions; and the success of the Frenchman's great game is commemorated on the pillar of Dupleix, and by the foundation of the city of *Dupleix-Futteabad*. But another storm is already brewing. The nobles who have slain the uncle, dissatisfied with the price of blood, destroy the nephew on his homeward march, and are themselves cut off in the struggle. All is again confusion and dismay. The fortune of France, however, is still in the ascendant. Bussy's authority commands general confidence, and promptly restores order. Another puppet is substituted, and ratifies the concessions made by his predecessor to his European patrons; and the march towards the Dekkan is quietly resumed."*

It was an anxious question for the Peishwa what line he should adopt at this momentous crisis. The crafty, enterprising, and experienced Nizam-ul-Mulk was indeed no more; and while his eldest son, Ghazi-ud-deen, though detained at Delhi, was preparing to assert his rights against Salabat, who at present was in the ascendant, there were in the background two other brothers who, as events soon showed, and as the Peishwa probably already suspected, were watching their chance of dividing still further the Mahometan interest in the Dekkan, and embroiling the fray by their ambition and turbulence.

Salabat himself was not a man of energy or ability. Externally, therefore, Balaji might well see reason to hope that, as usual, the mutual hostilities of the Moguls would favour the growth of his own power and territory. While, internally, he had escaped or

* The above paragraphs are condensed from a published lecture of my own, already quoted.

overcome some serious dangers, and his supremacy in the Confederacy was, openly at least, undisputed. Rugoji, who had at first opposed his succession as Peishwa, had been propitiated by the partition compact, which left that Chief free to pursue his own course in Bengal and the neighbouring Provinces. Sukwar Bhye had paid the penalty of her bold attempt to snatch at the Regency, and her terrible fate might operate as a warning to others. Tara Bhye seemed absorbed and satisfied with the charge of the young Raja, who as yet lived at large, and liberally provided for in the town of Satara; while his real or *soi-disant* grandmother remained in the fort adjoining that city, and garrisoned by the Peishwa's troops. A serious difference had indeed lately arisen between Balaji and his high-spirited and rash cousin Sedasheo—or the Bhow, as he was now commonly called; and which had proceeded so far, that the latter had, for a time, gone over to the Kolapoor Raja, and become *his* Peishwa. But this difference had been composed; and the deserter was reclaimed by being made Prime Minister at Poona.

Yet, on the other hand, there was still much smothered discontent. Popular opinion was strongly in favour of the Regency of Tara Bhye; and her influence was not unlikely to be exerted in order to convert the nominal into a real office, and a means of depressing, if not overthrowing, the crafty Brahmin with whom it had suited her purpose to co-operate for the moment against their common enemy.

These internal dangers were mueh more formidable when viewed in eonnexion with the present eharaeter of the Nizam's army, following, and politieal allianees. The Pondieherry magieian was easting his spells over the whole eountry. He had overthrown Nazir Jung: the fate of his ally Mirzapha had not arrested his poliey for more than a day; his brilliant agent and representative, Bussy, seemed equally eompetent to deal with military and with politieal emergeneies; the Freneh arms and diseipline were manifestly something totally different from, and far superior to, the hostile elements whieh the Marathas had hitherto eneountered; and it remained to be proved how far the Cossaek lanee could hope to withstand the European musket and bayonet, and above all, the quiek-moving and quiek-firing field-pieee.

To remain an inaetive speetator of the progress of Salabat, or even of the eontest between the sons of Nizam-ul-Mulk, for the sake of watehing and eounteraeting an old woman's sehemes, was not only inglorious, but was eontrary to the eharaeter, the interests, and the uniform praetice of his family, and of the people whom he aspired to rule, and eould rule only by indulging their restless and aequisitive temper.

On the whole, therefore, Balaji determined to side

with Ghazi-ud-deen, the elder claimant; to quiet Tara Bhye in his absence, by giving her the complete control of the Raja's person, and to march without delay against Salabat, before his authority should have gained the strength of well established rule. Accordingly he petitioned the Emperor to appoint Ghazi-ud-deen Subahdar of the Dekkan; for this formality might prove of no little efficacy in the approaching war of succession; and withdrawing his garrison from the fort of Satara, he rashly hoped that thi proof of confidence would appease an angry and jealous woman.

On reaching Aurungabad, he levied on Salabat's Governor there, who, though professing to yield to force, was really in the interest of the elder brother, a contribution of fifteen *lacs* of rupees; and hastened to confront the French Nizam and his European allies. But before a shot had been exchanged, he learned that the mine which had been preparing, and which his own conduct had contributed to fire, had exploded behind him; and patching up a hasty truce with Salabat, he returned by forced marches to Satara, accomplishing 400 miles in thirteen days. He arrived in the nick of time to meet a most serious crisis, and to succeed once more, though not without recourse to measures which would hardly have been adopted by his bolder and wiser father.

Ram Raja had explicitly agreed to leave the whole

government in the hands of the Peishwa on certain conditions, which were never fulfilled. No sooner was Balaji well on his way to Aurungabad, than Tara Bhye, in a personal interview, endeavoured to arouse the spirit of the youth, and induce him to throw off the political thraldom to which he had pledged himself. Finding him hopeless, the fiery and overbearing Princess lured him into the fort; rated him furiously as an impostor and a changeling; placed him in close custody; and secure of the sympathy and obedience of the present garrison, which consisted of Marathas of the old stamp, who revered the memory of the earlier state of things, and were opposed to Brahmin domination, she opened a fire upon the Raja's people, as they hung about the gates unprepared for so warm a reception; and then proceeded to turn the fort guns upon the town, and the quarters occupied by the Peishwa's troops. She had, moreover, invited Dunnaji Guikwar to carry out the plan which Trumbuk years before had been prevented, by the late Peishwa's promptitude, from accomplishing, and in a happier hour to march on the capital, and rid it and the State of the Brahmin clique. Just at this juncture accordingly, Dunnaji's approach, at the head of 15,000 men, was announced. The Peishwa's party marched out to meet him, and though more numerous were repulsed. The Guikwar and the Bhye met, secured several forts, and were joined by the new *Prithee Needhee* (the inheritor of Sreeput's office and jealousy of the Peishwa's assumptions, and who had already opposed and been coerced by Balaji); and as Satara was well provisioned, prepared to stand a siege of the fort, until large reinforcements expected from various quarters should arrive

But at the critical moment they received a check; and while still hesitating, they were threatened by the Governor of the Concan in their rear, and by the Peishwa, who suddenly appeared in their front. Negotiations as usual were entered into; and while these were in progress, Balaji enticed the Guikwar to encamp near him, under a solemn promise which he immediately after broke; and presently assaulted and pillaged his camp, and made Dunnaji himself prisoner. By this treacherous step, which deterred the other opponents of the Peishwa's power from rising in rebellion, the military danger was for the present averted (1751).

But the Princess still occupied the fort; maintained a defiant tone; and kept the Raja in close, indeed, in unhealthy confinement. "His prison," says Grant Duff, "which still exists, was a damp stone dungeon, and his food was of the coarsest grain." Nothing is more curiously illustrative of the strange and commanding character of this remarkable woman, and of the singular and inconsistent feelings and ways of the

Marathas, than her conduct and influence at this period. She had no longer an army to execute her decrees, yet she could afford to brave the Peishwa and his victorious forces. She claimed the Regency, and the popular verdict was in favour of her claim; though not an arm was raised in her support outside the gates of the fort of Satara. Her pretensions seemed based on the story, that Raja Ram the Second was her genuine grandson: yet she was known to have declared her own belief that he was nothing of the kind, but a base-born changeling. And how she treated the youth whom she had brought forward in the interests of her own ambition, has been stated. Nor does it seem to have occurred to her people, that it was absurd to obey the priestess who had broken her own idol. She could not deny or resist the power of the Peishwa outside the limits of her present residence: yet she refused all overtures to surrender and "having assembled her garrison, she required an oath from every man, that he would stand by her to the last," * though, with prudent confidence, or suspicious insidiousness, she offered to dismiss all who declined to take the pledge of resistance *à l'outrance*. We are not told that anyone came forward to test the good faith of her offer.

Certain it is that Balaji shrank from the danger of proceeding to extremities against her. Several cir-

* Grant Duff.

cumstances seem to have brought about this curious political dead-lock. Besides the wide-spread jealousy of Brahmin encroachment, and the antecedents, abilities, and imperious temper of Tara Bhye, the native notions on succession and adoption, and the superstition which was equally strong and general among them, will go far to account for the situation. In the present state of things, whether Raja Ram were or were not the true son of the Second Sivaji, there could be no doubt that the aged Princess represented the original right of her husband, the first Raja Ram; and that, whether in ordinary cases of property an adoption by her, without his sanction or that of his son, would be strictly valid or not, there was very much to be said in favour of recognising her right to continue, by such a step, the person of the Founder of the whole Community, and as a corollary of the same act, to become Regent, as she had actually been after Ram Raja the First's death.

Thus her claim went further back than the question of the present Raja's parentage. She was rather the perennial fountain of honour, that was to ennoble, if necessary, a new family, by artificially mingling its blood, in the rite of adoption, with that of the ruling race. Shao's deed, handing over the power to Balaji, she would of course treat as Harold treated William the Bastard's alleged donation from the Confessor.

But, moreover, not only have women frequently

exercised political functions among the Marathas, but such was this aged but vivacious lady's temper and bearing, that all quailed before her as *uncanny*: and while some thought her a good spirit, and others an evil one, there was a very decided disinclination among the Peishwa's soldiers to incur more than mortal perils by acting against her.

For the time therefore, in form, the contest ended in a sort of drawn battle. The government of the State and the command of the army remained with the Peishwa; and though he afterwards released the Guikwar, it was only on the latter's binding himself in the most absolute manner to very humiliating terms: he was not only to accept the Peishwa's lead, but to yield permanently the right to half the revenues of Guzerat, and to fulfil other stringent stipulations. The Princess, on the other hand, was left in possession of the fort of Satara, and retained the custody of the unhappy puppet Raja, and whatever *prestige* attached to that fact.

But Balaji was in truth the real gainer. He had driven the Bhye both to discredit, and to set the example of imprisoning, the unfortunate representative of a great name. And though, more than once afterwards, he experienced some trouble and more anxiety, from her connexion with other politicians, both Maratha and Mogul, and even with Bussy; yet he at last induced her to submit to his *de facto* supremacy, on the understanding that "the control of the Raja's person and establishment should remain at her disposal." And with a final and neat touch of Brahmin artifice, he compassed his own desire that the *roi fainéant* should continue withdrawn from the eyes of the people, whom such a spectacle might too distinctly remind of the Peishwa's usurpation, by urging the Bhye to release him, which, as he expected, she therefore took good care not to do.

Thus ended the third and final attempt to wrest the power out of the hands of the Peishwa, who henceforth was the undisputed head of what may now be strictly called the Maratha Confederacy, until many years of the present century had elapsed, when the triumphant English abolished the office; and formally released the other members of the League from all obedience to their whilom superior.

CHAPTER X.

CULMINATION OF THE MARATHA POWER.

THE Marathas were now once more united under the acknowledged and tolerably defined supremacy of the Peishwa, as head of a Federation of great chiefs. The older families had mostly dropped out of consideration, or retired into the background. Moorar Rao indeed represented the Ghorepurays, and he acted, from time to time, with the Peishwa's army. But he could hardly be considered a member of the League; and he was reckoned as a feudatory and dependent of the Nizam. The Raja of Kolapoor continued to administer his small territory, but he had little political or military power. The Bonslay, whose seat was in Berar, was gradually, with the concurrence of the Peishwa, and in pursuance of the agreement which had been entered into between them, extending his influence, his exactions, and his dominion north-eastward through Gondwaneh to Bengal. The Guikwar, it was arranged, was to divide with his conqueror half the revenues of Guzerat, the Mogul capital of which Province was not yet in Maratha hands. But Baroda, the modern residence of this chieftain, had already been occupied by his troops. Holkar and Sindia were domesticated in Malwa; but were prepared to act with the Peishwa's forces in levying dues, and seizing territory further north, and to take part in revolutions at Delhi itself. The imprisoned Raja of Satara had now sunk into utter insignificance, and his name was hardly mentioned. The Peishwa, having his capital at Poona, and possessing most of the original Maratha country, presided over the whole community; projected profitable expeditions in all directions; employed one or other chief, so far as their common interest led to such concerted action, though his actual power over any, except perhaps Sindia and Holkar (who were more intimately connected with him by old and grateful ties) was small; intrigued and interposed, both at Hyderabad and at Delhi, watching his chance of aggrandisement, and the dangers threatened by the increasing prosperity of the French; connected himself, after a time, with their enemies—the English, and, with the help of our countrymen, reduced the strength and seized some of the fortified ports of his old enemy Angria;

committed the civil government of his home territories to his cousin, under whom much improvement took place in the condition of the people; sent forth his armies under his brother, who extended the Maratha fame to new regions, and made specious conquests in the North, but at vast cost, and to the embarassment of a State which was not accustomed to find itself a pecuniary loser by its campaigns:—attained, in short, the zenith of his power, which I am about now to endeavour to trace in its diverse and fitful course, as it hastens with accelerated velocity to a bloody setting.

The French, indeed, though allied at one time with Sivaji's people in the Carnatic Plain, held them in check in the Dekkan. But the heyday of Bussy's greatness was short; and his recall by Lally will be seen to have given to the Peishwa's cousin and lieutenant an easy victory over the Nizam; a victory which almost annihilated the fabric reared with such care and skill by Asof Jah; and at the same time tempted the successful leader to engage rashly in a contest of a very different character, and beyond his powers, and thus precipitated his own ruin, and the downfall of the supremacy of his people.

It will be remembered that the Peishwa connected himself with Ghazi-ud-deen, and marched against Salabat and Bussy, but was recalled hastily to oppose Tara Bhye's schemes. After treacherously taking the Guikwar prisoner, and leaving the Princess blockaded in the fort of Satara, he resumed his campaign. This proved a memorable and eventful one, though no decisive results immediately followed from it. The feeble character of Salabat; the intrigues, jealousies, and quarrels among his officers; and the untrustworthy and mutinous temper of his native soldiers, chiefly on account of their pay being in arrear, frustrated all Bussy's efforts to break the Peishwa's power, and penetrate to its centre. In vain the skill, discipline, and gallantry of the French contingent astonished and overawed both friends and foes. In vain the new-fashioned and well-served field-pieces of the Europeans arrested the impetuous onslaught of the Marathas; dealt destruction among their ranks; and, in a night attack, while they were engaged in deprecating the wrath of the gods during an eclipse of the moon, put them to a panic flight, in which, however, the confusion and consternation were more notable than the loss. In vain Bussy urged an advance on Poona, and arrived within no great distance of that place, ravaging the whole country with fire and sword, in a manner that must have brought sensibly home to the villagers the miseries which their countrymen had so long, with impunity, inflicted on others. Though the Peishwa thus saw the nursery of his power invaded, his capital threatened, his numerous and fine army surprised, routed, and thinned, by antagonists whóm his superstitious countrymen might well regard with some of the same profound misgiving, with which the Spaniards were contemplated by the warlike and hitherto irresistible Mexicans; and might well fear, as in that case, that the Empire of the Continent was destined to pass into the hands of the white-faced children of the great Ocean:—yet, for the present, at least, the arts, if not the arms of the subtle Brahmin, and the well-timed, though independent enterprise of another Maratha potentate, proved more than a match even for Europeans, inspired by Dupleix, and led by Bussy.

The Peishwa's followers, in fact, under all the disadvantages arising out of the new system, fought, on the whole, magnificently. On the march they swarmed in the boldest manner round Salabat's army, and seriously impeded its operations, charged the French guns, and regaining their confidence after the late surprise, made a general and tremendous attack, which would certainly have prevailed, but for the murderous and rapid covering fire of the European artillery. If they learned to fear the French, not less did the latter learn to respect such resolute and persevering, though irregular and ultimately unsuccessful valour.

But meanwhile Balaji had his emissaries and confederates in the Nizam's camp, who kept him well informed of the state of affairs there, and succeeded in producing division of counsels, and personal differences. The Moguls were jealous of each other; but worse still for the interests of Salabat, they already began to entertain that common and deep grudge against the brilliant and ostentatious Bussy and his Europeans, which soon after broke out in a conspiracy, the object of which was to expel them altogether from the Dekkan.

And now the prudence of Balaji's concessions to the Bonslay, and the efficacy of the confederate bond as a means of resisting a common enemy, were strikingly shown. While the Peishwa was in vain striving to retard the steady advance of the Moguls and the French towards Poona, and urgently pressing the immediate march of Ghazi-ud-deen to the South, and the return thither of his own brother, Rugonath, who had gone off to Guzerat, and of Sindia and Holkar, who were in Hindostan; Rugoji was already in motion. He had previously (as we have seen) extorted from Aliverdy Khan the cession of "the whole province of Kuttack, as far north as Ballasore,"* and a stipulated amount in lieu of the *chout* of Bengal and Behar (another notable Maratha encroachment). He now suddenly burst into hostility in Salahat's rear, and created a decisive diversion. "He surprised," says Grant Duff, "and took Gawel-gurh and Nur-

* Grant Duff.

nallah, made himself master of Manikdroog, occupied the districts dependent on these forts, and * * * * not only laid the whole country between the Payn Gunga and the Godavery under contribution, but drove out the Mogul thannas, and established his own."

The alarm excited by these summary and hostile proceedings, coinciding with the increasing disaffection of his troops, and the bad spirit shown by many of his officers, induced Salabat to take Bussy's advice, and concluding an armistice with the Peishwa, to return homewards (1752).

Thus, though Balaji's campaign had been by no means reassuring as to the eventual prospects of his people when opposed by Europeans, he had reason to congratulate himself upon its immediate issue, and upon the collective efficiency of the Confederacy, the result of his policy.

In the North, meanwhile, new successes had attended the national arms. Rugonath had, indeed, been prevented from effecting at this time what he did afterwards in Guzerat, by the necessity of returning to reinforce the Peishwa during the late campaign. But Holkar and Sindia had been invited to co-operate with the imperial Vizier, and Nawab of Oude, Sufder Jung, against the Rohillas; and had invaded their territory, defeated and driven them into the Kumaon hills, and been rewarded with a grant of the greater part of the conquered districts (1751). The promise of further concessions, in return for their assistance against Ahmed Shah Abdali, and the subsequent call to accompany the Peishwa's ally, Ghazi-ud-deen, to the southward, had led them to evacuate Rohilkund, after a very short occupation; but not (it is surmised) without exacting, according to their custom of contriving to be paid by both sides for the same act, a previous *douceur* of fifty *lacs* of rupees, as the price of their withdrawal.

And now the long impending contest between the sons of Nizam-ul-Mulk bade fair to be brought to a decisive issue. Ghazi-ud-deen advanced with a large army, the Mogul troops at Burhanpoor going over to him; Sindia and Holkar contributing their contingents; and the Peishwa's soldiers swelling his numbers to not less than 150,000 men.

In return for this assistance, the eager claimant of the Subahdary of the Dekkan consented to curtail his future territory, and granted to the Peishwa all the country westward of Berar, between the Tapty and the Godavery. Anticipating the ensuing catastrophe, I may mention here that Salabat afterwards, though unwillingly, confirmed this grant, which thus marks another advance in the flood-tide of Maratha greatness.

As usual, before arms were resorted to, diplomacy was active. And after every effort to evade his elder brother's claim, Salabat was forced to confess, that he could find no material flaw in it. A *coup de main* was required; and a woman's hand, though not (as Orme states) Ghazi-ud-deen's own mother's, administered to the unfortunate Prince, in the treacherous security of a friendly entertainment, a dish —"*post quod, nil amplius edit!*"

The perpetrator of this third murder of a descendant and would-be successor of Nizam-ul-Mulk, within five years after that ruler's death, was the mother of Nizam Ally, a younger son; the same son who afterwards dethroned and murdered Salabat, in whose interest the present crime was committed.

So bloody were the annals of the successful usurper's family! So quickly matured, and luxuriant, and bitter were the fruits of the ambition which, both by precept and example, the wily statesman had fostered in his children!

The establishment of Salabat's undisputed authority as Subahdar of the Dekkan, was almost immediately followed by the artful conspiracy on the part of his minister to get rid of his French allies, which Bussy not only foiled with characteristic readiness, vigour, and address, but converted into an occasion of obtaining an ample territory for his countrymen on the eastern coast, in *jaghire* (1753). This memorable chapter of Franco-Indian history has been related by Orme with his usual fulness, clearness, and spirit; and it needs now only to be mentioned, that other authorities attest the excellent and liberal dispositions made by Bussy for the government and prosperity of the Provinces thus entrusted to his care, in requital of the services of the French contingent.

Meanwhile the ascendancy of the Maratha arms was asserted in various directions. Twice, within a short interval the Peishwa's army overspread the Carnatic Bala Ghat, or Upper Country; levied large contributions; stormed such places as ventured to hold out, slaughtering their garrisons, and (much in the late Prussian fashion) compelling open villages to pay, by seizing and roughly handling their head-men.

Seringapatam, the capital of Mysore, which was still under Hindoo rule, was only freed from their importunity by the payment of a subsidy, the recognition of the Maratha revenue claims, and humble promises to meet these demands for the future with punctuality.

In Guzerat, too, Rugonath's interrupted plan was now resumed. In concert with Dummaji Guikwar, who had at length made his peace with the Peishwa and been released, he proceeded to demolish the last relics of Mogul dominion in that Province, besieging and, after a spirited defence, compelling the surrender of Ahmedabad (1755), the imperial capital, and dividing the spoils and the custody of the city with his confederate, in a manner too illustrative of

Maratha joint warfare to be omitted. "The revenue," says Grant Duff, "was to be equally divided between the Peishwa and Guikwar, but the whole garrison was furnished by the Peishwa, except one gateway, which was occupied by the troops of Dummaji; the latter, however, paid six thousand rupees annually, to assist in defraying the expenses."

Then, attended by younger members of the Sindia and Holkar families, Rugonath pushed on northwards, to turn to account the grants last extorted, in his extremity, from the titular Emperor. The imperial territory immediately around Delhi was now subjected to the two capital exactions of the *chout* and the *surdeshmookee*. The Rajputs, Hindoos of the Hindoos, and old allies of the Peishwa's house, were laid under contribution. And even the warlike and turbulent Jats, so closely connected, both in origin, character, and fortunes with the Marathas, were after some resistance, obliged to "yield an acknowledgment," as it is gently expressed; though an acknowledgement, however trifling in amount at the moment, was, with such tax gatherers, a dangerous pretext for indefinite encroachment at a later time.

The death about this period (1753) of Rugoji Bonslay, though followed by some dissension between his sons, did not permanently weaken the League; and Janoji, the eldest, was not only formally recognised by the Peishwa as successor to the office formerly held by Rugoji in the Maratha State, but promptly showed his disposition and ability to maintain the hereditary character of his house, by a successful raid into the French coast Provinces. This raid, too, has been described by Orme. The new chief, however, was not so successful in an attack upon Salabat's territories.

If the military renown of the French did not avail to secure the immunity of their districts, still less did the effete majesty of the imperial sanctuary any longer serve to overawe the insolent and ever active invaders.

The murdered Ghazi-ud-deen had left behind him at Delhi a son who, though only a youth, had already his full share of the ambition traditional in his house; and at once entering the path which his grandfather had so skilfully traced, and in which his father had been so summarily arrested, he assumed, like them, the title which the founder of the family had borne, and was henceforth himself known as Ghazi-ud-deen. Mindful, no doubt of his father's political leanings, he lost no time in calling to his aid Holkar and Jyapa, the latter a younger member of the house of Sindia; and after ungratefully displacing his patron and benefactor, Sufder Jung, the Vizier, and involving him in a tedious and indecisive struggle with the Emperor, he proceeded to procure first the appointment of a connexion of his own, then obtained, as the result of a new contest, the high office of Vizier for himself; a step facilitated by a sudden attack by Holkar, without orders, on the imperial army, which was routed and plundered of its baggage.

Thus did unauthorized Maratha audacity begin that direct interference with the concerns of the Court, which was ended only by the great victories of the English under Lord Lake, just half a century afterwards. Relying on such support, the young Vizier next affected the king-maker; deposed and blinded the ill-fated Ahmed Shah; and placed on the throne a new puppet, on whom, with cruel irony, he conferred the title of Alumgeer the Second (1754). Such is the Nemesis of history! Alumgeer the First, or as we commonly call him Aurungzib, wore out his life in a desperate effort to stamp out the Maratha plague, which his vaulting ambition and mistaken policy had engendered and disseminated. Alumgeer the Second has no policy, and probably no ambition: but his elevation marks precisely the period when that plague, having long raged uncontrolled throughout the body of the Empire, has at length reached its heart, and may be said to have extinguished its life!

Sufder Jung, the displaced Vizier and Nawab of Oude, turns his face to the wall, and quits a world now hopelessly out of joint, and hastening swiftly to decay. And the historian of the disintegrating power sums up the state of things with concise force in the melancholy words,—"Violence, rapine, and anarchy continued to increase in Hindostan."

While Maratha influence was thus radiating in so many directions, and penetrating to such distant regions, its concentrated vigour nearer home was equally notable. Thus one of the late expeditions which had scoured the Carnatic upland in quest of *chout* and other dues, had pierced the forest girdle of Bednore, and dipped into the ample treasures there amassed through peaceful government and commerce, and which were to be soon afterwards rifled by Hyder Ally. Thus, again, at this period it was that the English, under Watson and Clive, and by the orders of the Bombay Government, co-operated with the Peishwa's forces in reducing Angria's long-abused and piratical power, capturing his strongholds, and burning his fleet (1756). The details of this expedition will be found in Orme.

And thus, again, (what Orme does not give) there is a curious Treaty concluded between the Bombay Government and the Peishwa, and which exhibits the formidable character and high pretensions of the same people.

Moreover, not only had the Peishwa's uncle, Chimnaji Appa, humbled and weakened the Portuguese; but at this time there was a serious project on the part of the Marathas, if not actually disclosed, at least plainly hinted at by them to the English, for conquering Goa, and expelling altogether the descendants of the earliest European coast-settlers, who had once been so famous and powerful. Among the many consequences of the great catastrophe, which was so soon to overtake the pushing and light-fingered military pedlars, not the least interesting, however slight its direct political importance, was the circumstance that thus, and thus alone probably, was so curious a historical fossil and instructive a social phenomenon as the present Portuguese settlement at Goa preserved for later study and description.

The Nizam's Court, during this interval, was torn with faction; and the jealousy against his European allies, which had so long smouldered, and once already had broken out openly, again manifested itself in a positive order to Bussy, extorted from the unwilling Salabat, discharging the Frenchman from the Nizam's service, and directing him to withdraw his soldiers from the Dekkan (1757). The remarkable scenes that followed; Bussy's calm resolution and deliberate retreat; the friendly and chivalrous attendance of a Maratha escort which accompanied the French, until it was gratefully dismissed when the danger of pursuit seemed over: the hot chase that was given by the Nizam's people as soon as the Marathas had retired; Bussy's gallant, determined, and skilful stand at Hyderabad; the extreme danger in which he was involved; the timely arrival of his reinforcements from the eastward; his ultimate triumph, and the restoration of his influence:—these and other particulars are interwoven into a most attractive narrative by Orme.

But in two or three circumstances the Thucydides of Anglo-Indian story seems to have been mistaken.

1. The Marathas who escorted Bussy on his retreat from Aurungabad were not, it appears, in the service of the Peishwa, but in that of the Nizam;—like the older corps of the same people who, long after Sivaji had appealed to the common sentiment of nationality, had remained subjects of Bijapoor, the Empire, or Nizam-ul-Mulk respectively.

2. Whereas Orme states that the Peishwa requested Bussy to enter his own service, there is good evidence that the fear was herein father to the thought on the part of the Bombay Government: but no clear proof that Balaji made the offer, much less, of course, that the Frenchman at all encouraged it. That the Peishwa was quite ready to play off the rival Europeans against each other, if he could do so prudently, is obvious enough. But, connected as he was with the English on the Malabar coast, and inveterate as was the hostility between our countrymen and the French (in spite of the short truce about this time), on that of Coromandel; it seems hardly likely that

one so cautious should have risked encountering the enmity of both parties, by contracting with each relations which must have committed him to strife with the other.

3. Orme represents Bussy as actually intending originally to march to the French district on the coast, but compelled by the activity of the pursuit, and the non-arrival in time of his reinforcements, to make his celebrated halt at Hyderabad. But Grant Duff, a military critic of experience in war, is decidedly of opinion, that Bussy, from the first, designed the Nizam's modern capital as his rallying point, and that herein he showed strategic wisdom: whereas, had he set off with the purpose of reaching the "Northern Circars," he would have adopted a course unwise both in its end, and in the means which he used to compass it. The question seems to be one of general probability, and perhaps not capable, with our present materials, of positive proof.

Another indication of the wide-spread activity and high pretensions of the Marathas during this culminating epoch of their career was afforded, by the Peishwa's twice addressing, and forwarding through the Bombay Government, letters to the king of England. And it was observed on the second occasion, that the dubious state of our affairs in the Carnatic Plain, and our recent disasters in Bengal, emboldened him, in corresponding with the local Government, to take a less cordial tone than he had hitherto adopted. But still more illustrative of the same circumstances, and still more mortifying to our countrymen, was the exaction from Mahomed Ally of the *chout* for the Arcot Province. This the Madras rulers did their best to prevent, but in vain. Mahomed Ally was thoroughly afraid of his terrible neighbours; and the hold of the English over him and his dominions was not yet strong enough to justify the rejection of a claim, which they were in no condition at the moment to oppose by force of arms.

Mysore was still a Hindoo Principality; though Nunjiraj, the Prime Minister and early patron of Hyder Ally, had already reduced the Raja to a political nonentity, and was soon to be himself in turn superseded by his ambitious and unscrupulous Mussulman client. In tracing the early history of Hyder Ally, it will be necessary to revert rather more in detail to the Maratha expeditions against Seringapatam and the dominions of the Mysorean Raja. But, in pursuance of the general design of noting in each direction the development of the predatory society, it may be here mentioned, that the Hindoo capital was besieged, several important districts were occupied, and no less than thirty-two *lacs* were exacted on one occasion alone, from this as yet petty State, by the Peishwa's followers.

On the other hand, as coming events are said to cast their shadow before, it was on the same occasion that the future usurper, tyrant, and aggrandizer of Mysore signalised himself, both by the craft and the warlike energy and skill which he brought to bear against this hitherto irresistible people; and thereby facilitated his own acquisition of supreme power, and provoked the lasting resentment of the partially baffled invaders.

Another expedition was planned by the Peishwa, which, had it been accomplished, would probably have altered the whole history of the Peninsula. It was resolved to conquer Bednore—also (as I have said) a Hindoo State. And the reduction of Bednore, at this crisis, would (Colonel Wilks thinks) probably have prevented altogether the rise of Hyder Ally. Certain it is, that the great and rapid extension of that adventurer's power was, by his own admission, in no small measure due to the vast treasures and other military resources, which he obtained from the possession of Bednore. Circumstances, however, prevented the execution of the order by the Peishwa's general, and he soon had ample occupation and food for thoughtful anxiety elsewhere.

Bussy's influence was still predominant at Hyderabad. But the term of his domination was at hand; and Lally was already on the seas, impatiently enduring the tedious voyage, that was to end in the speedy recall of his lieutenant from the Dekkan, in a convulsive struggle with the English, and in the complete and final destruction of the French polity in India.

The beginning of the end, however, had already set in. The Nizam's two younger brothers, Nizam Ally and Basalut Jung were intriguing and agitating to secure their share of place and all its attractions. Salabat's ministers were united in their jealousy of the French. Bussy detected a conspiracy to coerce and imprison, if not to murder Salabat; and lending himself to native arts, the Frenchman seized, by an act of gross treachery, the impregnable rock fortress of Dowlatabad, which was in the keeping of the Prime Minister and his own bitter enemy, Shanaveze Khan. Here Bussy proposed, if necessary, to secure the person of the Nizam. But new commotions, the result of complicated plots, arose. Nizam Ally murdered Bussy's Dewan, and fled to Berar. The Prime Minister, in turn, who was supposed to be an accomplice of the fugitive, was slain by a French sepoy: and just as Bussy was balancing the prudence of leading the Nizam in pursuit of his guilty brother, orders arrived, couched in Lally's characteristically imperious tone, insisting upon the immediate return of the French troops and their commander to the Eastern coast (1758). A force indeed was to be still quartered in the Northern Circars. But this was promptly attacked and dispersed by Colonel Forde from Bengal. In vain the Nizam and Basalut Jung, whom he had made his Minister, moved to the support of their hard-pressed allies. Instead of aiding the French, the brothers were panic struck by the advent in their rear of Nizam Ally, at the head of a large army which he had collected in the North, and with which he had on his way gained an important victory over a Maratha force.

The English, as against a common enemy, showed themselves friendly to Nizam Ally. This hastened a pacification and alliance between Salabat and our countrymen, whereby the French connexion with the Dekkan was finally severed; the English acquired a large and fertile district in *enam* (and not as the French held their wider Provinces in *jaghire*), and, moreover, contrived to exempt themselves from the obligation of rendering military service, which had been the occasion of the grant to their enemies. Deserted by his old, and undefended by his new allies, Salabat soon fell under the complete control of his resolute and unprincipled brother, Nizam Ally, and was fain to make him Dewan in place of Basalut, whose leanings were French, and who retired to his appanage of Adonee.

From this hasty glance at the circumstances under which Bussy's ascendancy at the Nizam's Court was replaced by that of Nizam Ally, and the English connexion superseded the French, the misfortune that at once overtook Salabat, and the crowning triumph of the Maratha arms in the South, will be more easily accounted for. For the English were neither able nor willing at that time to step into the place of those, who had lately exercised so precarious and invidious an influence in the upper country. Girding up their loins for a death-grapple with their old European enemies on the Coromandel coast, they left their new ally to take care of himself, after extorting from his combined hopes and fears territory and commercial privileges of much importance and value.

The Peishwa's brother, Rugonath Rao, had lately returned from the North, where he had gained fallacious successes at a heavy cost; and hence a serious difference had arisen between him and his cousin, Sedasheo, which had ended in the exchange of their respective functions, Rugonath assuming the civil government, the Bhow (as he was now generally called) taking the command of the army.

The latter step had been angrily and scornfully proposed by Rugonath; and thus all that followed was proximately due to a family dispute in the Poona Durbar, in which the ladies and others are said to have taken a warm part. The Peishwa might have forgiven, but he had certainly not forgotten, the early waywardness and desertion to Kolapoor of his cousin; and though Sedasheo had since served him faithfully, and had honestly exerted himself to bring forward into public employment Balaji's sons, yet their mother was very jealous of him; and Rugonath and his party took the Bhow's free criticisms on the unprofitable and—from a Maratha point of view—degenerate character of the late operations in the North, much amiss.

Once embarked on his new element, Sedasheo lost no time in pushing his voyage, and showing himself a vigorous and daring pilot. But, before he set out, his career was very nearly cut short by assassination. It is not clear how far any members of his own family were concerned in this nefarious project. But he had opposed the entertainment in the Peishwa's service of a certain Mozuffer Khan, who, partly from jealousy of a relative, whom the new general took into his employ, and whom the quick suspicion of Mozuffer contemplated as a rival, devised this plan for furthering his own ends, and not improbably also those of others. The Bhow was saved by the presence of mind of a Sillidar, and escaped with a slight wound. Mozuffer and his agent were executed.

I must pause a moment in the narrative to give a rather more particular idea than has yet been conveyed of the new commander, and of the circumstances in which he proceeded to enact his eventful and chequered part.

Sedasheo was the son of that Chimnaji Appa, who had throughout his life zealously and ably seconded the policy of his brother, Baji Rao; and had gained great successes against the Portuguese, conducting to a triumphant issue the most remarkable and protracted siege in which the Marathas were ever engaged. One result of this achievement seems to have been, to impress on both father and son the importance of regular infantry and artillery as opposed to cavalry, in which last arm their nation had hitherto specially excelled, and to which their progress had been mostly due. The later operations and triumphs of the Europeans, both French and English, had tended very greatly to foster the same notion, that the strength and efficiency of an army must depend, in a great measure, if not principally, on its disciplined infantry and guns. The Nizam and his brother had adopted the same view, and though properly applied, it might be true enough, it will be soon seen that, under the actual circumstances, it was calculated to bring disaster alternately upon both of the rival native Powers in the Dekkan.

Thus Nizam Ally had employed Ibrahim Khan Gardee, an artillerist who had been trained under Bussy. But after a time, Ibrahim transferred his services to Sedasheo (to the disgust, as has been mentioned, of Mozuffer), and became the Campo Basso of the Bhow, in a career destined to end as tragically as that of Charles the Bold. The Maratha horsemen, however, were still in full vigour, and as numerous as ever; and the question remained to be decided, how far the traditional and approved type of Maratha warfare was to be modified or abandoned in favour of a new system, more scientific and pretentious, but less unquestionably adapted to the genius of the people, and the capricious and impulsive temper of the chiefs.

Sedasheo was bold to temerity, but had as yet gained little military experience; indeed he had rarely commanded an army in the field. He was of an overbearing disposition, and had a special grudge against Holkar, who had crossed him in some of his arrangements in the Dekkan. He was, moreover, bent upon proving himself, in refutation of Rugonath's taunts, an enterprising and practical general, and not unlikely to make serious mistakes, both from too much dependence on his pet nostrum—artillery, from yielding too much to personal considerations in the choice of his advisers, and from the elation of spirit likely to follow any early successes of moment, that might confirm his extremely good opinion of his own judgment and talents for war.

Again, though he had shown himself no incompetent administrator, and the condition of the country had improved under his rule; his experience and associations seem to have been of a local and contracted character, and he showed little disposition to understand or deal gently with the prejudices and, in spite of the decay of the Empire, the strong imperialist sympathies of the natives, both Mussulman and Hindoo, of Hindostan; in this respect resembling far more the savage Vandal of a corresponding period in the world's history, than the wise Ostrogoth or the politic Frank.

For the rest he was, though a rival of Rugonath, faithful to the Peishwa and his family, genial and, within the sphere of his experience, sensible and clear-sighted, energetic, and a firm believer in the invincibility of his people, at least when opposed to Asiatics.

Such was the general to whom, at the age of thirty, and in the very zenith of the Maratha power, the fortunes of that power were to be now entrusted.

His first operations were crowned with such brilliant success, almost realising indeed the latest and baffled scheme of his uncle Baji Rao, that his head may well have been turned, and his fate and that of his people thereby precipitated. Being probably well aware that Salabat and his now all-powerful brother, Nizam Ally, were ill prepared to plunge again into war, he procured the betrayal to his agents of Ahmednuggur, once the capital of a powerful kingdom, and the aim of Acber's prolonged hostilities in the Dekkan. To leave such a city to its fate would redound to the eternal disgrace of the Nizam. The brothers accordingly marched in haste against the insolent Hindoo, taking with them a lumbering siege train. But their army was ill appointed, and they committed several serious faults: in particular they twice divided their forces, and at length, in fatal reliance on their artillery, suffered themselves to be caught and hemmed in with a small party by a mighty host of 40,000 horse; while Ibrahim and his field-train pressed on to answer with their improved weapons and skill, that arm of the Mogul host, which had so often already proved ineffectual against the insidious and locust-like squadrons of the Marathas.

It was the old, old tale, so often repeated on occasion of encounters between the same antagonists. But a new danger threatened the Moguls; a new instrument of terror now befriended the assailants. While their flying cavalry cut off supplies, confined the Nizam's soldiers to their lines, harassed and diminished their already scanty numbers when they attempted to break out and escape; and while the heavy artillery of the Moguls did little execution against the floating clouds of Maratha horsemen, Ibrahim's light field-guns were plied with terrible effect upon the dense masses of Salabat's cavalry; and the iron entered no doubt still further into the souls of the haughty Mussulmans, from feeling that artillery, in which they had hitherto peculiarly trusted and gloried, was now turned, in a more effective form, against themselves. Unable to extricate themselves, the Nizam and his brother were summoned to surrender at discretion. And though they refused to do so directly, their conduct practically amounted to much the same thing. For the exulting Bhow received Salabat's seal of state, which implied that to his arbitrament was left the imposition of the terms of peace.

They were not only hard and humiliating, but virtually concluded the long rivalry between the Houses, by transferring to the Maratha a very large part of the remaining dominions of his opponent. The whole Province of Bijapoor, almost the whole of that of Aurungabad, and part of Beder, together with the famous and impregnable fortress of Dowlatabad after which the Peishwa had long been hankering, and others destined to become famous in our later wars with the victors on this occasion, were conceded unreservedly (1760).

The revenue thus acquired amounted to sixty-two *lacs* annually, of which (in the usual fashion) forty-one were distributed among the chiefs and officers, whose joint exertions had contributed to an issue, in which the Maratha Power attained in the South its maximum elevation. But a dark cloud was gathering in the Himalayas, which was destined soon after to pour a devastating flood upon the northern plains, and submerging the now proud conqueror and the bulk of his levies, to extinguish for ever the dawning hope of Maratha sovereignty over the Peninsula.

CHAPTER XI.

THE RISE OF HYDER ALLY.

WHILE the last of the long series of invaders, who have assailed India by the familiar north-western route, is gathering his forces for the encounter, we may pause to tell a story of a very different kind.

An account of India, on the eve of the British Conquest, would be most incomplete without a pretty full summary of the rise of Hyder Ally. While the personal adventures of the man are remarkable; the natural history of usurpation, in all its stages, was never more curiously illustrated than in the course of those adventures. And moreover, the complexion of the times; the inter-dependence of the various political elements which had arisen out of the ruin of the Empire; the development of a character, and the first rudiments of a system, which in their maturity, were destined to be, for many anxious years, the astonishment and the terror of our countrymen, both in India and at home; are all exhibited in Hyder's early history, in a manner that seems not to justify, so much as to demand, a more detailed narrative than would otherwise be commensurate with the general proportions of the present sketch. And it is only, it appears to me, by thus, occasionally at least, realising in their minuter circumstances the inevitable evils from which the establishment of British rule has delivered the country, that a sound judgment of the comparative merits of that rule is likely to be formed.

The general interest of Hyder Ally's career, I have elsewhere endeavoured to intimate in a passage which will be found below;* and proceed now to trace the opening stages of that eventful course.

* "In the case of Hyder we see an illiterate Mahometan adventurer win his way to supreme power in a Hindoo community, by a boldness and an originality of artifice, which while we condemn we cannot but admire; frequently overpowered by the force of external circumstances, yet rise superior to each reverse, and more indomitable and threatening from each disaster; secure internal tranquillity by a system of administration equally simple, effective, and awe-striking; extend the limits of the kingdom, until it stretches nearly from sea to sea, and includes a large part of Southern India; grapple with the jealous and formidable hordes of Maharashtra, in campaigns that wear throughout an air of the marvellous, and carry us back in association to Alfred's combats with the Danes; meet at last on no unequal terms the armies of England, and emerge victorious from the strife; pitted in a second encounter

Hyder's earliest recorded ancestor, on the paternal side, is his great grandfather; and amidst much uncertainty about him, it seems clear, that his name was Mohammed Bhelole; that he migrated from the north of India to a town in the district of Kalburga; was a devotee; built a small mosque and a caravanserai appendant to it; thus acquired some wealth; married his son, Ali Mohammed, to the daughter of one of the ministrants at the famous mausoleum at Kalburga; and died at his new home, in the odour of sanctity.

Ali Mohammed, like his father, moves on southward; and after a time takes service at Sera, in the capacity of a revenue *peon.* Here he has a son, Futteh Mohammed, Hyder's father. He afterwards migrates once more to Kolar, where he, too, acquires property, partly in agricultural pursuits, partly in some official employment; and there, in due time, dies. After this event Futteh Mohammed experiences various fortunes; but first becomes conspicuous by his conduct in the assault of a fort near Balipoor (1720). On this occasion he rallies a for-

against our ablest General (Clive perhaps excepted), and though more than once defeated, in the end almost victorious over him. Thus subtle, vigorous, terrible to his life's end, he leaves behind

'A name at which the world grew pale,'

and a reputation second to that of none of the military adventurers, whom we have encountered in the East."—*The Mussulman, &c.*

lorn hope which has been repulsed, and the fort is taken; when Durga Kooli Khan, *soi disant* Subahdar of Sera, makes him on the spot a Naik, or captain, of *peons*, or irregular infantry.

He, too, has a turn for ecclesiastical architecture; and at Kolar, where he resides for some time, he erects a mausoleum, on the death of his first wife, and a mosque and tank, with gardens attached to them. And the early history of Hyder Ally's family has been illustrated by a record kept at this mausoleum.

The accounts of Futteh Mohammed's motions and commands are very contradictory. But it seems probable that he served successively in the Sera district, in the Carnatic low country, at Mysore (whither he is said, by a native writer, to have been invited by a nephew, named Hyder, who had established himself there under the Hindoo government), and again in the Sera district. He attained, apparently, considerable reputation, and filled military offices of some importance. And though the literal accuracy of some of the descriptions given of his functions by the native biographer of his son is very questionable; yet it is evident, that that son was not the obscure pretender to social position, that it was the fashion, in his own day, among our countrymen to represent him; but that Futteh Mohammed had gained a name and station, which would be likely to prove an advantage as well as a stimulus to the son in later times. But the sudden and untimely death which overtook Futteh in a night attack on a besieging force at Sera, plunged his family into misfortunes, out of which Hyder Ally emerged in a new scene, and under new auspices; and thus he came to bear the aspect of a mere adventurer, the carver of his own fortunes, from the beginning to the splendid position which he eventually occupied.

Such were his antecedents on the father's side. Religion, civil duties, warlike achievements, had blended in the tissue of his family annals, to reappear hereafter in stronger colours and more imposing proportions. His mother's life, like his own, opened in storm; and her ancestors had been the victims of the persecution for conscience sake, which his son was one day to inflict so freely. She was a *Nevayet*, one of a fair-haired race, descended from some members of the illustrious house of Hashem, who had been driven by religious intolerance from Irak, as early as the eighth century of our era; and had migrated to India, where they jealously refrained from intermarrying with the natives, and thus (we are told) preserved the purity of their complexions.

Her parents, on a journey from the Concan eastward, had been robbed, and her father murdered, on the frontier of Bednore. The mother, with a son and two daughters, reached Kolar in great distress.

Her desolate circumstances overcame her family exclusiveness; and she allowed Futteh Mohammed to marry her elder daughter; and after the death of that lady without issue, gave him to wife the younger daughter, Hyder's mother.

The boy who had accompanied his parents in the ill-fated journey from the Concan was Ibrahim Sahib, later a considerable person. Hyder had an elder brother, Shabaz.

Before the final struggle in which Futteh Mohammed fell, Abdul Russool (the son and successor of Durga Kooli Khan,) his employer, had placed Futteh's wife and two sons in the fort of Great Balipoor, as hostages for their relative's fidelity. This proceeding implied no peculiar suspicion, but is a frequent practice in the East, and was habitually followed, both by Hyder himself and his son.

Abdul too had been slain in the battle, and the fort fell into the hands of his son, Abbas. He, taking advantage of the widow's unfriended state, in the moment of her deepest distress, tortured the boys, and not improbably herself, for the purpose of extorting money from her. Shabaz now eight, and Hyder three or four years old, are *said* to have been immured in a huge kettle-drum, which was then beaten vigorously—*pour les encourager tous deux!* The reverberation was no doubt painful enough at the time to the tender children. The echo of that sound lived in Hyder's memory with such distinctness, that more than thirty years afterwards he delivered his hoarded vengeance against his persecutor, with all the venom and fury inspired by a recent wrong!

In this emergency, the widow and her sons were befriended by Ibrahim Sahib, Hyder's maternal uncle, who was then engaged as a commander of *peons*, under the *killedar* of Bangalore. As the young Shabaz grew up, he obtained a similar appointment at Mysore, and gradually acquired reputation and authority, till he had under him 200 horse, and 1000 peons. Hyder meanwhile, who had accompanied his brother, led an idle and irregular life, until his twenty-eighth year. "He would frequently," says Colonel Wilks, "absent himself for weeks together, secretly immersed in voluptuous riot, or passing with facility, as was the habit of his whole life, to the opposite extreme of abstinence and excessive exertion; wandering in the woods while pursuing, not without danger, his favourite amusements."

So do events and characters present, amidst strange contrasts, equally remarkable resemblances. Here, as on many other occasions, we are forcibly reminded of Sivaji and his abnormal training, complex character, and subtle power of turning circumstances to account, in the pursuit of an ever-expanding ambition.

It was at the siege of Deonhully that Hyder Ally first displayed, as a volunteer in his brother's corps, his dawning aptitude for the game of war, in which he was destined to become so great a proficient. As with Sivaji, his hunting had not been thrown away as a preparation for campaigning. "He was observed on every service of danger to lead the way, and to conduct himself with a coolness and self-possession seldom found in a young soldier."*

It is worth notice that he did duty not only on horseback, but with the infantry, in the trenches. And Nunjiraj, one of two brothers who had usurped the conduct of the Mysore government, and reduced the Raja to a phantom sovereign, took the promising youth under his special protection, and gave him the command of 50 horse and 200 foot; authorised his increasing this contingent; and entrusted him with one of the gates of the captured fortress. Here Hyder Ally accordingly took up his abode, and soon augmented his numbers, recruiting, for his personal service, 300 Beder *peons*, men specially accomplished in plundering on their employers' and their own account. An excellent opportunity for the display of their talents and the aggrandizement of their master soon occurred.

Nazir Jung, on his advance against Mirzapha and Chunda Sahib, summoned the Mysore army to attend him. Hyder and his brother marched in obedience to this summons; and the panic and confusion that

* Wilks.

followed the murder of Nazir on the field of battle, by his own tributary, "the Pathan Nabob of Kirpa," were precisely adapted to the tastes and the talents of Hyder Ally and his recent recruits. They watched their opportunity, as the treasurer was hastily preparing to carry off his charge from the turbulent scene, and contrived to intercept two camels laden with gold; and with this, and a large supply of arms, acquired in an equally irregular manner, they stole back securely to Deonhully.

Soon after followed the two famous sieges of Trichinopoly. In the course of the first, Mahomet Ali, casting about in all directions for assistance, but totally regardless of the consistency and good faith of his engagements, while the English were bearing the brunt of his defence, solicited the support of Mysore, with a secret undertaking to give up the city to that State, when the French should have been compelled to raise the siege. On this condition, unknown to the English, Nunjiraj, as Commander-in-Chief, against (it would seem) the opinion both of his own brother, and of the Raja, eagerly embraced the offer; and, as far as numbers and equipment went, fulfilled the contract in no grudging spirit. A large army—horse, foot, and artillery—went with him; a well-filled military chest, and supplies of all kinds. But, in the end, the ill success of this large venture, and of the more protracted and disastrous operations involved in the second siege, contributed greatly to embarrass his government, destroy his reputation, and assist his ungrateful client in supplanting him.

Hyder's part in the first siege is described in glowing, and no doubt exaggerated terms, by his native biographer, Meer Ali Hussein; and may be here left to the imagination of the reader. But we have more authentic information of his conduct towards the end of the second siege, which was brought on by the refusal of Mahomet Ali, backed by the English, to execute the secret compact. The imbecility both of the arts and the arms of Nunjiraj, was conspicuous throughout this eventful period. But the French and the Marathas again and again reduced the place and its English defenders to extremities, from which they were as often delivered by the vigilance of Dalton and other officers, the ability of Lawrence, and the gallantry of the British soldiers, especially of a band of heroes—"the Grenadier Company"—who covered themselves with glory on many a well-fought field. At length, however, the retirement of Moorar Rao to the North, and the supercession of M. Dupleix, followed by M. Godeheu's pacification, left Nunjiraj in helpless isolation; and though he vapoured, and talked of conquering the English single-handed, he was obliged to abandon the contest; and his departure was hastened by a sudden and pressing summons to help his brother against a new enemy at Seringapatam.

It was towards the end of this second siege that an event occurred which specially concerned Hyder, and illustrated both his knack of helping himself on every occasion, and his relations with a rival, whose pretensions bade fair to interfere seriously with his own advancement.*

The great and constant difficulty experienced by the English was to provision the garrison. Their supplies were drawn mainly from the country of Tondiman, a chief whose woody district lay south-east of Trichinopoly, at no great distance. On the occasion in question, a large convoy was advancing, and had neared the outskirts of the woods, escorted by a numerous but inadequate force, including the Grenadier Company. An incompetent officer was unfortunately in command, who made the worst possible disposition (according to Orme and other authorities) of his soldiers, and when attacked, completely lost his presence of mind.

The Mysoreans and the Marathas lay in wait for the convoy, their cavalry posted on each side of the road out of the wood. Among the former were Hyder and his horsemen, and Hurri Sing, a gallant Rajput partisan, the *protégé* and favourite of Deoraj, as Hyder was of Nunjiraj. In the attack that ensued, Hurri Sing led the way, and greatly distinguished himself. The Grenadier corps was almost annihilated; the stores were lost; a terrible hand-

* Shabaz, Hyder's brother, was killed in an early engagement.

to-hand combat ended in the slaughter or capture of the troops *en masse;* and though there is no reason to think that Hyder had been behind hand in fighting, he characteristically was the first to seize the English guns.

The Rajput had always underrated his rival's courage, and denied his claim to promotion for military service, attributing his success to courtly arts. He was indignant at the thought, that where he had himself been foremost in the fray, and had broken the force of the enemy, his despised colleague should snatch from him the most honourable trophies of victory. The dispute waxed hot and long. It was settled by Hyder's resigning one gun, keeping three, and no doubt making a careful note of the transaction, with a view to a more decisive settlement another day.

Disastrous as the sieges proved to Nunjiraj and the Mysore State, they greatly improved Hyder's prospects. He learned much from his association alternately with the English and the French. And latterly he procured from the latter arms, equipments, and artificers,—perhaps also thus early stray soldiers, if not officers, willing to share his rising fortunes. How far he had, as yet, contemplated distinctly the project of making himself master of the government is perhaps doubtful. But his course in that direction was steady and uniform. He was totally illiterate. But his memory was extraordinary; his power of calculation was equally remarkable; his discernment of character unfailing; his ingenuity inexhaustible; and he had the most perfect confidence in himself. His plans were ably seconded and improved upon by a crafty Brahmin accountant, whom he had already made his *dewan,* or general manager; and who, under the name of Kunde Rao, was destined to play an important part in his history. Colonel Wilks gives an account of Hyder Ally's arrangements at this period, which is so curious and instructive, that it is subjoined entire in a note.*

* "The consultations of these two persons produced a system, regularly organised, by which the plunderers received, besides their direct pay, one-half of the booty which was realised; the other half was appropriated by Hyder, under a combination of checks, which rendered it nearly impossible to secrete any portion of the plunder. Moveable property of every description was their object; and, as already noticed, they did not hesitate to acquire it by simple theft from friends, when that could be done without suspicion, and with more convenience than from enemies. Nothing was unseasonable or unacceptable; from convoys of grain, down to the clothes, turbans, and earrings of travellers, or villagers, whether men, women, or children. Cattle and sheep were among the most profitable heads of plunder: muskets and horses were sometimes obtained in booty, sometimes by purchase. The numbers under his command increased with his resources; and before he left Trichinopoly, besides the usual appendages of a chief of rank, in elephants, camels, tents, and magnificent appointments, he was rated on the returns, and received pay for 1,500 horse, 3,000 regular infantry, 2,000 peons, and four guns, with their equipments. Of the horses, 500 were his own property; and the difference between the sum allowed

Nunjiraj had been summoned to make head against the new Nizam. Salabat Jung had lost no time in turning to account his connexion with M. Bussy. Mysore was technically one of his tributary States. And as Nazir Jung had called its army into the field, so the present Subahdar of the Dekkan demanded its money-dues. Arrears being taken into account, these amounted to a sum which, after the recent outlay on the Carnatic war, Mysore was in no condition to pay.

Deoraj determined to resist, and keep the Nizam at bay behind the walls of the capital, until his brother could join him.

Bussy had reluctantly consented to lend his aid against Mysore, for that State was in alliance with the French at Pondicherry. But he had personally negotiated to render general service to the Subahdar of the Dekkan. Such was one of the many political complications of the time. And Bussy was not a man for half measures. His rapid and skilful approaches disarranged all Deoraj's cal-

by government, and that disbursed in the pay of the man, and the provender of the horse, was Hyder's profit. In consideration of his furnishing the cannon and their draught, the muskets and accoutrements of regular infantry, he was allowed a certain sum for each gun, with its equipments, and for every hundred men; and was permitted to make his own agreements with the individuals at inferior rates; they also, as well as the rest of his troops, regularly accounting for one-half of the plunder they acquired."—(*Wilks*, vol. i. pp. 351-2.)

culations. The Marathas, too, were said to be approaching, to assert *their* claim to tribute at this most unseasonable time. It was necessary to come to terms at once. By the greatest exertions and sacrifices a large sum was raised; more was promised; and Salabat retired.

Meanwhile Nunjiraj had, by forced marches, arrived within twenty-five miles of Seringapatam, when tidings of this arrangement reached him. He proceeded to discharge a large part of the forces, which the impoverishment of the State would no longer enable him to maintain. Hyder took the opportunity of enlisting the choicest of the discharged troops in his own service. Thus he carried with him to his next command 5,000 regular infantry, 2,500 horse, 2,000 peons, or irregular foot, and six guns.

That command was at Dindigul, of which he was appointed Foujdar, or civil and military governor combined. This place the Mysorean Government, availing itself of the confusion of the times, had seized some years before; and the disturbances in the Carnatic had prevented Mahomet Ali's expelling the intruders. Kunde Rao remained at the capital, watching over his master's interests there.

Several Poligars around Dindigul had refused, as usual, to pay tribute, on the ground of its excessive amount. Hyder at first affected to sympathize with them; promising to intercede for a reduction of their dues. Thus he secured a peaceable and safe passage for his troops, into the heart of the country. He then systematically swept off the cattle, reselling it at high prices, frequently to the owners themselves. This he followed up by a regular attack on the unfortunate Poligars, in which, after a long and obstinate struggle, he was completely successful. Lastly, he proceeded to make great capital out of his successes, in his dealings with the Government. The account given below, and carefully substantiated by its author from the testimony of eye-witnesses, will give a lively idea of his impudent conduct on this occasion, the better worth notice in connexion with similar tricks, on the part of others, soon afterwards at Seringapatam, and with the virtuous indignation which his partial biographer, Meer Ali, ascribes to him, on detecting those artifices.*

* "Nunjeraj on the receipt of Hyder's dispatches, with a long list of killed and wounded, sent a special commission with rich presents for Hyder and the officers who were represented to have distinguished themselves, and Zuckhum puttee for the wounded. This officer was soon made to understand his business. Zuckhum puttee is an allowance to wounded men, as some compensation for their sufferings, and for the purpose of enabling them to defray the expenses of their cure; for an Indian army has neither hospitals nor surgeons provided by the State. The allowance on this occasion was fourteen rupees a month, until the cure should be completed. Hyder marshalled his wounded men, to be inspected by the commissioner: sixty-seven was the true number; but about 700 had

His civil administration was equally well-adapted to the end which he seems now to have definitely proposed to himself, that of securing funds sufficiently ample to sustain an independent force, adequate to turn the political scale in his own favour.

"It was at Dindigul," again remarks Colonel Wilks, "that he also first obtained from Seringham, Trichinopoly, and Pondicherry, skilful artificers, directed by French masters, and began to organize a regular artillery, arsenal, and laboratory."

Other writers, as I have already intimated, antedate much of this careful provision for the coming struggle.

Kunde Rao and Hyder himself took credit for the

their legs or arms bound up with yellow bandages, and acted their parts with entire success. The money was paid to Hyder according to the muster, and to the probable time of cure reported by the attending surgeons, at the rate of fourteen rupees per man per month. To the really wounded he gave seven; and of the presents brought for the officers of the army, he made a distribution equally skilful, while each officer was made to believe that he was the person most particularly favoured by Hyder. During these operations Kundè Row was perpetually sounding the exploits of his master to Nunjeraj, exaggerating the disturbed state of the country, and the necessity of augmenting the forces; which was accordingly authorized from time to time, and assignments on the revenues of other districts were added for that purpose to his other resources. Special commissioners were always deputed to muster the new levies; and on one occasion, Jehan Khan saw exhibited the manœuvre which he calls a *circular muster*, by which 10,000 men were counted and passed as 18,000."—*Wilks*, vol. i., pp. 353—4.

largeness of the force, which he contrived to maintain out of his allotted revenues; and it was true that his skilful arrangements and his untiring eye made his actual numbers far more serviceable than would have been the full muster, on the old system. But serviceable for what? and for whom?

Thus passed nearly two years (1755—1756,) Hyder consolidating his power in Dindigul, increasing his army, procuring through Kunde Rao further grants of provincial revenues in payment of his troops, and the reputation of an able administrator and skilful manipulator of soldiers. His talents, however, in the field of regular warfare were as yet questionable, and were denied by his rivals and detractors. Deoraj looked with no kindly eye upon him: Deoraj's favourite, Hurri Sing, continued bitter and contemptuous in his criticisms of "the *naik*."

But, at the end of that time, a serious political difficulty recalled him to Seringapatam. The Raja had shown a disposition to throw off the yoke of the brothers, and was listening to advice that he should imprison them. (To put a Brahmin to death would have been an extreme measure in a Hindoo Court.) This advice was betrayed to the subjects of it. Deoraj tried the mild plan of remonstrance. The Raja took a high tone, and was surrounding himself with soldiers on whom he could depend. His wife—a daughter of Nunjiraj—was then urged to poison her husband. Thus much seems clear; and that she received the proposal with indignation and horror. But how far it was made directly by Nunjiraj himself; or whether Deoraj assented to it at all, is uncertain. This plan failing, Hyder's patron, entirely in opposition to the opinion and wishes of Deoraj, made a vehement and insulting attack on the palace; violated the sacred seclusion of the women's apartments; and forcibly replaced the Raja's attendants by creatures of his own: and to fill to the brim his miserable father-in-law's cup of bitterness, compelled him to assume the mockery of a public approval and sanction of the late proceedings.

Deoraj thereupon indignantly assembled his family and followers; and leaving the city, settled below the Ghats, at Sattimungulum. There, being in want of funds, he directed the revenues of several districts which had been granted to Hyder—to be paid to himself. Kunde Rao recommended his master to return, and fight his own battle at head quarters.

But another public calamity combined to render his presence at the capital necessary. The threatened visit of the Marathas came off in March, 1757. Again a large contribution was demanded. Again the impossibility of payment was urged. Again Seringapatam was besieged. And again, Europeans being employed by the assailants, the determined and vigorous sallies led by Nunjiraj himself availed not; and he was soon obliged to make terms. Little money and few jewels being forthcoming, large districts in the northern regions of Mysore were pledged to the Marathas. The main army had departed; but 6,000 horsemen, and the Peishwa's civil collectors, had been planted in these districts, when Hyder reached the capital.

He urged that had *he* and his troops been more promptly summoned, the fortune of the day might have been very different. And he recommended the forcible expulsion of the Maratha garrisons, when the monsoon should come on, and the swelling of the rivers give a long reprieve from the renewal of the invasion. *Then* he would be ready to help. Meanwhile, the revenues might be withheld, on various pretexts, till the plot was ripe. His advice prevailed. And he next proceeded to arrange matters on his own behalf with Deoraj. A body of Hyder's troops had, on the invitation of the Nair Raja of Palghat, been sent under Mukhdoom Sahib to assist that Prince against his enemies; and are said to have been the first Mahometan corps that ever entered the country, though the chief of Cannanore was certainly a Mussulman. The Rajas of Cochin and Calicut yielded to the invaders, and engaged to purchase their retirement with twelve *lacs* of rupees. But they proposed to pay by instalments; and Mukhdoom, like

21

his master, was a strict man of business in money matters. He declined to quit the country until the whole sum was discharged. The Rajas then applied to Deoraj, and offered to hand over the entire claim to him, if he would rid them of the presence of the obnoxious Mussulmans.

Hyder arrived on the scene at this crisis, and arranged that Deoraj should receive the sum in question, on restoring the revenues of which he had lately despoiled the negotiator who, in consideration of the expenses of the campaign, should be credited by the State with three *lacs* in addition. Hurri Sing was then sent into Malabar. Thus again the Rajput conspicuously crossed the path of his rival.

Hyder now returned to Dindigul, and resumed his local projects of ambition. His present object was, to add Madura to his own districts. But here he came into collision with Mahomet Issoof, another remarkable man, and our ablest partisan and organizer of Sepoys, who, with inferior members, gave him a decisive repulse. Hyder, however, rarely abandoned an object on which he had set his heart. He was still meditating a repetition of the attempt, and had already received French reinforcements under M. Astruc, when again he was called off to the capital by urgent affairs.

The government was bankrupt, and the army,

clamorous for arrears of pay, had adopted the quaint practice of sitting in *dhurna* at the gate of the unlucky minister, whom his ambition and misconduct, and the public troubles connected with the Nizam and the Marathas, had placed in the strangest of political positions. His brother and late confederate in the conspiracy against the royal authority was in passive and sullen opposition. Nunjiraj now wielded ostensibly the whole civil as well as military force of the State, under a pageant but impatient sovereign. Yet Nunjiraj himself was, by the binding power of an Oriental custom, being literally starved, as well as blockaded, by his exasperated, but patiently tormenting soldiery.

Hyder, with all the troops he could muster, marched promptly to the capital (1758). He met Kunde Rao by appointment at Sattimungulum; and they jointly persuaded Deoraj to be reconciled to his brother, in the face of the great danger that now threatened their common power. The old man's strength was fast failing. He was already suffering from dropsy. He returned as far as the town of Mysore, while Hyder and his *dewan* went on and arranged terms with Nunjiraj, who had staved off for the moment the *dhurna* attack, by selling the provision stores of the capital. The humiliated and embarrassed minister consented to make ample apologies to the Raja for his outrageous conduct: and the guns of the fort announced the reconciliation. Deoraj was honoured with a pompous procession, which went forth to meet and escort him to Seringapatam, his brother and Hyder conspicuous at its head. In less than a week afterwards he died. Suspicions of foul play were of course entertained, Colonel Wilks thinks without reason. The event, however, was, to say the least, a very opportune one for Hyder at this crisis.

The military difficulty still threatened the surviving minister. Perplexed, worn out with anxiety, really grieved at his brother's death, and overweeningly confident of Hyder's attachment to himself, he devolved entirely the task of settlement on his astute *protégé*. This was a great opportunity, and one which Hyder Ally was the last man to neglect. His abilities were precisely suited to such an emergency. Personally quite fearless, resolute, engaging, humourous, cunning, and well versed in the arts by which Government was made the victim of military extortion; he contrived at once to satisfy real claims, and to relieve the Raja and Nunjiraj of a mass of debts which were grounded on imposture, and of a host of turbulent followers, who were of little or no use in serious warfare.

The importance to his prospects of his conduct on this occasion is forcibly delineated by Colonel Wilks. "Hyder," he observes, "throughout all these transactions, had been enabled to assume the character of a general benefactor. The gratitude of Nunjeraj was due for his conduct in effecting the reconciliation, and for the zeal and exertion which relieved him from much embarrassment: the troops considered him as their only hope for a liquidation of arrears; the Raja beheld as yet only his preserver and protector from the violence of Nunjeraj; and all orders of men began to look up to Hyder for the restoration of public prosperity."

Indeed he might probably have seized the supreme power at once, without difficulty. For his troops, being the only soldiers who could be trusted to carry out his plans, were in actual possession of the fort. But his time, he knew, was not yet fully come. And he was too prudent to strike prematurely or openly. But he did not neglect to execute a plan essential to the promotion of his ambition, one which, no doubt, he had long meditated, and which the death of Deoraj, and his own commanding position at the present juncture, emboldened him to attempt.

Hurri Sing was encamped securely at Coimbatore, on his return from the Malabar coast. Hyder despatched Mukhdoom with a large force, professedly to return to Dindigul, really to fall upon the Rajput by night, and cut him off, with his army, in cold blood. This was done thoroughly.

It is but right to mention, that Hyder's native panegyrist, while he misdates this incident, endeavours, by connecting it with the *dhurna* proceeding, to apologise for it. But the apology is as lame as the act was atrocious. And while we recognise Hyder Ally's ability, and his habitual abstinence from purposeless cruelty, we may confidently conclude, from an examination of his whole career, that he would not hesitate for a moment at committing a crime, that was to remove an avowed enemy, and speed his own advancement to supreme power.

It is equally clear that he had no false delicacy in pressing his claims to reward for the valuable services, which, by address and good fortune combined, he was able to represent himself as having rendered both to his patron and to the State.

Thus he easily obtained, at this period, a grant of the revenues of Coimbatore, in liquidation of the three *lacs* stipulated with the defunct Deoraj, as a reimbursement for the expenses of his recent operations in Malabar. To which, by way of recognising him in the character of a public benefactor, and prospective champion on the exposed frontier, was now added the command of the fort of Bangalore, the second city in the kingdom, with the enjoyment of the revenues of the districts dependent on it. Those districts had been assigned to the Marathas. And they would not be likely to leave him, without a severe struggle, in quiet enjoyment of what had been pledged to themselves.

Accordingly, as had been foreseen, they returned after the rains, under Gopal Hurri and Anund Rao (1759). They at once re-occupied the open country, and proceeded to invest Bangalore with their multitudinous cavalry; while with their infantry they took Cenapatam, a place of considerable consequence, as covering the approaches to Seringapatam, at only forty miles distance, and still nearer to Bangalore.

And now Hyder had an opportunity, not only of redeeming his pledge to Nunjiraj, that he would, on their return, grapple with the formidable invaders, but of refuting the sceptics who still questioned his military talents; and of performing services which should—*parvis componere magna*—place him in the same relation to the Mysore Government, as Cromwell had attained to the English through his campaigns in Ireland and Scotland. To triumph over the Marathas, was to become virtually master of the State. *Then* he might discard Nunjiraj, and domineer in turn over the Raja, as Cromwell had purged the Long Parliament, dismissed the Rump, and tyrannised over the people, whose nominal authority the Commons had usurped, to fall before their own instrument.

Part of the recent settlement with the soldiers had been effected by their officers discharging the arrears, on the understanding that Government should repay these advances. But this was as yet impossible: and most of the officers refused to enter on this new and arduous service, until their claims had been satisfied. Matters were thus brought to a dead-lock; and the terrors of *dhurna* again overhung the minister. Hyder, who was not improbably fomenting underhand this passive resistance on the part of the officers, tendered his services, and was appointed Commander-in-Chief. He also curried favour with the soldiers by undertaking to guarantee the payment of what might still be due to *them;* knowing, but ignoring the fact, that *that* was not the hitch. Many high-born chiefs resigned, in consequence of his appointment. That when left thus to his own resources he would fail signally, was as confidently anticipated by his enemies, as by his admirers, that he would prove equal to the occasion.

His first care was to screen the capital, which he did by placing Meer Ibrahim, his maternal uncle, in Mallavilly, and Lutof Ally Beg, a valiant Mogul, at Madoor. Lutof Ally, in obedience to orders, affected fear, and thus lulling the Marathas into security, made a sudden and successful dash at Cenapatam; so sudden, that he recovered it almost without loss to either party. Then Hyder massed his troops under cover of this place, and lured Gopal Hurri to break up the blockade of Bangalore, and lead his formidable squadrons against forces numerically very inferior. But Hyder gave him no advantage, and profited much by his own experience of European warfare. He threw up an entrenched camp, a secure barrier against the sudden and furious assaults of the Maratha cavalry. He kept quiet with his main army during the day; though his wild horsemen were ever on the move, scouring the country, and excelling the Maratha feats of horsemanship and plundering. But when the mantle of night favoured his stealthy approaches, and his disorderly and ill-guarded opponents were buried in slumber, he fell upon them with the flower of his well-trained and well-appointed soldiers; and smote them with the fire-arms that they had learnt to dread, rather than to use. Nor was this all, nor the worst. So far his warfare was European. But bolder and more threatening and effective grew his horsemen, until they fairly beat the enemy in their own characteristic mode of fighting.

To be out-galloped and out-plundered by irregular cavalry; to be starved in their quarters, and reduced to inactivity, when they had come to overspread the land like locusts, and (as the Madras Government had formerly said of them) to "peel it to the bones;" this was indeed a novel and serious experience for Marathas!

Yet this did Hyder accomplish through his unrivalled *Kuzzaks.* In short, three months sufficed to establish his reputation in the field; to disgust Gopal Hurri and his people with a war so entirely reversing their previous impressions of the defensible resources of Mysore; and to bring about a peace, which was as skilfully negotiated by the victor, as the war had been ably conducted.

The Marathas abandoned all claim to the ceded districts on payment of thirty-two *lacs.* To be quit of such an enemy, at such a price, was at once an advantage and a burden to the exhausted State. But a compulsory *benevolence* produced half the money; and Hyder's personal security obtained the loan of the rest from the bankers in *the enemy's* camp. So high an opinion had they formed of him and his influence in the course of the short campaign. On the other hand, Hyder obtained "the direct management of the pledged districts, as the fund from which that remainder was to be liquidated. He accordingly despatched without delay his own agents and aumildars to these restored districts."*

Thus, step by step, did his abilities and services enable him plausibly to absorb the revenues of the State, and thereby render his own assumption of the direct administration more speedily inevitable.

On the departure of the invaders, the fortunate general returned in triumph to Seringapatam, where

* Wilks.

his reception was magnificent, and he was the theme of universal applause. Nunjiraj, on his appearance at Court, rose to do him honour, and publicly embraced him. The Raja saluted him with the title most dear to his ears—Bahadur. His bitterest and most irreconcileable enemy, the Rajput, he had removed. Deoraj was no longer alive to misdoubt and watch him. His old patron still retained the fullest confidence in him. The military sceptics were answered: his enemies cowered before him, or eagerly pressed forward to pay him insidious honour. Like Cromwell, he had an efficient and devoted army, to do his bidding. Many of the fortresses of the country were in his hands. He had wealth in abundance to buy off opposition, and to secure secret service. He knew that, in spite of the formal reconciliation, Nunjiraj was unforgiven by the Raja. He knew that the *zenana,* in its secret recesses, harboured in the person of a Dowager Queen, a ready agent for the work of undermining the power of the man, who had murdered her husband, and violated the sanctity of her private apartments. He knew that he could command this powerful and secret influence. He felt that the time was come at last for striking the blow that he had long contemplated; and possessing himself of the power and station to which all his steps had tended. But true to his character he still struck in the dark. His approaches to the throne were as devious and insidious as his attacks on his enemies in the field.

The expenses of the Carnatic war, the Nizam, the Marathas, and Hyder together, had so effectually drained the resources of the State that the military difficulty soon recurred. Advantage was taken of this state of things to execute the plot which had been concerted with the Court, for the ruin of Nunjiraj. The "wire-pulling" began by a formal deputation to Hyder, as Sipahsalar, or Commander-in-Chief, on behalf of the army, demanding a settlement of arrears. This demand was met by expressions of sympathy, and a distinct intimation, that Nunjiraj was the responsible finance minister. This was of course followed up by a strict renewal of the *dhurna* operation, but with a significant improvement on the former experiment. The complainants, instructed by the initiated, insisted respectfully, but firmly, on Hyder himself joining them in this purgatorial session. Nunjiraj at once understood the move; and his spirit sank forthwith to the level of his fortunes. Hyder, in a private interview, induced him to go through the form of a voluntary and unconditional resignation, and even himself to suggest the next step. The minister announced to the troops, that his administration was at an end; and that they must now look to the Raja for their money, and exempt *him* from the further penalties of *dhurna*.

The hint was unmistakeable: and the Palace was immediately beset, and laid under the same singular embargo. But the Court was in the secret, and was prepared to play its part in this grotesque, but important political melodrama. Kunde Rao was summoned to an audience in the Palace. On emerging, he notified the Raja's pleasure, that Hyder should selemnly and publicly swear to "renounce his connexion with the usurper;" and, that this being done, the ex-minister should be handsomely provided for, and the military grievance redressed. Hyder thereupon, with an appropriately rueful countenance, took the oath that was to sever his interests from those of his beloved patron. Then he, in turn, visited the Raja, and presently pledged himself to the soldiers, amidst general expressions of satisfaction, to effect the settlement of their claims.

This pledge, and the further charge of providing regular payment for the army in future, enabled him to appropriate a still larger portion of the public income: and he now held the *jaghire*, or government share of the revenue, of half the Mysore territory. But the transformation scene was still incomplete. Kunde Rao was now made *dewan*, or finance minister to the Raja; and he still continued to hold the corresponding office in Hyder's personal service; a confusion of relations which not improbably suggested its own termination in the way least agreeable to his promoter, who of course still considered and treated the Brahmin as his own creature. Nunjiraj had revenue assigned him to the amount of three *lacs;* two on account of troops which he was bound to maintain for the service of the State.

He settled at the *town* of Mysore, the *old* capital. But this was thought ominous, and he was ordered to move nearer to the frontier. Hyder, on announcing this order, still further trampled on the pride of the fallen minister, and enriched himself, by appropriating the two *lacs* granted on account of the troops, and exempting Nunjiraj from the obligation of maintaining them. The latter replied by a sullen and reproachful defiance. "I have made you what you are: and now you refuse me a place in which to hide my head. Do what you please, or what you can. I move not from Mysoor."* Thereupon, in the conscientious and punctual discharge of his duty to the Raja, Hyder was compelled to take strong measures, and besiege the disobedient subject. He never excelled in siege operations. But on this occasion he moreover wished, probably, to make political capital out of his protracted labours. At the end of three months Nunjiraj surrendered, and was settled at Cunnoor, westward of Mysore (1760). The Raja visited the scene of hostilities; admired the works, and the prowess of his new Commander-in-Chief;

* Wilks.

and graciously rewarded the victor with a further accession of revenue and territorial authority. Kunde Rao viewed this last transaction as Chancellor of the Exchequer to the Raja, rather than as Hyder's personal *dewan;* and opposed it In a dispute that followed, we have the first muttering of the storm, which was shortly to sweep away for a time the ambitious and fortunate favourite, more summarily than he had himself disposed of Nunjiraj.

Such is, in substance, Colonel Wilks' well-informed and critical account of this famous revolution. So much was obviously enacted behind the scenes, that we are here peculiarly at the mercy of the historian, and liable to mistake assumptions for facts. But this writer, beyond question, is not only our best, but a most competent guide through this, as through so many other labyrinths of Eastern story.

Undisputed, and, as he believed, secure in his political ascendancy, Hyder now turned his attention to extending the limits, and increasing the resources and reputation of Mysore. Two claims to the exercise of his warlike energies at once presented themselves. The French required, and urgently sought, his assistance. And a discontented subject of the chief of Kirpa invited him to re-conquer a district which had once belonged to the State, whose destinies he was henceforth to sway. He closed, in the first instance, with the latter proposition, and sent Mukhdoom Sahib to reduce the Baramahl, and when this should have been accomplished, to negotiate with the French.

The Baramahl forms a sort of intervening fringe of hilly country, separating the Eastern Ghats from what the English habitually, though inaccurately, termed *the* Carnatic. It was guarded by twelve fortresses on the heights, some of which played an important part in the war which, not many years after this period, we waged against Hyder. It had been wrested from Mysore by the "Patan Nabob" of Kirpa; who, in turn, two years earlier than the time at which we have now arrived, had lost half of it to the Marathas.

Mukhdoom's first task was to reduce the Poligar of Anikul, and seize his fort, thus securing an entrance into the Baramahl, and an undisturbed roadway towards Pondicherry. The Baramahl was then occupied quickly and easily; and the Mysorean general visited the French capital, and, on behalf of his employer, concluded a treaty with Lally (June, 1760). Thiagar, a place well situated for communications between Mysore and Pondicherry, and lately taken by the French, was to be made over to him. And he was to furnish 3,000 good cavalry, and 5,000 regular infantry, to oppose the English. It was also agreed, that in the event of success, Madura and Tinnevelly, if not Trichinopoly too, were to become Hyder's; and that the French were to aid him in investing them. Though the course of events nullified the last article, it deserves mention, as excusing the nervous anxiety which Mahomet Ali and the English seem to have afterwards felt at Hyder's conquering career in Malabar, and his threatening pause afterwards in Coimbatore, so near their own frontier, and as if meditating a swoop on the south-eastern provinces, upon which from Dindigul he had so early cast a longing eye. And this anxiety it probably was which principally tempted the English at least to rush precipitately into war with their dangerous neighbour; when, according to Colonel Wilks, they engaged in it "exclusively in the character of dupes."

Occupying Thiagar on his march, Mukhdoom led his first instalment of troops to Pondicherry. He was advancing with the remainder, and a large convoy much required by his famished allies, and for which he drove a hard bargain, when he fell in with and totally defeated an English force sent to oppose him. Coote was as yet unaware of what he was one day to understand too well—the new life which had been breathed into the Mysorean army by Hyder. And he had made very inadequate provision accordingly. On hearing of this achievement, Hyder's delight was so great, that he increased his contingent considerably beyond the terms of the contract; and was intending to take so active and extensive a part in the Anglo-French war, that he might have altered its whole character, when his own condition suddenly became not less critical than that of his unfortunate ally.

Few historical coincidences are more remarkable than the precise synchronism of Lally's final contest with Coote, the Maratha strife with the Abdali, and Hyder's struggle with Kunde Rao. All involved issues decisive of the fortunes of Powers, that at one time or another, and almost simultaneously, aspired to supremacy in India. And so far from being isolated events, the three crises were singularly and closely connected in the way of cause and effect. The surrender of Pondicherry extinguished for ever the political independence of the French in India; though as auxiliaries of Mysore they continued long afterwards to play an energetic part. The defeat of Paniput for the time almost crushed the Marathas; and though afterwards most formidable, they never regained the position they had formerly occupied among the native Powers. Kunde Rao's alienation brought on the most dangerous catastrophe of Hyder's life; the turning point of the fortunes of his house. It is singular that three such wars should have been waged simultaneously in the Peninsula. It is not less singular to think, what course events might have taken had one or other of these wars been postponed. Had Kunde Rao held his hand for a time, possibly Pondicherry might not have fallen at all. Had the Abdali marched somewhat later into India, or been defeated, Hyder would almost certainly have failed to effect a junction with Mukhdoom, and would then have been beaten in detail, and finally destroyed. Such momentous complications invest with new interest the platitude, that war is an uncertain game.

The counter-revolution, like the change which gave occasion for it, began by a Court intrigue. The Queen Dowager discovered too late that Hyder's little finger was likely to prove, in the end, thicker than the loins of Nunjiraj. And she observed with satisfaction, that in the absence of a large part of his army, he was himself cooped up, with a comparative handful of followers, in the island of Seringapatam; while the rest of his troops, and his already famous artillery, were posted on the northern shore. The monsoon had filled the river, and made the fords impassable; and the bridges were commanded by the fort. The Marathas were hovering in force near the frontier, and marauding as usual; but were quite ready to take service with any one who would pay them.

Before the great Idol of the capital the Queen swore Kunde Rao and the Raja to a well-concerted plot for cutting off the obnoxious upstart. Resentment at his patron's exorbitant greed of revenue, ambition, and religious sentiment, contended in the Brahmin's breast with fear, and perhaps with gratitude. But he elected to follow that patron's example, and betray him in turn, though in a ruder and more obvious manner. It is noticeable, that the Brahmin is the more violent; the Mussulman more supple and insinuating. A bargain was soon struck with the Maratha commander, who was to send 6,000 of his horsemen to Seringapatam by the twelfth of August.

Hyder, on that memorable morning, was quartered on the ground, where later stood the *Dowlut Baug*. His family were with him, Tippoo being now in his ninth year. Another son was born on that very day, amidst a scene of tumult, which not inaptly prefigured the twice-repeated terror of English warfare on the same island. The fort gates continued closed. But before the sun was up a tremendous fire of artillery was directed from all the adjacent works against the unsuspecting *Sipahsalar* and his followers. He sent instantly for Kunde Rao; but that worthy was shortly after descried superintending the operation. The fire does not seem to have been very effective; and the soldiers and Hyder's family found shelter, though no comfort. In this extremity, though he saw his army on the northern shore routed, and his artillery captured, by a large body of troops from the fort; and though he expected to be attacked each moment in his quarters, Hyder was calm and thoughtful as ever. Hussein Ali gives an account of his proceedings which, however little confidence can be placed in the statements of so inaccurate and eulogistic a writer, is not intrinsically improbable.

"He immediately manned his defences with musketeers, and also without the knowledge of any one despatched a number of men, and seized all the Ambakars (watermen) of the river Cauveri, with their baskets, and made them prisoners. Then, having placed his infantry and cavalry in readiness round his house, he sent for the writers of his different departments, and made them write out distinct lists of what he was possessed of in valuable cloths, elephants, camels, arms, rich stuffs, utensils, &c., and arranged all this business by mid-day."

It is added, that Kunde Rao attacked his encampment; which I doubt. It is certain that the Marathas, as usual, did not come up to time, and that a parley ensued between the rivals in ambition and treachery. Hyder, ever ready to adapt his tone to his needs, ascribed all his past prosperity to his *dewan;* confessed that, deserted by *him,* he should be utterly undone; and implored his old servant not to break the bruised reed, but to advise and help one, who was prepared to obey cheerfully the commands of the now all-powerful minister. Kunde Rao, in turn, gracefully acknowledged his own obligations to the suppliant; assured him that he was not personally hostile, but was only officially executing the Raja's orders. If Hyder would promise (the Brahmin did not even demand an oath) to retire permanently from Mysore, he should be permitted to escape unmolested on the same evening. And it seems that Kunde Rao was not content with mere words, but that he actually left the landing-place on the northern bank of the river unguarded—thus almost literally making a bridge for a flying enemy. Perhaps he could not trust his own troops against such an adversary, and began to despair of the arrival of the Marathas. Or he may have counted on the extreme probability of Hyder's flying towards Bangalore, and being thus intercepted and disposed of by their advancing squadrons.

Whatever the explanation of so remarkable a proceeding, on which in fact the fate of his opponent at this moment depended, Hyder was not slow to profit by it. He packed up in bags as much money and as many jewels as his hundred horsemen, with two officers, and two camel-drivers (all trusty persons) could carry; and leaving his infantry and his family on the spot, crossed the river in the coracles, the horses and the camels swimming. Then each took up his burden, and all rode off at such speed that in less than twenty-four hours after the garrison guns had opened on them at Seringapatam, they had evaded the Marathas, and reached Anicul, a distance of seventy-five miles. Many horses broke down, and were left on the way. But spare ones—Tartar fashion—had been provided. And all the men and treasure reached their destination. Hyder rode the same horse throughout. Kunde Rao at dawn visited the fugitives' quarters; and, experiencing no opposition from the deserted infantry, removed Hyder's family into the fort, and placed them under a guard; but treated them kindly. Their lord had probably felt that they would be safer in his rival's hands, than in attempting to follow his own desperate and impetuous fortunes.

Bangalore would have been his most natural and powerful rallying point. But though its commandant was an old friend, Kunde Rao's desertion seems to have made Hyder cautious, if not distrustful of Kubbeer Beg. And he knew that there were Hindoo irregulars in the fortress, and that it would be well looked after without delay, in case of his arrival or attempt to gain it. He had no inclination to be trapped there. While at Anicul, Ismael Ali, his brother-in-law, was in command; and of him he was sure, as well as of finding there a small force of cavalry, which was under marching orders for Arcot. Ismael was sent off immediately to Bangalore, and found Kubbeer Beg staunch. Fortunately, the soldiers' pay was just due. The unsuspecting Hindoos were mustered on the glacis to receive it; while the trustworthy Mussulmans took charge of the gates. Hardly was this precaution completed, when Kunde Rao's orders to keep the place in the Raja's interests arrived. Hyder's activity had again, so far, saved him: and he shortly afterwards entered the second city in the kingdom with the Anicul horsemen, and, as Meer Ali expresses it, "made himself easy." He certainly needed rest. For he had ridden ninety-eight miles in twenty hours.

But great as had been his exertions to take time by the forelock, and great the success that had so far attended them, easy he could not be at the prospect before him. Colonel Wilks observes at this point:—

"Hyder was now left, as it were, to begin the world again, on the resources of his own mind. The bulk of his treasures, and his train of artillery and military stores all lost; the territorial revenue at the command of Kunde Rao: and the possessions on which he could rest any hope for the restoration of his affairs, were Bangalore on the northern and Dindegul on the southern extremities of the territories of Mysoor: with Anicul and the fortresses of Baramahal. The sole foundation of a new army was the corps of Mukhdoom Ali; and its junction was nearly a desperate hope."

But his prompt and decisive arrangements show how fully he understood the situation, and was prepared to improve it. He borrowed, on his personal security, from the rich bankers of the city money to the amount of £40,000, which he afterwards repaid faithfully. He lavished largesse freely, to attach the soldiers more firmly to his interests. He strengthened the works with new batteries, and manned them with zealous partisans. He recalled Mukhdoom Ali from Pondicherry, and directed him to restore Thiagar to the French, and to conduct its garrison, and those of all other places on his route, to Bangalore. He issued a general invitation to all soldiers of fortune, who were swarming in the country, from its lately disturbed state. He lured many of his old comrades from Kunde Rao's own army: and many more joined him from the garrisons which had been turned out of his fortresses in the lost districts. Jaseen Khan, one of his favourites and familiars, and a good officer, came in shortly with his men.

But his most important accession, at this period, and one that tended more than all else to restore his *prestige*, was that of Fuzzul Oolla Khan. He was a man of high birth, son-in-law of Dilawir Khan (Nawab of Sera, and already mentioned), and had a high military reputation. So princely were his pretensions, that on throwing in his lot with Hyder he stipulated, that he should be considered his equal in rank, though serving under the Mysorean; and that this equality should be attested by the new recruit's habitually sitting upon the same "saddle-cloth, carpet, or musnud" (according to the oriental practice of squatting, tailor-like, on the ground), with other marks of distinction. To all this Hyder consented; and it was duly observed, until the pair quarrelled in later days, when the then firmly-established ruler of Mysore requited his present ally with characteristic ingratitude. This aristocratic follower brought with him a large number of soldiers; and his example was very influential with others.

But Kunde Rao was mustering and concentrating his forces, and showed no lack of ability in the disposition and employment of them. He sent on the Marathas, now reinforced to 10,000, under Gopal Hurri, Hyder's old antagonist, to intercept Mukhdoom on his march to Bangalore. Another large Maratha force, under Visaji Pundit, with whom Kunde Rao had contracted for those now under his orders, was hovering not far off, on the slopes of the Ghats overlooking the Villenore valley. Mukhdoom advanced successfully as far as Anchittydroog. But there he was brought to a stand, and compelled to apprise Hyder, that he could not proceed, unless reinforced. Fuzzul Oolla was dispatched with every man that could be spared, 4,000 in all, many of them raw recruits, and with five guns. He made a desperate attempt to force a junction with Mukhdoom, but in vain. His young soldiers, after a furious and almost successful combat, broke and fled to the woods; he was consequently repulsed; all his guns were taken; and he himself escaped with the utmost difficulty back to Anikul. Mukhdoom's junction with his chief appeared now quite hopeless; and Colonel Wilks remarks, "the career of Hyder seemed again approaching its close."

But that was not to be. Once more fortune favoured him. The news of Paniput, and the order of immediate recall, reached the Maratha Commander-in-Chief just at this juncture. Hyder had, all along, been negotiating with him. But Visaji now closed on easy terms, which (ignorant as yet of the great catastrophe that had overtaken the Maratha arms in Hindostan) the Mysorean eagerly accepted, but could not comprehend. In return for the cession of the Baramahl, and the small sum of three *lacs*, Visaji agreed to retire with all his forces, and leave Kunde Rao to settle his account with Hyder single-handed. But it is worth while to mention, that in true Maratha style he had already arranged with the English to withdraw, and thus seal the fate of Lally and Pondicherry, in consideration of the more liberal allowance of twenty *lacs*. In pursuance of his orders, and of this double bargain, he moved off to join the muster against an invader, who was already really on his way back to Afghanistan.

Hyder suspecting, both by the easiness of the

terms, and the unusual promptitude of the Marathas, that all was not well with them in their own affairs, made no haste to surrender the Baramahl; and when apprised of the cause of this moderation and urgency, flatly refused to do so.

The English, meanwhile, were sorely perplexed at the symptoms of instability in the Mysorean counsels. Hyder, after his elevation and his treaty with Lally, had lost no time in sending a force to annex the long-coveted district of Madura. Thereupon, the English had besieged Caroor. Now they were informed by Kunde Rao, that the aggressive adventurer was no longer in power; and that the Raja had no wish to quarrel with them. And as the withdrawal of Mukhdoom's troops seemed to countenance this view, they contented themselves with letting the garrison of Caroor depart, and retaining that place, till they had leisure to come to a more definite understanding with Mysore. Dindigul still held out for Hyder; but the whole country thence to the Baramahl was in Kunde Rao's hands.

Hyder, who began to be pinched for supplies, sent a large detachment into Coimbatore; and to cover it marched south-westward across the Cavery; and near Nunjundgode came in sight of his rival's army. Pondicherry had now fallen, and 300 Europeans, whose occupation in the French service was gone, joined him under MM. Hugel and Alain, before he marched. Two-thirds of these were cavalry; and a small native force accompanied them.

The issue of the contest was staked by each commander on the conduct of comparatively scanty numbers. Hyder had 6000 horse, 5000 foot, and twenty guns; Kunde Rao about 1000 more of each arm, and twenty-eight guns. The old comrades seemed loth to close in the deadly grapple, but each tried to out-manœuvre the other; and both in this and in several skirmishes which ensued, the Brahmin appeared to have the decided advantage. At length a real battle was fought, and Hyder was defeated with heavy loss; but effected an orderly retreat to Hordanhully.

His case was now again desperate. Out-manœuvred, defeated, waiting impatiently for reinforcements, but receiving none; pressed closer and closer by the superior numbers and skill of his opponent, (who, whatever his former disposition to compromise, now displayed the most energetic determination); his supplies failing; his followers at length disposed to believe that his star had set for ever;—whither could he turn for assistance?

A bright thought struck him, which only his unlimited confidence in himself, and in his unparallelled power of deluding others, could have tempted him to indulge. He would visit Nunjiraj in his seclusion; cry *peccavi!* to him; make his peace with him; and induce his early patron to join him against the present wielder of the power, which Hyder had wrested from the old man, only to forfeit it so soon afterwards to his own instrument, and become a new and memorable example of the vicissitudes of fortune, and a companion in adversity of his former victim. Nunjiraj would be flattered; and would perhaps transfer his indignation and hatred to the new usurper of the authority, which he considered rightfully his own. With a small escort the daring and subtle politician left his army in the night; evaded the enemy; and early next morning reached Cunnoor; and unarmed and alone threw himself at the feet of Nunjiraj. His consummate hypocrisy quite won the heart of the desolate recluse, and induced him to espouse the desperate cause. The ex-minister's influence was still considerable. He had also retained some of his troops; and, since the civil war began, had been increasing them, probably expecting that some sudden turn of fortune might again enable him to reclaim his old position.

Kunde Rao, however, was very vigilant, and managed so well, that he prevented Hyder and his new ally from joining the main army. More and more difficult became their situation; till again it grew desperate. And again Hyder's cunning was called into requisition. His present stratagem was a very common-place one, habitually practised indeed in the East; but one which, in a state of society where mutual confidence is so small, constantly proves successful. And it answered its end perfectly in the present instance. Hyder wrote letters in the name, and authenticated with the seal of Nunjiraj, to Kunde Rao's chief officers, assuming the existence of a plot on their part to betray their leader. And he took care that these letters should fall into his enemy's hands. The Brahmin, treacherous himself, and the former confidant and present opponent of an arch-traitor and intriguer, was appalled at the supposed revelation; and without making a single inquiry, fearful for his immediate safety, mounted his horse, and rode off in haste to Seringapatam.

The panic that invariably overtakes an Oriental army, when deserted by its general, ensued. Hyder had been anxiously watching his opportunity. His scouts soon announced the state of things. He fell upon the disorganized host in front and rear at once, and inflicted on it a terrible defeat, "capturing the whole of the enemy's infantry, guns, stores, and baggage."* Most of the infantry readily rejoined his service. The horse had escaped by flight. They afterwards rallied, and were reinforced by a body of foot, at the southern part of the island of Seringapatam. Hyder again came upon them un-

* Wilks.

expectedly at midnight, and slaughtered them wholesale under the very guns of the fort, carrying off 700 horses and much booty. Then he deliberately spent some time in collecting forces, revenue, and stores, and in reducing the country below the Ghats.

Kunde Rao still had some 5000 or 6000 cavalry, chiefly Marathas, and a body of infantry. These were all quartered, as before, on the island, near its southern bank. Hyder, after a time, assembled his whole army, mounted the Ghats, and coolly sat down on the main land, just opposite to the troops on the island. Here he pretended to be absorbed in negotiation. But the river being at this time fordable, he each day drew out his men, as if for practice, in the evening; and, after a week had elapsed, suddenly converted this movement into a rapid dash across the river; and, taking the enemy completely by surprise, made himself master of most of their baggage, stores, and horses.

This was the *coup de grâce* to Kunde Rao's cause. Hyder now encamped across the island; and intriguing with the civil and military officers, and terrifying the Raja by the calm tender of demands, which he knew could not be satisfied, while yet there was no means of opposing them, drove the wretched sovereign, in fear of his life, to terms which amounted to a virtual abdication.

Nunjiraj had now served the turn of his ally, and

was dismissed to a seclusion and insignificance more complete than before.

The conqueror had sworn to the Raja that he would not put Kunde Rao to death, but that he would "cherish him like a parroquet." And he kept his word literally, imprisoning his ill-fated rival in an iron cage, and feeding him upon rice and water.

Hussein Ali thereupon breaks out in a high moral strain, a little out of place in one who was cognisant of the prosperity, which from this period attended almost uninterruptedly, and to the end, the master dissembler and traitor in the rapid vicissitudes which have just been related. "That dispenser of good to the world, having regard to his oath, instead of impaling or dismembering him, which he richly merited, put him into an iron cage, like an inauspicious crow, and sent him off to Bangalore.

"Verily, if a man eat salt from the table of his master's benefits, and ungratefully betray him; the true avenger of ingratitude, in a short time will cause him to be taken in the net of his own perfidy."

Such was the early life of the Jugurtha of Southern India in the last century. Its details are so little known to our countrymen, are so characteristic, both of the man and of the times, and form so eventful and complete an episode in the general history, that it seemed desirable to enter into them with some minuteness. But we must now return to the North, and follow the tide of Maratha warfare, as it surges fiercely onwards towards the fatal plain of Paniput.

CHAPTER XII.

THE PANIPUT CAMPAIGN.

In tracing the circumstances which led to the catastrophe that I am about to relate, it will be necessary to go back, for a moment, from the period which we reached at the close of the tenth chapter; and to repeat, that in the year 1754 Meer Shahabodeen, or Ghazi-ud-deen as he was afterwards called, had with the aid of Holkar and Sindia made himself Vizier and master of Delhi; and afterwards, deposing and blinding the Emperor, Ahmed Shah, had placed on the throne a tool of his own, with the title of Alumgeer II.

It must also be remembered that the Afghan king, Ahmed Shah Abdali, (the last the name of his tribe) had already several times invaded the North-West Provinces of the Empire; and had conquered and entrusted to the government of a former Viceroy of the Mogul, Meer Munnoo, the extensive, but half-desert region then called Mooltan and Lahore, but which we should now term, with some geographical vagueness, the Punjab (1752). On the death of Munnoo, his widow, with the Abdali's sanction, acted as Regent for her infant son; and, on *his* death, had just compromised a dispute with an officer, who sought to supplant her authority, by agreeing to share it with him; when the restless and vainglorious young Vizier, who had been engaged to marry Munnoo's daughter, advanced with an army to claim his bride. She was given up to him; but he persisted in invading the Province, and sent off the mother a prisoner to Delhi (1756).

Hardly had the rash youth thus re-annexed the territory, and committed it to Adina Beg, a miscreant who had first invited the Afghan to cross the Indus, when that formidable chief returned for the fourth time, inflamed with anger and bent on revenge. Never was

"Quicquid delirant reges, plectuntur Achivi"

better illustrated. Ghazi-ud-deen's cringing tone procured him a free pardon; but "Delhi," says the Maratha historian with terrible brevity, "was plundered, and its unhappy people again subjected to pillage, and its daughters to pollution." Similar horrors befell other places, abridged however by a pestilence, which led the invader to retire. He left his son, Timour Shah, as Viceroy of the Punjab; and, on his own authority, promoted to one of the highest offices at the Imperial Court Nujib-ud-Dowla, a chief of the Rohillas, then recent Afghan settlers in Hindostan.

No sooner had Ahmed Shah departed, than the insolent and infatuated Vizier degraded the Rohilla, of whom he was jealous; allied himself with Rugonath Rao; with *his* help recovered Delhi and the custody of the Emperor's person (1757); and but for Holkar's secret aid, Nujib-ud-Dowla would have perished, instead of escaping to play a conspicuous part in the battle of Paniput.

This might have seemed enough to provoke anew the wrath of the Abdali. But the cup of his anger was to be now drugged with still more stimulating ingredients. The alternating impertinence and servility of the young Mogul Vizier he might despise, however distasteful might be the interposition of Rugonath Rao at the capital.

But when the Punjab fell anew into disorder; when Adina Beg, unstable as water, and ever shifting his connexions, broke out into rebellion; raised the now martial Sikhs, and invited Rugonath, at the head of a vast Hindoo army, to invade the Province; and when accordingly that enterprising, but rash and ill-fated chief, destined throughout an adventurous life to bring eventual trouble on all his supporters, accepted the invitation; routed the Afghan governor, and entered Lahore in triumph (1758):—Ahmed Shah's indignation knew no bounds; and he prepared to measure his full strength against that of the southern adventurers, who thus crossed his track of conquest, and challenged his power, much as Bajazet had presumed to match himself against the invincible Timour.

Meanwhile Rugonath, having spent, instead of acquiring immense sums, in the course of this remote expedition, and in over-running and occupying so sterile a country as the confines of the Indian Desert, and having, like a later politician, "with a light heart" committed his countrymen to a strife, of which the issue was to prove little less than ruinous; having lastly feebly garrisoned the straggling territory with a Maratha detachment;—returned to give an account of his proceedings to the Peishwa; and in a Hippocleides vein to toss off the responsibility of the ensuing struggle upon his critic and cousin, the still rasher and less experienced Sedasheo.

Other proceedings of the Maratha leaders in the North also tended to raise the now inevitable storm, and to leave them to encounter its full fury in perfect isolation. Holkar had co-operated in the Vizier's measures against the low-bred but powerful and warlike Hindoo Jats. Rugonath had made war on the proud and princely Rajputs; had occupied Ajmir, and exacted tribute from the oldest and haughtiest of the Houses, that of Joudpoor. Now Duttaji, (a son of the original Sindia—who was dead,) still impelled by the minister of evil counsels, the Vizier, again overran the country of the Rohillas; drove those kinsmen of the Abdali to the hills; and becoming involved in hostilities with the new Nawab of Oude, who, though he hated both the Rohillas and Shah Ahmed, dreaded the Marathas still more, thus contrived not only to sustain, in the person of his lieutenant, a defeat at Shuja-ud-Dowla's hands; but to exasperate afresh, at such a crisis, both those Mahometan Powers, and revive the bitter memory of the former Maratha conquest of Rohilkund.

A hasty truce was indeed patched up and duly sworn to, both with the Nawab and the Rohillas, on tidings that Shah Ahmed was already on his way (1759). But each party knew full well how far such a convention was likely to stand in the way of particular interests, and tribal or religious affinities.

The author of all this mischief, meanwhile, Ghazi-ud-deen, having put an appropriate finish to his short but meddlesome and eventful career as king maker, and general embroiler of the politics of the North, by murdering his own creature, the wretched Alumgeer, and setting up a new titular Emperor, a grandson of his present victim's great namesake;—fled to Sooraj

Mull, the Jat Raja, and hid himself in one of that Prince's forts, while the mighty contest proceeded, that he had done so much to bring about.

The opening events of the campaign were of evil augury to the Marathas. Their detachment hastily evacuated Lahore on the advance of Ahmed Shah. While Holkar and Duttaji Sindia retired along the right bank of the Jumna, before what they believed to be the invader's main body; he had in reality crossed to the opposite side with the bulk of his army, to receive the ready accession of the Rohillas; and recrossing far down near Delhi, he suddenly assailed Sindia's flank, and cut off two-thirds of his force. Duttaji fell, but his half brother Mahadaji, famous in after times, escaped. Holkar retreated in hot haste beyond Agra; thence made a successful attack on a convoy which was proceeding to the Afghan army; but though he rapidly placed the Chumbul as well as the Jumna between himself and the enemy, they pushed on with such speed, that they overtook and defeated him in a bloody battle.

Such were the sobering tidings that greeted the Bhow shortly after his triumph over the Nizam. But, flushed with victory, he saw in them only an occasion for winning new laurels, and eagerly demanded permission "to recover the lost reputation of the Mahrattas in Hindoostan, and drive the Afghans beyond the Attock."*

* Grant Duff.

Balaji granted the request; and confided to the care of Sedasheo his own son Wiswas Rao, the heir apparent to the Peishwaship.

It was proposed to assemble by degrees the whole available force of the Confederacy; and in spite of late occurrences and unfriendly relations with those peoples, to call upon both Rajputs and Jats to make common cause against the threatening Mussulman. But the nucleus of the whole host was the Peishwa's army, which, though not much more than thirty thousand strong, consisted of picked levies, in the finest condition, and splendidly appointed. Twenty-two thousand were cavalry; ten thousand artillery and infantry, trained in imitation of the new European fashion, and commanded by Ibrahim Khan Gardee, Bussy's old follower.

From an eye-witness Colonel Grant Duff gathered an account of the gorgeous array in which the ill-fated Bhow moved out to his doom, which is well worth transcription, and will give a lively idea of the change that had come over the people since the days when Sivaji enforced among their ancestors his stern, simple, and business-like dispositions.

"The equipment of this army was more splendid in appearance than any Mahratta force that ever took the field. * * * The lofty and spacious tents, lined with silks and broadcloths, were surmounted by large gilded ornaments, conspicuous at a great distance; immense parti-coloured walls of canvass enclosed each suite of tents belonging to the principal officers; vast numbers of elephants, flags of all descriptions, the finest horses, magnificently caparisoned, and all those accompaniments of an Indian army, which give such an imposing effect to its appearance, seemed to be collected from every quarter in the Bhow's camp. Cloth of gold was the dress of the officers, and all seemed to vie in that profuse and gorgeous display characteristic of wealth lightly acquired. It was, in this instance, an adaptation of the more becoming and tasteful array of the magnificent Moguls, in the zenith of their glory."

To enumerate the swarm of distinguished chieftains, heads of families, and experienced officers, who contributed, as in the French hosts at Crecy, Poitiers, and Agincourt, to give *éclat* to the gathering, and national significance to any reverse that might be sustained, is unnecessary, and would not be melodious. But it may be mentioned that the levies of Holkar, Sindia, and the Guikwar joined the Peishwa's army as it neared the Chumbul, with those of many minor chieftains. The Rajput Princes sent bodies of cavalry; the Jat Raja appeared in person with 30,000 men. "It seemed," says Grant Duff, "the national cause with all Hindoos." Soldiers of fortune, irregulars and Pindaries (the ominous word is already familiarly applied to a familiar phenomenon) poured in from all quarters, So vast was the concourse, that no exact estimate of it at this period seems attainable. But mismanagement and dissension soon thinned the ranks, though what remained was far too numerous a host to be handled deftly by such a general as the Bhow, especialy against such an antagonist as the Abdali – a man of war from his youth; a cool, determined and methodical commander; the absolute disposer of his own motions, and well acquainted with the condition and feelings of his enemies.

The incapacity of the Maratha general, arising not only from inexperience, but from the moral defects and dangerous prejudices which have been already noted, and which late events had tended greatly to confirm, at once began to make itself felt.

Three different races had successively distinguished themselves in India, by carrying on war in three different manners. The imperial armies had been conspicuous for the trained aptitude and martial spirit of their high bred officers, the stature, strength and number of their soldiers, the size and fine condition of their horses, the imposing array of their powerful though cumbrous artillery, the ostentatious magnificence of the whole *mise en scène,* and last, not least, for the harmonious co-operation of Hindoo and Mussulman under the same banner. The Marathas had been unrivalled for celerity of movement, promptitude and completeness of information, and all that is thus gained. To attack at discretion, unexpectedly, and with full effect; to evade retaliation, and baffle pursuit; to supply their own wants with facility, and with equal facility to incommode their antagonist, by operating on his communications, surprising his convoys, and reducing him to actual or imminent starvation; this had been their *forte*, and the cause of the terror they had so long inspired. Of late the French had revolutionized the whole game of war in India, by the introduction of disciplined battalions and light field-pieces. At this very time was being trained, in Hyder Ally, a general who was to solve successfully and with terrible effect the problem, how to combine the three systems in one comprehensive and well adjusted method of operations.

But the Bhow was, if I may venture to say so, a sort of anticlimax to Hyder. Instead of assimilating what was best in each system, he selected that which was least appropriate to his circumstances, and constructed altogether a machine elaborately adapted to defeat its own ends.

He adopted Mogul luxury, cumbersomeness, state, dilatoriness, deficiency of information. Maratha family feuds, personal grudges, a peddling, vulgar disposition to raise money by means abhorrent and insulting to all who cherished the memory of departed imperial greatness; such were the original incentives which his early associations had implanted, and which no large converse with the world outside Maharashtra had removed. And these presently led him to abandon the special and felicitous peculiarities of Maratha warfare, and to lose the services of his other Hindoo associates. Lastly, the sepoy battalion, and the European field-piece were admirable instruments when managed by those who had introduced them, and directed by a competent commander. But, as usual, it was not the mechanical appliance, or the theoretical system, but the discerning eye and calculating mind of the skilful master that must determine the success of their application: and neither Ibrahim Khan nor the Bhow himself was a Bussy, a Clive, or even a Dalton. Nor, had they been so, could the marvels of Indo-European warfare have been reproduced with levies exclusively composed of natives, exclusively officered by natives, and but slightly tinged with the reflection of the bright light that had recently arisen on the Coromandel coast.

The pomp without the dignity, the large-mindedness, or the unity of the Empire; the waywardness without the mobility and vigilance of the Maratha; the form without the spirit of the European levies; and all presided over and misdirected by a *tête monté* neophyte, jealous of his subordinates, contemptuous in his bearing towards his allies, underrating his able opponent, and obstinately bent upon pursuing his own caprices and crotchets, in defiance of the evidence of facts:—what could be expected to come of so unhappy a combination?

Sooraj Mull, the Jat prince, at once detected the weak point in the character of the armament. The cavalry obviously could not act freely while compelled to attend the slow motions of the infantry, guard the heavy cannon, and protect a gipsey-like host of women, children, and camp followers. He therefore urged that these encumbrances should be got rid of, by placing them in some of the many fortresses available in the neighbourhood. Holkar seconded this proposal. But the jealous, suspicious, and self-opinionated Bhow, proud of his supposed monopoly of European skill and appliances, and misliking the suggestion, as proceeding from the lips or mind of Holkar, against whom (as I have explained) he had an old grudge; perhaps also anxious to retain the Maratha families as pledges of the fidelity and energetic action of some of the chiefs, refused to adopt the advice.

He marched in full force to Delhi, and after some opposition, occupied that city; and immediately proceeded to shock the feelings of the Hindostanees generally, as well as of the Mussulmans from other parts of the Peninsula, by proposing to place, or (as one account says) actually placing Wiswas Rao, the Peishwa's young son, on the throne. For Stilicho or Gelimer to have raised an Arian Goth or Vandal to the imperial dignity, would hardly have done so much violence to the sentiments of the Catholics of Italy, as did such a step to those of the Mahometan or even the Rajput adherents of the house of Timour.

He next further insulted both the Moguls and the Rajputs, whose Princesses had habitually intermarried with the Emperors, and who had been the constant and favoured attendants in the stately audience hall of the palace, by stripping it of such costly decorations as had escaped previous spoilers, or had been supplied to make amends for earlier acts of the same aggravating kind; and ended by breaking up, in imitation of Nadir Shah, the throne itself.

The remonstrances of Sooraj Mull and Holkar were superciliously disregarded; and the immediate and disastrous result of these wanton acts was, that both the Jat and the Rajputs retired with their forces, and left the infatuated and impracticable Maratha to wage the tremendous contest with his own army alone.

Thus deserted by the Hindoos, the Bhow sought aid from the Nawab of Oude, whose favour he had already endeavoured to gain by the notable proposal, that the latter should be Vizier under Wiswas Rao! But the Mussulman, little as he loved either the Abdali or the Rohilla, and, though he gave fair words, and continued up to the last moment to negotiate publicly—as mediator—and to carry on a private correspondence with Sedasheo, lost no time in joining Shah Ahmed with a powerful contingent (July, 1760); and opened his real mind, and that of his Maratha correspondent, and would-be confidant, to his co-religionist.

Jealousy of the Maratha power, and the character and conduct of the Bhow, combined with the outraged feelings of the son of the imperial Vizier, and the prejudices of Islam, to frustrate this last hope of securing efficient aid in the North.

Sedasheo then tried another expedient; but succeeded only in showing the shiftiness of his own policy, and in angering yet more those who already denounced the insolence of the low-bred robbers, by presuming to determine afresh who should be the occupant of the throne, which he had actually destroyed. He made a new Emperor—this time a scion of the Mogul House; and again declared Shuja-ud-Dowlah Vizier. This, in itself a *brutum fulmen*, was at once dissipated in the crash of battle that began now to set in.

The Bhow stormed a town favourable to the Abdali. Ahmed Shah seized the first opportunity of fording the Jumna (Oct., 1760), on the abatement of the monsoon; and while the negligent and incredulous commander of the Marathas was still shutting his ears to the tidings, made good his passage, and the next morning engaged the outposts of his opponent.

At this crisis Holkar again strongly urged the propriety of returning to the old style of fighting, in which his people had proved so formidable; but in vain. The Bhow "had a plan;" and that plan was inconsistent with Holkar's recommendation; though a separate effort made by the old and wily partisan leader proved so successful as to lend much countenance to his advice.*

Glued to his artillery corps, and reckless of the dispiriting effect of placing such an army in a purely defensive attitude, Sedasheo took up a position at

* The following, somewhat condensed, is Sir John Malcolm's general estimate of Holkar:—

"Mulhar Row was seventy-six years of age when he died; he had for more than forty years of his life been a commander of reputation, and during the latter part of this period was certainly one of the most distinguished in the Mahratta confederacy. * * * * For simplicity of manners and manly courage, no Mahratta leader stands higher in the opinion of his countrymen; nor were his talents limited to those of a soldier. His administration of the countries subject to his direct control was firm, but considerate. * * * * The principal virtue of Mulhar Row was his generosity. He had personally no regard for money; he was wont to declare (probably with truth) that he understood nothing of accounts, and he listened with impatience to those ministers who recommended the diminution of his frequent largesses. To his relations, and indeed to all Mahrattas, he was uncommonly kind. It is stated of this chief, that in his conduct to the Paishwah, and in the performance of all his duties as a member of the Mahratta confederacy, he did that from the heart which Madhajee Sindia did from the head: the one was a plain, sincere soldier; and the other added to great qualities all the art of a crafty politician."—*Central India*, vol. i., pp. 155—6.

Paniput—a place where the fate of India has been decided in several memorable engagements. He then proceeded to construct an elaborately entrenched camp. "He dug a ditch," says Grant Duff, "fifty feet wide and twelve feet deep, and raised a rampart, on which he mounted cannon, round both his own camp and the village of Paniput."

He had traced a charmed circuit, which ominously enveloped the people whom he led; and which, far from defending them, sapped rapidly, as by enchantment, the ardent and confident spirit that had hitherto sustained and rendered them invincible!

Ahmed Shah surrounded his camp with the slighter protection of a sort of breast-work of prostrate timber.

In point of numbers the armies were not very unequally matched. Of regular and serviceable soldiers, the Abdali had about 80,000; that is 42,000 cavalry, and 38,000 infantry, with 70 guns. The Marathas had 70,000, including 55,000 horsemen, and 15,000 infantry; but not less than 200 guns. Thus the Afghan's superiority in men might seem to be counterbalanced by the greater number of cannon on the other side. But the difficulty of mobilising and working so many guns, and the necessity of guarding an entrenched camp, full of women and children, greatly impaired this ostensible advantage.

The *physique*, too, of the Afghans, if not of the

Oude men, was in some respects, and for certain purposes, as decidedly, though not obviously, in their favour, as that of the Germans over the lithe and impetuous, but less tenacious and stout-built Frenchmen in the late war. Rapidity and *élan* were the Maratha's *forte*. He shone in the dashing charge, and the initial and overwhelming shock of battle. But in the prolonged "tug of war," in the dull thudding impact, which was to secure the final victory as the result of reiterated and protracted exertions, he might—mountain-trained as he was—meet more than his match in the tall and stalwart invaders from the confines of the mighty and bracing Himalaya.

Much, then, would depend on the character and circumstances of the stricken field in which these redoubtable rivals should ultimately engage; and on the skill and care with which the Afghan, if he were to stand before the terrible onslaught of the Maratha cavalry, should be able to devise means for stemming that hitherto irresistible tide of battle, until his own dogged strength and physical stability should have time to tell.

It must be added, that irregulars doubled the above number of the Abdali's army; and that the Marathas are said to have had upwards of 200,000 of such inferior soldiers and Pindaries, or half soldiers, half *looties*.

Thus far as to the armies. The contrast between

the commanders was striking and complete. I have already endeavoured to sketch the character of Sedasheo, and to exhibit the effect of his incompetency, both in the political and in the military aspects of the campaign. His civil administration in Maharashtra had been meritorious. But he was simply out of his element in the North, and at the head of an army, and opposed to such a general as the Abdali.

On the other hand, in an age of remarkable men, who by their abilities and energy had raised themselves to a conspicuous station, and who played an influential part in the complicated drama of imperial dissolution, Ahmed Shah was one of the most remarkable. By birth the noblest of the Afghans, and the son of a statesman, whose diplomatic services in Persia had kindled the admiration of the wild tribes of a wild country, Ahmed had been chastened by early suffering, trained to war in the army, and under the eye, of the great master of the art, Nadir Shah himself.

After Nadir's assassination Ahmed returned, with the Afghan contingent, from Persia to his own country; and was, after a strange and protracted debate, and on the decisive motion of a religious devotee, unanimously elected King of the whole nation, at the early age of twenty-three. He soon justified the choice by his politic conduct. He repressed the mutual hostilities of the turbulent and jealous clans; extended the sphere of his influence by associating in the Confederacy outlying, alienated, or doubtful members; bound together his heterogeneous subjects by wise regulations, and caused them to respect a ruler, who was equally determined to hold his own, and to concede and secure what was due to those under him; and he employed abroad warlike energies, which would otherwise have been expended in sanguinary domestic dissensions and dangerous rebellions. Thus he overcame the natural disadvantages of his precarious position, and in the course of a few years made himself one of the most considerable potentates in Asia.

But this was not all. To bridle and unite the fierce and lawless Afghans, and to rival the military exploits of Nadir, were proud achievements for the King and the Conqueror; and would alone have entitled him to the place I have assigned him.

But as a man and a religionist, he occupies a still more eminent position. He may be said to stand alone in the dark group of astute and determined, but selfish, low-toned, and utterly worldly adventurers, whose persevering ambition attained indeed its reward, but at whose performances, under the influence of that ambition, the unsophisticated reader is apt to stand aghast, as at those of an oriental Cæsar Borgia.

Paradoxical as it may appear, and though his name is indissolubly associated with scenes of carnage (the irrepressible result of the ferocity of his people,) which savour more of Timour than of Thomas à Kempis; yet, certain it is, that Ahmed Shah was not only a man of cultivation, but a devout mystic, and a religious poet of no common order. Persian influences had, no doubt, operated on him; and his young mind had not improbably been much impressed by the terrible fate which had overtaken Nadir, in the midst of his theological aberrations and religious persecutions. However that may have been, the sincerity and fervour of his spiritual aspirations do not seem to be open to question, and found utterance in such strains of psalmody as the following:—

"I cry unto thee, O God! for I am of my sins and wickedness ashamed;
But hopeless of thy mercy, no one hath ever from thy threshold departed.
Thy goodness and mercy are boundless, and I am of my evil acts ashamed;
'Tis hopeless that any good deeds of mine will avail, but thy name I'll my refuge make.
When I my iniquities review, I say, O that I were but a mere blade of grass!
The lusts of the flesh and the devil are so implanted within me, that, O God! I can nothing do.
Though I strive to the utmost, there's no escape for me out of the devil's evil will:
If it be possible the heart from evil to guard, how shall the eyes be protected?

O Ahmad! seek thou help from the Almighty, but not from pomp and grandeur's aid." *

Such was Ahmed in the solitude of his chamber! But when from the *Sufi* penitent we turn to the professional soldier, all is changed; or rather the same earnestness of character which sent him in private to the Throne of Grace for pardon, comfort, and strength, impelled him, when in the field, to "do with his might what his hand found to do;" and rendered him one of the ablest and most successful, because one of the most thoughtful, deliberate, and steadfast of generals.

Of his military qualities some idea may be formed from the subjoined passage, on occasion of his election: †—

To this much more might be added. But this is enough, especially in contrast to such an antagonist as the Bhow.

At this crisis, Ahmed Shah took the just measure

* Quoted in the *Calcutta Review*, No. 101, Article I.; a very interesting and well-written paper on *Ahmad Shah Abdali*.

† "Such a chief was found in Ahmad Shah, a man in whom the enthusiasm of youth had been sobered by imprisonment and the vicissitudes and responsibilities of a soldier, early called to high command, but restrained by the bonds of the sternest discipline; who was thoughtful and far-seeing in planning, but who, in carrying out his plans, exhibited the patience of the most unwavering resolution, with the swift decision of one habituated to watch the changes of a battle, and to turn them to account."—*Calcutta Review, ut supra*, page 7.

of the Maratha disposition; and, though his own army began to grow extremely impatient for action, and to suffer severely from the failure of supplies adequate to the wants of so large a body of men, he absolutely refused to engage in a general battle, or to make any attempt to storm the Maratha entrenchments, and thus expose himself to a disheartening repulse. Negotiations, and private messages from the Bhow to the Nawab of Oude still continued; and his ally never failed to inform Ahmed of the purport of these secret communications. Thus, and in other ways, he learned, what indeed the nature of the case might have told him, that the vast colluvies of predatory troops, interrupted in their usual practice of making war support war by preying on the country around; little habituated either to want, or to the thrifty use of such stores as they could still command; exasperated by the seditious clamour of Ibrahim Khan's mercenaries for arrears of pay, which the increasing poverty of the Bhow would not allow him to satisfy; hampered by the presence of a vast mass of worse than useless *looties*, women, and children; disheartened by their stationary attitude, and distempered by the quarrels of their chiefs:—might indeed determine, in their desperation, to force a battle upon him, but were playing his own game every day that they remained cooped up in their camp.

Twice, indeed, within a short time, he had reason to respect, if not to dread, the prowess and fury of his antagonists; and he might well hesitate to meet the full array of their host, until despondency, discord, and famine should have materially diminished its strength. On the first occasion Holkar, at the head of 15,000 horsemen, broke into the Afghan camp; and cut down 2000 men before the arrival of reinforcements induced him to retire, with the loss of half that number. On the second, Bulwunt Rao, Sedasheo's Dewan and a good officer, assailed the Abdali's Vizier in the open field, as the latter was on his way to a mosque; and 3000 of the Rohillas whom Nujib-ud-Dowla led to the rescue fell, before Bulwunt himself was killed; when the Bhow, on whom the shadow of coming fate seemed fast settling, and benumbing his faculties, retired to bewail his friend, in the seclusion of his own tent.

Thus the armies for some time contented themselves with watching each other, or with witnessing single combats, which, in old Homeric fashion, came off by mutual agreement at a place midway between the hostile levies, and marked out by a sort of barrier.

The Rajputs and the Jats, though they had abandoned the contest, still in some degree befriended and mitigated the distress of their Hindoo compatriots, by transmitting to them occasional supplies, both of money and provisions. This, however, was but a feeble palliative; and too often the enemy, retaliating the inveterate Maratha practice, intercepted the intended succours.

Ahmed Shah was equally confident, imperious, indefatigable, and vigilant in the prosecution of his restrictive plan. "He was on horseback," says Elphinstone, on the authority of an eye-witness, whose narrative is said to have been authorised by Holkar, "for the whole day, visiting his posts, and reconnoitring the enemy; and never rode less than fifty or sixty miles a-day. At night he placed a picket of 5,000 horse as near as he could to the enemy, while other parties went the rounds of the whole encampment. 'His orders were obeyed like destiny,' adds Casi Rai 'no man daring to hesitate or delay one moment in executing them.'"

Such, in his sterner mood, was the remarkable northern chief selected by Providence to curb the insolence, and break the power, of the rash and domineering Southrons.

And thus, hemmed in, chafing, fasting, wasting, and, in Prince Bismarck's too expressive phrase, "stewing in their own grease," the unhappy warriors, so lately triumphant in all quarters of India, now brought to bay under such an accumulation of disadvantages, at length insisted on being led forth to conquer or to die. A large body, who had sallied of their own accord in the night, upon a desperate quest after food, had been already intercepted, and slaughtered without mercy. There remained provisions sufficient only for one hearty meal. But the improved modern plan, of surrendering *en masse* on such considerations, never seems to have entered the thoughts of these licentious, but, even in their desperation, thoroughly determined warriors.

The inevitable hour had struck. The Bhow gave the word, calmly and sadly (January 6, 1761.) The army ate once more; and then quitted the camp that had been, for two long and weary months, its prison, and had tamed its spirit, like the dank and gruesome precincts of an unfamiliar and hideous charnel-house.

They emerged, not now proudly and confidently mindful of the long and successful resistance offered by their fathers to the imperial tyrant; nor of their own widely diffused triumphs; nor of their recent and crowning victory over their neighbour and constant rival, the Nizam; nor their faces jubilant with the exulting joy of battle: but plunged in the deepest dejection, anticipating the all but certainty of defeat; attired and dishevelled as if doomed to destruction; and anxious only to escape from their long captivity, and exhibiting to the last their renowned valour, to sell their lives as dearly as possible.*

* "The ends of their turbans," says Grant Duff, "were let loose, their hands and faces anointed with a preparation of turmeric,

The Bhow had committed his wife and some of the chief families to Holkar's care, as to that of one who had the best chance, should he survive the fray, of finding favour in the eyes of the influential but vindictive Rohilla, Nujib-ud-Dowla. He also sent a last and touching appeal to Casi Rai, which reached its destination not long before the armies closed in the tremendous strife. "The cup," he wrote, "is now full to the brim, and cannot hold another drop. If anything can be done, do it, or else answer me plainly at once; hereafter there will be no time for writing or speaking." These desperate measures taken, he led forth his army, and disposed it in order in the open plain.

The artillery was posted in front of the line, and preluded with a general discharge, which was kept up and answered by the enemy's guns, until the impetuosity of both armies carried them past their batteries, which seem thenceforward to have taken little part in the battle.

The Bhow, with his young nephew, Wiswas Rao, and Jeswunt Rao Puar, occupied with their immediate followers the centre of the line; and in front of them floated the *Bhugwa Jenda*, the great standard of the nation, associated with the proudest

signifying that they were come forth to die, and everything seemed to bespeak the despondency of sacrifice prepared, instead of victory determined."

recollections of Maratha achievements. Sindia commanded on the right; the Guikwar on the left, with whom was now joined Ibrahim Khan.

Meanwhile the Shah, at first incredulous of the tidings, that his opponents were actually advancing to try the chances of a general engagement, had ridden forward to reconnoitre; and at length certified by the loud and prolonged roar of the artillery, he coolly removed a pipe from his mouth, and remarked to Shuja-ud-Dowla, "Your servants' news is very true, I see." He then lost no time in marshalling his own forces.

His Grand Vizier, Shah Wullee, was posted in the centre, with the bulk of the Afghans, 10,000 of whom were horse. Three Rohilla chiefs, and two other considerable leaders, led the right wing; the left was intrusted to the Nawab of Oude and Nujib-ud-Dowla. The Rohilla Prince knew too well, by repeated experience, what it was to encounter the impetuous shock of Maratha cavalry. He, therefore, with admirable forethought and great labour accomplished a task which probably, in the end, determined the fate of the battle. As he moved forward he threw up a number of hasty earthworks, behind which his men, if repulsed, might successively rally, and escape being swept off the field.

The event soon proved the wisdom of this precaution. The Marathas in the centre, raising their noted and inspiriting battle-cry, thundered down in one terrific and overwhelming body on the Afghan host opposed to them; and, their momentum undiminished by a counter-charge of cavalry, poured right onward, like an irresistible flood, through the stationary mass, breaking and scattering it in their headlong career. Then followed a desperate, clamourous, and hand-to-hand struggle. So thick was the dust-cloud that instantaneously overspread the scene, so wild the tumult, that the combatants could recognise each other only by the rival shouts of defiance. *Hur! Hur! Mahadeo!* was answered by the fanatic *Deen! Deen!* a sound terrible and bodeful of death to many an Englishman and Englishwoman in our own day!

The Vizier, finding his redoubted soldiers, though still struggling in detail, giving ground on all sides, and in imminent danger of being utterly routed, leaped from his horse, accoutred in full armour, and was imitated in this gallant but dangerous proceeding by many of his officers. But this display of confident bravery availed not; still his men were borne backward, and a panic began to prevail among them. "Our country," exclaimed the agitated general, "Our country is far off, my friends; whither do you fly?" But in vain he appealed to his troops, the bulk of whom had already deserted him. He was left for awhile with but a handful of men.

While thus the battle raged in the centre, the Marathas on the left, covered by a prudent manœuvre of Ibrahim's (who had wheeled two battalions to his left rear, so as to protect his flank), and ably seconded by the Khan's personal exertions, had sustained not less successfully their old reputation. Ibrahim was himself wounded, and more than half his men had fallen. But the Afghan right also was borne down in a desperate charge; and nearly 8,000 Rohillas lay dead or wounded on the field in that quarter alone.

The battle had already lasted from early in the morning until noon, when Ahmed Shah, who had remained in the rear, surveying with the eye of an experienced general the darksome and shifting tempest of war, and issuing his orders with consummate calmness and precision, ascertained that his left alone, with the help of the extemporised earthworks, continued still unbroken, though in much danger of being outflanked and ridden down. He now took measures for a great and supreme effort to restore the battle. He had prudently retained a considerable reserve, a precaution which the Marathas had entirely neglected. In addition to this, he hunted out of the camp every soldier who had, on any pretence, loitered there, and had not yet been engaged. His right was speedily succoured, and rallied. Ten thousand horsemen were entrusted anew to the Vizier, who was ordered to charge again and again the victorious Maratha centre. Nujib-ud-Dowla and Shah Pusund Khan, an Afghan officer, with a picked band of his countrymen, were directed to support these attacks, by assailing the Bhow's less successful right division.

The conflict then became more equal, and was waged with great severity and horrible carnage for two hours more. Holkar alone, it was thought, did not put forth his full strength. But, despondent and enfeebled as his countrymen had been when they marched forth to battle, they seem to have displayed, when once actually engaged, not only the most determined and effective valour, but an amount of physical endurance in the long and arduous contest, that was truly wonderful. Though fainting, famished, and overmatched by the stout northern mountaineers, they still fought on with the energy of despair, and the animating fury of national and religious hatred.

But at length Wiswas Rao fell mortally wounded; and the unhappy Bhow, probably overcome by a sudden access of family feeling, and discerning in this blow the hand of inevitable fate, dismounted from his elephant; gave, or is said by Holkar to have given him, some indefinite directions; and, plunging into the thickest of the fight, in all probability perished almost instantly, though a question was afterwards raised, whether he were indeed dead at all, and had not made his escape.

As on so many other occasions, the disappearance of the leader produced, almost instantaneously, the irretrievable rout of his army. What was the real import of the Bhow's communication to Holkar must ever remain a mystery. As at Balaclava, we can only conclude that

"Some one had blundered."

Holkar himself immediately left the field and fled, promptly followed by the Guikwar.*

Then the whole army broke, and in vain attempted to flee also. But a wholesale butchery added its horrors to those accumulated throughout the pro-

* Sir John Malcolm remarks on Holkar's conduct (*Central India*, vol. i. p. 153) :—

"The early escape of Mulhar Row, on a day so fatal to his nation, has given rise to some reproaches; but his advocates ascribe his safety to his superior knowledge as a leader, which made him, when he saw the action lost, keep his party together, and retreat with an order that none of the others preserved.

"This account will be more probable, if we credit the statement given of his quarrel with his commander, on the morning of the day on which the battle was fought. He had, it is affirmed, intreated Sedasheo Bhow to delay the action for one or two days;* but the latter, whose pride and vanity exceeded all bounds, impatient of the advice, exclaimed, 'Who wants the counsel of a goatherd?' If the anecdote be true, we cannot wonder that a chief of Mulhar Row's character should not have anticipated success."

* Sedasheo Bhow used to allow his attendants to exclaim, "Purseram Ootar," or an Incarnation of Vishnu, as one of his titles.

tracted and envenomed conflict. The field was cumbered with the Marathas slain in their flight. The trenches of the Bhow's camp were choked with the carcases of those who had crowded into them, and had been trampled to death before they could extricate themselves. The ferocious victors beset the camp all night. On the morrow, they divided amongst themselves as slaves the women and children, and slaughtered in cold blood, and at leisure, all their male prisoners, piling the heads in heaps around their tents. The peasants in the neighbourhood killed great numbers of the fugitives. "Of the fighting men," says Grant Duff, "one-fourth only are supposed to have escaped, and of the followers about an equal proportion; so that nearly 200,000 Mahrattas perished in the campaign."

The Jat prince treated the fugitives with much kindness. Wiswas Rao's body was found, and the barbarous chieftains assembled around the Afghan sovereign at first insisted that the corpse of the king of the unbelievers should be stuffed, and carried back to Cabul. But, by Shuja-ud-Dowla's intercession, it was eventually burned. A headless trunk was displayed as that of the Bhow. But it remained uncertain whether the body were actually his. Sindia was taken, and fell a victim to Nujib-ud-Dowla's vengeance. Ibrahim Khan, too, was one of the captives, and was executed for the unpardonable offence of having fought the battle of the infidel against the followers of the Prophet.

The tidings of this terrific calamity were too much for the Peishwa. He speedily sickened and died; and for the time the spirit of his people was completely broken.

With the change of a few proper names, Scott's verses on the overthrow of his countrymen at Flodden exactly suit the occasion.

> "*Nerbudda* heard the ceaseless plash,
> While many a broken band,
> Disorder'd, through her currents dash,
> To gain the *Dekkan* land;
> To town and tower, to down and dale,
> To tell red *Paniput's* dismal tale,
> And raise the universal wail.
> Tradition, legend, tune, and song,
> Shall many an age that wail prolong:
> Still from the sire the son shall hear
> Of the stern strife and carnage drear,
> Of *Paniput's* fatal field,
> Where shiver'd was *Maharashtra's* spear
> And broken was her shield."

CONCLUSION.

WITH the battle of Paniput, the native period of Indian History may be said to end. Henceforth the interest of the story gathers round the progress of the Merchant Princes from the far West. The Mogul Empire, as a palpable entity, has vanished; though as an idea, a tradition, a diplomatic assumption, it continues to haunt the minds, and complicate the political relations both of Natives and of Europeans. There is still a titular Emperor, but he is a fugitive adventurer. The Subahdar of the Dekkan also survives; but he is fast sinking into the Nizam of Hyderabad. The portentous incarnation of predatory energy, which has eaten out the heart, and decked itself in the trappings, and for awhile has threatened to assume the authority of dismembered imperialism, lies prostrate and bleeding under the Afghan knife. The star of the *Feringhee Sahibs* is in the ascendant, and is destined to rule the empyrean, though not unchallenged, or without eclipse.

The English have now not only freely engaged in the quarrels of the Country Powers, but have just, for the first time, obtained a secure and commanding position along the whole shore of Eastern India, and far up the Valley of the Ganges.

On the Coromandel coast, the long duel between the French and our countrymen is being terminated by the surrender of Pondicherry.

While, in Bengal, Clive has recently gained the battle of Plassey, and entered on his career of King maker, and Founder of our Indian Empire.

A new candidate for dominion has indeed arisen in the South, and is already revolving schemes incompatible with the security and extension of our authority in that quarter, and which will even threaten, at times, our expulsion from the country. And the Maratha Hydra, though crest-fallen, stunned, and maimed, is fated to revive, and to try conclusions once and again with the ever encroaching conquerors of Suraja Dowla, of Lally, and of Tippoo. In the Eastern Himalayas, too, is nestling a brave and hardy race, who will severely tax hereafter the military energies and resources of the British. And though the Afghan does not now linger to enjoy the fruit of his hard-won victory, the bloody trophies of Paniput foreshadow the deep humiliation of England eighty years afterwards, at the hands of Ahmed Shah's exasperated and ferocious countrymen.

Already, lastly, around the banks of the Indus a remarkable community of fervid religionists and formidable warriors is clustering, which after many terrible vicissitudes, is just emancipated from all external control; and which, organised, disciplined, and held in check through long years, by an ambitious but wary chief, will, after his death, pour like the resistless floods of the same region, over the adjacent British Provinces, and once more emperil our power, already shaken to its foundations by the Afghan disaster.

Still, throughout these and minor convulsions, the figure of the Englishman is ever the most prominent: his heavy hand and his scheming brain eventually carry the day in all directions: the sequence of his fortunes gives a new unity to Indian story: and the character and operation of his system of direct government, or of indirect influence, are the all-important circumstances upon which the fate of the people depends.

The memorable struggles which have intervened between the accession of Aurungzib and the death of Balaji Baji Rao have facilitated and inaugurated the British Conquest; and neither the military, the political, nor the moral aspects of that great achievement can be properly understood without a previous knowledge of the eventful and complicated prelude.

INDEX.

ERRATA.

Page	Line	
v.	23.	*For* "ancestors" *read* "descendants."
ib.	24.	*For* κτῆμά *read* κτῆμα.
31	3.	*Read* "Ye are brothers! Ye are men!"
53	6.	*For* βασιλέα *read* Πρίαμον.
64	12, 13.	*Dele* "As the English—called it."
91	25.	*For* "Ajit" *read* "Raj."
143	13.	*Dele* "Colonel."
212	9.	To *Asof Jah* add in a note—"A title assumed by Nizam-ul-Mulk when he finally settled in the Dekkan."
219	*ad fin.*	The parenthesis should have been printed below, as a note.
220	6.	*Read* "to give way to, &c."
225	18.	*For* "prince" *read* "princess."
246	5.	*For* "the claim to" *read* "the claim for."